D0418505

The Origins of
Modern Europe

The Origins of Modern Europe

THE MEDIEVAL HERITAGE OF
WESTERN CIVILIZATION

R. ALLEN BROWN

THE BOYDELL PRESS

First published 1972

Reissued 1996
by the Boydell Press
an imprint of Boydell & Brewer Ltd
PO Box 9, Woodbridge, Suffolk IP12 3DF, UK

ISBN 0 85115 665 7

A catalogue record for this book is available
from the British Library

Printed in the United States of America

TO PHILIPPA AND GILES

Contents

Maps

Introduction

Not long ago, if memory serves, a British Minister of Education (if such an official still exists) proclaimed in public that it was more important for school-children to know 'all about' Vietnam than the Wars of the Roses. This horrific statement, as remarkable in its source as in its content, reflects at least two of the heresies of our philistine age. The first derives from a fashionable but false academic liberalism, the treason of the clerks, and in the field of history takes the form of a belief that it does not matter what you study, so long as you study it. This would seem to be the academic variation on the vogue theme of everyone doing his or her own thing. In fact in history, if we wish to understand, some periods, some places, some people even, are more important than others—more relevant, if we may at once introduce another vogue word of our time. The truth is that Charlemagne and Pope Gregory VII are more relevant to us in the West, if we wish to comprehend our present condition, than Che Guevara and Ho Chi Minh. For history, like charity, should begin at home. It is meet and right that historians and students of history in the West should make the history of the West their primary concern. We are all of us, on both sides of the Atlantic, heirs and members of Western civilization, whether we like it or not, conditioned and moulded by that inheritance, as also by our own individual local contexts (which still matter even in a rootless world), whereby our attitudes and even our potentialities are controlled. There can be little hope for us if we do not know first our own origins, nor understand the way we came to be the way we are, which is to know ourselves. This, surely, is the sovereign benefit of history, over and above its use, like any other subject taught in youth, as a mere means of training the mind. History, said Bacon, makes men wise, but it will not do so if the syllabus consists of isolated, unrelated bits and pieces drawn from all over the world, with little relevance to ourselves. It also must be true that in the creation of the whole modern world we know, Western civilization and Western values, good and bad, for better or for worse, have so far been the most important factor. For this reason also, therefore, they merit our first attention. World history, moreover, even if thought desirable, can scarcely be much more than the sum of its component parts, each preferably written by its own participants, and, even so, those who wish to understand humanity, and who think the proper study of mankind is man, may still prefer to compare one culture with another rather than attempt a total history likely to be both superficial and to impose arbitrary patterns on the defenceless past.

The second heresy of our time aptly implied by the ministerial remark above is even more pernicious. It is that the most recent, the most modern, period of history must always and of necessity be the most relevant to the understanding of the present. Nothing could be further from the truth. Though you may, if you wish, have Instant Food, you cannot have Instant History, which is a manifest contradiction in terms. Yet, though one would have thought it the very reverse of the historian's creed, the arrogant, and at bottom ignorant, belief in the supreme and near-exclusive relevance of modernity seems to become ever more prevalent, even amongst historians, to make of history in some places little more than a study of current affairs in depth, and to show alarming signs of becoming a closed system as the curricula of new universities become vested interests, are aped by older universities who should know better, and as the wheel comes full circle with the student-beneficiaries of this Higher Education coming in their turn to teach. No one wishing to absorb the contents of a book would start at the end and never go back to the beginning: you cannot come in at the end of an historical process and claim understanding. The historian's particular task is to study origins and subsequent developments in order first to understand and then explain, and it is very likely that the origins, the foundations, will control all that comes after. The statement seems so obvious as to stand almost for a Universal Truth, and yet it is precisely the crucial period of origins and foundations, the so-called 'medieval' period of European history, that is nowadays increasingly missed out in the teaching of our schools and universities—or, worse perhaps (since a little knowledge is a dangerous thing), put in as an introductory sop to culture, 'background' to the serious stuff to come.

If our primary concern is, without apology, to study and to know the history of Western civilization which is the conditioning context of our lives, so also it is imperative that we should do this in some depth and begin at the beginning, if true understanding is our aim. Western civilization is derived from Western Europe which was Latin Christendom, and this begins in the 5th and 6th centuries A.D. with the amalgamation and the fusion of the classical culture of the declining Roman Empire, the Germanic customs, habits and attitudes of the invading 'barbarian' races, and Christianity, subsequently Latin Christianity. These are literally the elements, and thereafter developments came so thick and fast that by about 1300 at latest the pattern of the future and our present had been set. Indeed one is tempted to go further and declare that all that matters most in the history of the West had happened by then, and further still by suggesting that all that has happened since is a continuing decline and anticlimax. Of all centuries these, from the fifth to the thirteenth inclusive, are the most 'relevant', for this is where we come from, here are our roots, this is the period *par excellence* of origins and foundations, the springtime of the West (never to come again), present promise and wealth of the future beyond the eye's scope. Here, for a start, is Christianity, manifesting itself not just as a religion but as a Christian society, so that it would be insulting to the most general of readers to remind him of his debt to that, whether acknowledged or not, in a thousand-and-one ways every day. (When we say 'Goodbye', do we not also say 'God be

with you'?). Christianity also manifested itself in the form of the
Latin, Roman Church under the Papacy, and this, while still
with us, not only finds its origin and foundation in this period,
but its apotheosis also. As for the classical inheritance of Greece
and Rome, the barbarians, it has been well said, came not to
destroy the Roman Empire but to enjoy it: the learning of the
ancients was not in the event lost but was first preserved by
scholars like Boethius and then revived by the Carolingian
Renaissance, the Ottonian Renaissance and the Twelfth-Century
Renaissance so that the better-known Renaissance of the fifteenth
century holds nothing like the crucial position in our history
traditionally ascribed to it. Medieval civilization which has made
us what we are is, in fact, the amalgamation of classical and
Germanic cultures, with reverence for the former paramount
throughout, even though the scholars of the age, as men will,
moulded their inheritance closer to their heart's desire, and made
of the past they revered something different and alive—just as
medieval Latin, the universal language of the West, remained a
living, changing language and not the dead school exercise of
the fifteenth-century Renaissance scholars and their modern
successors. Politically the period saw, as it were, the physical
creation of Western Europe in the form of Latin Christendom,
and the process involved also that division between eastern and
western Europe, very much still with us albeit in another guise,
yet then as now part politics, part faith. The Arabic, Moslem
world of Islam, which now shares the headlines of the press with
tensions and wrangles between East and West, also has its
dramatic foundation in these centuries, just as long before the
period ends that world was also weakened by a disunity for which
as yet no remedy has been found. Meanwhile any history of the
Arab peoples must begin in the Middle Ages as it must begin
with Mohammed, and if one wants to know (as who should not)
why modern India is separated from modern Pakistan it is, as
it nearly always is, to medieval history that one must turn for an
answer. All this, of course, is also the beginning of the 'Eastern
Question' which so plagues the student of 'modern' nineteenth-

century history, and even spoils the otherwise enjoyable task of reading a life of Disraeli.

Within the boundaries of Latin Christendom and Western Europe, expanding southwards into Moslem Sicily and Moslem Spain, eastward with the eastern movement of the German peoples (not for nothing in the last war did the Germans give the code name Operation Barbarossa to their eastern campaign against Russia), and broken out of altogether in the great adventure of the Crusades, the modern and familiar states of France and England originated, were developed and established—both monarchies, both with Parliaments, for these things are medieval institutions, like the universities and the English Common Law. Much of medieval history is taken up by wars between the two, but if this theme begins in 1066 it does not end before 1815 or later. In this respect the Middle Ages may be said to end only with the Entente Cordiale, and even that, of course, has medieval origins in a common heritage and histories inextricably entwined. Those who, as I write, oppose the Common Market should at least read medieval history before they cite historical precedent on their side. But in terms of political history, both of Western Europe and the world, the pattern of the future was no less surely moulded by the negative fact of the failure in the Middle Ages of Italy, and more especially Germany, to congeal, than by the positive fact of the success in this respect of England, France and ultimately Spain, and here it could be argued with success that the explanation of the two world wars of the twentieth century lies more in the policies of Pope Gregory VII in the eleventh century than in those of Bismarck in the nineteenth. One could go on for a long time to urge the 'relevance' of the medieval period to the future and the present, and indeed we have the rest of this book to ram the message home. Meanwhile even in these introductory pages one cannot and should not forbear to point out that the marauding Vikings discovered North America about the year 1000, half a millennium before Columbus followed wallowing in the wake of their long-boats, nor that the same intrepid seafarers, warriors and traders, chiefly in the persons of the Swedes, can claim to be the founders of the Russian state, no less, through their settlement at Kiev. And as for English history, it should certainly be proclaimed in ringing tones at the outset of a book such as this, that there has seldom been a date more insignificant than the *annus mirabilis* of 1485, and better educated is he or she who knows nothing even of those national monuments the Tudors and Stuarts than he or she in total ignorance of Alfred the Great and William the Conqueror. The truth is that, aware or not, one cannot in Western Europe escape from the so-called Middle Ages in daily life at almost any level, whether one reads a book or a newspaper, goes to university or to law, enters a church, walks through a town or village or drives through the countryside—and the like is true, *mutatis mutandis*, of the United States of America, where the sheriff (with his *posse*) survives even though there are no counts or earls. A man, albeit a sociologist, has no more business to write of modern society in ignorance of medieval feudalism than in ignorance of the industrial revolution, though never the less all do. How then, one annually asks oneself, ploughing through the desert of 'A' Level history papers, all beginning confidently at 1485 or 1715, and meeting the fresh faces of history students straight from school—how can they be thought educated, let alone historians, who know nothing of these things?

There is nothing new in what I have so far said, or nothing new at least in the attitudes, beliefs and ideals which underlie it. In a broadcast made in 1952 Professor Geoffrey Barraclough had this amongst other things to say: 'But, above all else, it seems to me, we need a new conception of these centuries which will bring home to us their relevance. Those of us who study them, study them not because they are medieval, but because we believe that knowledge of immediate causes and contemporary events may blind, and not illuminate, unless it is counter-balanced by a deeper understanding of the continuity of history, its enduring factors and its underlying currents. From this point of view the very concept 'The Middle Ages' is objectionable, because it cuts them off as remote and distinct, a separate period which has little bearing on our lives and fortunes today. Yet this was the time when the foundations of modern Europe were being laid . . . If we understood it better, not as medieval history, but as modern history, very modern history—in the sense that all history which means anything is contemporary history—we might understand ourselves better, and our problems and potentialities'.[1] Reading those words, which could be echoed elsewhere, again, one might suppose this present book unnecessary. The truth is that the danger at the present time is not of a new ignorance of the Middle Ages but the revival of an old one which one had thought dead. If this were just a change of fashion in academic places (where, in England, not so long ago, almost everyone who was anyone was a medievalist, with a certain irritation resulting in those who were not) it would not matter quite so much, but there are unmistakable signs that it is in fact a more serious matter all too symptomatic of our instant, materialistic age, interested predominantly in the immediate and the quick return. Schools, universities and other places where they teach are not immune from the prevailing attitudes of the society which they ought to lead, their chief weakness being, like that of the Church, that they only have the laity to recruit from. There is also added to the negative factor of a revived ignorance of the Middle Ages, which is bad enough, the positive factor of a revived arrogantly ignorant contempt, which is even worse, and worse still when we reflect (as annually I do reflect) that in the young at least, allegedly educated, this attitude and presumption can only have been inculcated by their teachers, themselves presumably the product of some history school. For this, though it may well reflect the values of contemporary society, there is also, as always, a measure of historical explanation, in so far as it is the revival of an attitude of the past, and is also conditioned and positively encouraged by our inherited method of dividing time and labelling periods of history. For to all intents and purposes

[1] Printed in G. Barraclough, 'Medium Aevum: Some Reflections on Medieval History and on the Term "The Middle Ages",' printed in his *History in a Changing World* (Oxford, Blackwell, 1957), pp. 62–3.

'the Middle Ages', *i.e.* the concept of an historical 'Middle
Age', a *medium aevum*, and hence a 'medieval' period, was first
invented or established by a third-rate German scholar called
Cellarius or Keller in the seventeenth century. He it is who is
ultimately responsible for that arbitrary division of the whole
history of the West into three periods: the classical period of
Greece and Rome, ending for him precisely in 476 with the fall
of the last Roman Emperor in the west; the modern period,
beginning for him equally precisely with the fall of Constantinople in 1453; and, in the middle, a middle age. All divisions
of the seemless web of history are wrong though none so wrong
as this, and its worst feature is the contempt implicit in it for the
middle period as a dark age when nothing that was good took
place, since for Cellarius and his successors the lights of classical
civilization went out all over Western Europe with the fall of the
Roman Empire in 476, and did not come on again until 1453
when the fall of Constantinople to the Turk brought about, for
them, *the* Renaissance of the fifteenth century. Hence 'medieval',
like 'Gothick', became a term of abuse and so remains amongst
the ignorant, so that, for journalists, publicists, politicians,
television pundits and other moulders of public opinion today, to
call anything 'medieval' is only a degree less insulting than to call
it 'feudal'. Hence too, in terms of English history, those 'A' Level
history papers emanating from the sixth forms of our schools,
arrogantly confident in their certainty that life begins in 1485,
and that 'the Middle Ages', before that happy date, were a dark
and stagnant time, peopled exclusively by thug-like barons
constantly in revolt, proud prelates equally over-mighty, super-
stitious monks building cathedrals with their bare hands in the
intervals of immorality, and a down-trodden peasantry of serfs,
villeins to a man, secretly longing for the advent of Henry Tudor.
It would be funny were it not so tragic.

There is, of course, as nearly all would now agree, much else
that is wrong with this tripartite division of Western history
into the three immutable periods of classical, medieval and
modern, although in practice, with modifications and scholarly

qualifications, we go on using them. It is difficult to know where
to begin in condemning them, but let us ask first if it can really
make sense to treat as one unified whole a 'medieval' period of a
thousand years, from *c*.450 to *c*.1450, subject like any other to
continuous development and constant change, and when the
men at the end of it were as far removed in time from the men at
the beginning as was Queen Victoria from Alfred the Great or
Gladstone from Guthrum the Dane? Then again, if there is to
be a medieval period when does it begin and at what point does it
end? The year 476 marks no clean break: it is easy enough to
see the Roman Empire declining, but difficult if not impossible
to say when it ends. A recent writer has suggested that from one
point of view 'the Roman Empire achieved its fullest development in the thirteenth century',[1] and what are we to do with that
Holy Roman Empire which survived until 1806? As to the end
of the Middle Ages, few would now subscribe to the simple dual
view that the fall of Constantinople in 1453 ushered in *the*
Renaissance of the fifteenth century, which itself stands as the
great and immediate divide between something called 'medieval'
and something else called 'modern'. And how can the fifteenth-
century revival of classical learning and culture be seen as an
epoch-making event when medieval civilization was based upon
the classical past and saw itself a continuation of it? It is entirely
symptomatic that Renaissance scholars believed themselves to be
using original classical texts when in fact they were using Carolingian copies. Further yet, if it made some sort of sense for Cellarius
in the seventeenth century to see the period from the Renaissance
to his own day as modern, can we really go on infinitely extending
the 'modern' period forwards and thus backwards, and still
regard it as one unified whole, like the 'medieval' period which
precedes it? Are the Tudors and the Stuarts really modern?
together with Charles V, Philip II and Louis XIV? Clearly we
should rethink it all, not least because of the dangerously misleading implications of the conventional divisions. Professor

[1] R. W. Southern, *Western Society and the Church in the Middle Ages*,
Pelican History of the Church, vol. 2 (1970), p. 25.

Barraclough, in the lecture already cited, having first remarked that in Western Europe 'all our history, from the decline of Rome, should be regarded as "modern", in the sense that it is the history of our modern civilization', went on to suggest the following subdivisions[1]:

  i. decline of Rome [*c*.400?] to 800 or 900 A.D.
  ii. 900 to 1300
  iii. 1300 to 1789
  iv. 1789 to the present.

The first, he suggests, is the period of the prehistory of the European peoples: the second is the period of the formation of the European societies: the third is the real 'middle ages'; and only the fourth (so far) is modern. Although in the present book, for the convenience of those whose habit or training leads them to start at the end or in the middle, we shall continue to use the terms 'medieval' and 'the Middle Ages' in their conventional and (unhappily) accepted sense, Professor Barraclough's divisions, together with their gloss, are infinitely preferable to those now still in use. They avoid the dangerous anachronism of seeing the sixteenth, seventeenth and eighteenth centuries as 'modern', and above all they place the emphasis where it should be placed, upon the fact that in the history of the West what is conventionally called the medieval period, and especially the centuries from 900 to 1300, are of all periods the most relevant to us now, as the time of the origins and foundations, growth and development, of modern Europe and the modern world.

'And now it is all gone—like an unsubstantial pageant faded; and between us and the old English there lies a gulf of mystery which the prose of the historian will never adequately bridge. They cannot come to us, and our imagination can but feebly penetrate to them. Only among the aisles of our cathedrals, only as we gaze upon their silent figures on their tombs, some

[1] *History in a Changing World*, p. 61.

faint conceptions float before us of what these men were when they were alive; and perhaps in the sound of church bells, that peculiar creation of medieval age, which falls upon the ear like the echo of a vanished world'. Thus James Anthony Froude in a memorable passage on the passing of the English Middle Ages.[1] Perhaps enough has been said already to suggest that those Middle Ages were no unsubstantial pageant but robust, not all gone but substantially remaining as a controlling factor in our lives. Perhaps they may yet go, if God is really dead; if the fever of nationalism proves permanent so that men continue blindly to support their own countries, right or wrong, like so many football teams; if something called the G.N.P. is all that really matters; if personal greed cloaked as national prosperity continues to rape both town and countryside to turn both into desert places; and if the young are taught to turn their backs upon any past beyond about 1870—or, at best, the Tudors and the Stuarts. But not yet. I write these pages in a medieval house set in a countryside not quite changed beyond all recognition, though the tractor has replaced the timeless horse in the furrow and the windmill is disintegrating. And if the end of the old world we have always known is really approaching, there must still be voices crying in the wilderness. And if a gulf threatens to be opened between us and our own past, which is our identity, by so much the more is it urgently necessary that history, especially medieval history, should be taught and written. For myself, I have always done both in the hope and the faith that by showing people things as they were one may influence them to make better things as they are.

Meanwhile there is also a further and particular reason for studying so-called medieval history, over and above its obvious and overwhelming relevance as the period of the origins and formation of the modern West. The Middle Ages have not gone in any absolute sense, but in a more superficial sense they have become remote by the sheer passage of time. It is not easy to recapture, ever, the first fine careless rapture, and those figures

[1] Quoted by A. L. Rowse in *The Use of History* (London, 1946), p. 56.

whom Froude sought sleeping on their tombs have become elusive now. Yet herein, it may be urged, is the particular excellence of medieval studies as an educative process. They are relevant but they are not easy, and to overcome the difficulties, which should challenge and not put off, requires the exercise of those very virtues and attainments which history confers (quite apart from a modicum of Latin, now in process of abandonment by our schools and universities), but to a higher degree than any more modern period. The benefits of history as a means of education, which make it perhaps the best of the humanities and therefore the best of subjects, are that it requires and bestows a sense of proportion, the ability to see the other person's point of view, above all the imagination, compassion and humility not only to understand but also to appreciate habits, customs and beliefs different from or alien to our own. All this especially of medieval history, though the differences to be penetrated do not reduce the relevance of the discoveries made. Though he may well be warned against the potential dangers of the assumption, the student of the nineteenth century, to take an obvious example, feels himself to be, and in an obvious sense is, closer to what he seeks. No great barriers stand between us and our understanding of nineteenth-century Parliaments and politics and parties, Factory Acts and Free Trade (though Newman may well be another matter). By comparison, the student of the medieval past has a mountain of wholly beneficial mental effort to scale before he can find his promised land. Especially is this so in countries nominally Protestant, for the Reformation and the Industrial Revolution are probably the great divides in Western history, and both have to be crossed to reach the Middle Ages. To understand and benefit from the world that there awaits him, the modern student, like the student of more recent periods yet more so, must attain the humility and the wisdom necessary to be freed from the standards and values of the present, to appreciate, it may be, that faith can be enviable and not pathetic, that it just is, in any case, a motive force in history, as may also be at times a love of war. But he must also make the salutary effort to comprehend the logic and appeal of monasticism and asceticism —timeless, yet far removed from the public image of today—and to catch some glimpse of the breath-taking vision of the twelfth-century Papacy as it was meant to be. He must touch the garments also of royal majesty, of anointed Christian kings ruling by the Grace of God (still, just, on our coins) as vicars of Christ on earth, with powers real or potential over church and state greater than any the second Tudor or his Cromwell dared to claim. He must enter a world also which turned upon personal relationships, where in consequence loyalty was so important as to be institutionalized, where the great man's household was the equivalent of the firm, and to take service was the way to the top. He must conceive of lordship on a scale we have not seen since, and, at the other end of society, not be so naïve as to suppose that Hod the peasant as a serf (in so far as he was a serf) was necessarily worse off than Hod the peasant as an agricultural labourer in the England of 1930. He must conceive of a world in many ways more united than the modern West, but also more fragmented, a world of localities, rooted to the soil. He may come to find that technological progress is not the only sort of achievement nor the only measure of intelligence, and he may even cease to believe in progress of that kind. Certainly one's experience is enriched, the rewards are great. They may even include at the end a sense of kinship, for when the cowls, the visors and the skirts are lifted these people are not so different from ourselves, and certainly not inferior.

> Christ! that I were back in my bed
> And my love in my arms again!

The verse is not contemporary but medieval, and one can almost feel the dark, cold wet of a winter dawn, the breath of horses, the torches and the candles not yet quenched for the reluctant day.

CHAPTER I

The Roman Empire:
decline and survival

In the beginning was the Word, but in the beginning also was the Roman Empire. We must begin with that since the origins of the medieval world, and therefore the modern West, are found in the fusion of Roman and Germanic, classical and barbarian elements, while the third element, Christianity, was also inherited from Rome. In so far as it is ever possible to separate one strand of the past from another (for history is indeed a seamless web in the sense that in it, as in life, everything tends to happen all at once), we shall deal mainly with secular affairs in this chapter and the next, and treat later and in its own right of the early history of the Church.

In this chapter, then, we shall see in chiefly secular terms the origins of the Middle Ages and the modern West, but in so doing we shall also see as part and parcel of it the beginnings of that division between Western and Eastern Europe, with the Near East and beyond, never thereafter healed. For if in the West the Roman Empire, in conventional terminology, 'fell', in the sense that it was overrun and settled by barbarian tribes in the fifth and sixth centuries A.D., in the East the Roman Empire, based upon Constantine's new capital of Constantinople (now Istanbul), did not fall but survived until 1453. Of course in this Eastern, Byzantine[1] Empire there were vast changes in the course of that millennium from the fifth to the fifteenth century, and of course, and not without reason, the West saw itself also as the heir of Rome. Nevertheless there was continuity of a much greater order in the former than the latter, two worlds with increasingly

[1] So called from Byzantium, the former name of Constantinople.

divergent histories emerged where one had been before, and the difference was to be sealed by two divergent forms of organized Christianity, Roman and Greek Orthodox. But if the Eastern Roman Empire never fell, it suffered heavily in this early period of origins *par excellence* from the inroads and conquests of the Moslems in the seventh and eighth centuries—a movement which also severely affected the emergent and hard-pressed West. That, too, must be the business of this chapter, and in it we may see the dramatic emergence of a third world, a third force, of the Moslem, Arab powers, and with it the beginnings of the 'Eastern Question' for the West. It is a matter of the foundations of a new, and to us familiar world being laid amidst the ruins of the old.

Ideally the historian of the West, and especially the early medievalist, should know as much of classical, ancient history as of any other period, both in order to understand the decline of the Roman Empire which is also the origin of the modern West, and also to appreciate as well the classical inheritance as the changes wrought upon it as men remoulded it to suit their needs and comprehension, or to bring it closer to their heart's desire. Certainly there are some basic facts about the late Roman Empire which must be stated now to comprehend the sequel. The first is its geographical and political extent. In Europe it comprised all Italy and Greece, with what are now the Balkan States, Switzerland, a part of southern Germany, all France which was Roman Gaul, the Iberian Peninsula (Portugal and Spain), and Britain (chiefly England and Wales) on the periphery of the Roman world. So much for Europe, but to east and south the Empire comprised the Near East and much of the Middle East (where the chief neighbour was the Persian Empire)— Turkey, Syria, the Lebanon and Israel, roughly in modern terms —and the whole of the north African littoral from modern Egypt to the straits of Gibraltar. A map (Map 1) thus shows not only that the Empire was huge, but also that it was a Mediterranean empire, entirely surrounding the Mediterranean Sea, *mare nostrum*, which was its centre no less than Rome herself. Rome was a sea-power as well as a land-power, and her empire an

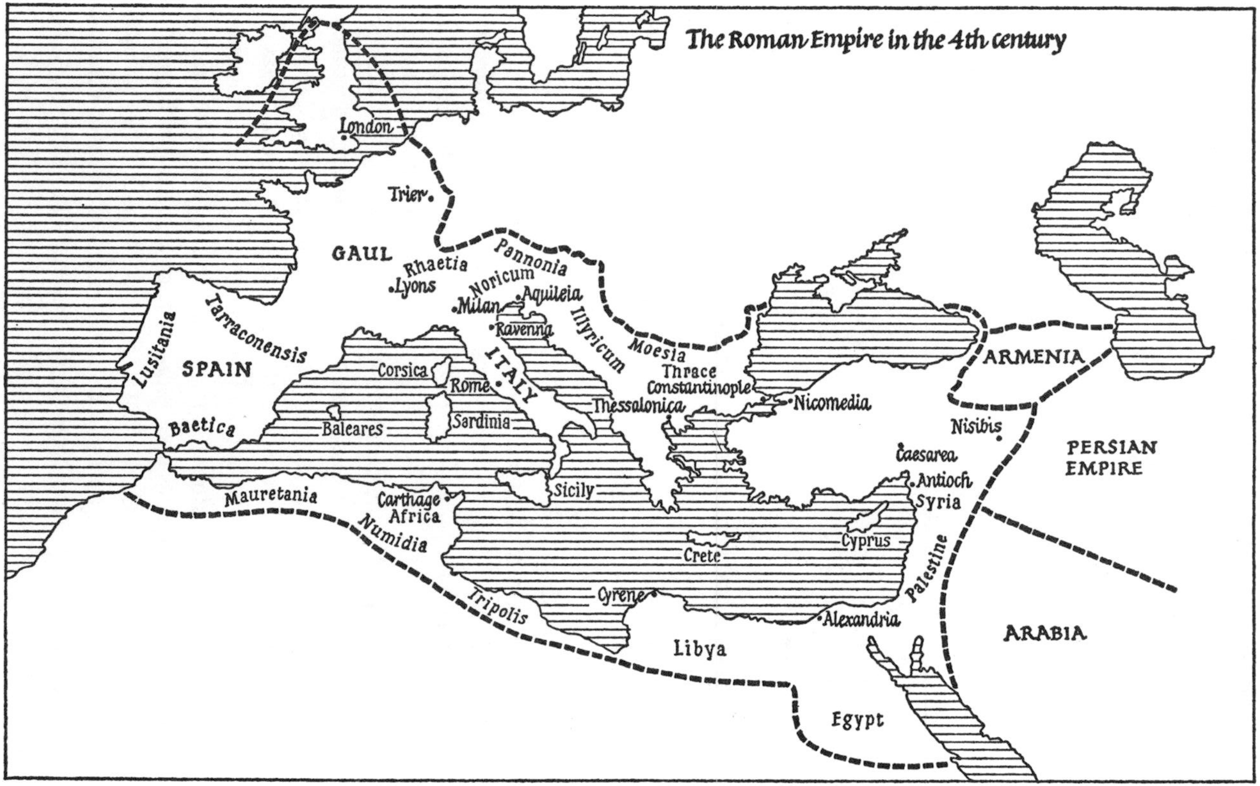

The Roman Empire in the 4th century

London
Trier
GAUL
Rhaetia
Lyons
Pannonia
Noricum
Aquileia
Milan
Illyricum
Ravenna
Moesia
Thrace
Constantinople
Thessalonica
ITALY
Rome
Sardinia
Corsica
Sicily
Crete
Balcares
Mauretania
Carthage
Africa
Numidia
Tripolis
Cyrene
Libya
Tarraconensis
SPAIN
Baetica
Lusitania
ARMENIA
Nisibis
Caesarea
Nicomedia
Antioch
Syria
Cyprus
Palestine
Alexandria
Egypt
PERSIAN EMPIRE
ARABIA

MAP I

economic as well as a political unit, made viable by the sea which held the whole together by trade and communications.

A second basic fact about the Roman Empire is its unity, which, if it was made possible chiefly by the centrifugal effects of the Mediterranean, did not thereafter depend solely on the *pax Romana* and the force of Roman arms. It rested also on a concept of the common humanity of all men, given expression in practice by, amongst other things but above all, a universal Roman law overriding all local custom. There was no racial unity, nor could there be, but neither was there any significant and disuniting localism. *Civis Romanus sum.* The citizens of Constantine's new capital city of Constantinople were no less 'Romans': the Roman Emperor Trajan was a Spaniard: St. Paul was a Roman citizen albeit of Jewish parentage, born in the Greek city of Tarsus in Asia Minor. Examples could be multiplied indefinitely. There was also religious unity of a real though negative kind in that there was no disunity. Roman pantheism was a type of toleration, for if not all gods were equal, all, including the gods of conquered peoples, could be given official recognition and Latin names, to be absorbed into the Roman system, so long as they too observed the *pax Romana*. What could not be tolerated was intolerance, as disruptive to society.

Therefore we may already see by anticipation that the entry into the late Empire of great numbers of barbarian peoples each retaining its own laws as sovereign, and the advent of Christianity with its monopolistic claims to be the sole repository of truth but in practice riven by dissension, cracked the seemingly timeless fabric of the Roman state, thereafter shattered by the loss of Mediterranean control. Yet it must also be added, again by anticipation, that the ideal of unity imposed and achieved by Rome took a millennium to wear off even in the West, and was given a perhaps inadequate expression by the 'Roman Empire' of Charlemagne and Otto the Great, and a much more adequate expression by the Papacy of the twelfth and thirteenth centuries, claiming supreme political as well as spiritual authority. It is in this latter sense that, in the words of R. W. 'Southern, it is not absurd to say that the Roman Empire achieved its fullest development in the thirteenth century', and the same writer points out that Hobbes' gibe in the seventeenth century about the Papacy being the ghost of the Roman Empire sitting crowned upon the grave thereof 'has a greater truth than he realized'.[1] It took in fact the Reformation and its divisions together with the aggressive nationalism that went with them finally to shatter the classical concept of unity expressed in the Middle Ages as Latin Christendom.

The essential point about the 'decline and fall' of the Roman Empire in the West is that all emphasis goes upon 'decline' to the extent that 'fall' becomes problematical, and is certainly not to be marked by any one dramatic event or date, such as the deposition of the last truly Roman Emperor in the West in A.D. 476. The process is a slow and gradual one: it is neither easy nor correct to say of any given stage 'This is the end'. Doubtless the barbarian invasions of the fifth century seemed dramatic enough at the time, but the invaders came, as we have seen, to enjoy rather than destroy the Empire, they were scarcely, as we have yet to see, a new phenomenon when they came, and in any case their final advent had been preceded by at least two centuries of internal imperial decline. There was economic decline, which may well have begun with the end of territorial expansion and the stabilization of the frontiers, for the Roman economy had come to be geared to conquest and expansion. The situation was made worse by recurrent plagues, and also and not least by the disastrous civil wars of the third century A.D. which did much harm to the central political power of Rome. It has thus, for example, been reckoned that there were more than fifty claimants to the imperial throne in the fifty years from 235 to 285 A.D. Partly, without doubt, as a result, the later Empire suffered from an increasing corruption of government. And it suffered also from an increasing shortage both of money and of men.

The shortage of manpower especially mattered most at the weakest point of Empire, the long northern frontier on the rivers

[1] *Western Society and the Church in the Middle Ages*, pp. 24, 25.

Rhine and Danube, the defence of which was most difficult and most expensive, and beyond which lay the barbarian, Germanic tribes, already known and described by Tacitus in the first century A.D. It is thus a truism that the barbarians were always there, and in fact, long before the invasions of the fifth century, there had been a constant and continuous intermingling, a prolonged, peaceful penetration of the Empire by barbarians which caused the complementary, dual process of the barbarization or Germanization of the Romans and the Romanization of the barbarian, Germanic peoples. Nothing could be more important for the future, and it is this above all which makes the decline of the Roman Empire in the West a slow and gradual process, which makes the border-line between the ancient and the medieval worlds so hazy, and which ensured that the origins of medieval and modern Western civilization would be part classical and part Germanic. This intermingling and peaceful penetration by peoples from beyond the pale, therefore, which precedes the events of the fifth century which in part are its culmination, deserves a little closer attention to see how it happened and with what effect. There were, for example, individuals in great number who, like Scotsmen into England in the eighteenth century, crossed the border southwards to find a place in the sun, attracted to the Empire and its higher standard of living, and to make good in its service. There were hostages also, taken continually and on a large scale in war, brought into the Empire to be affected by it and to affect their captors, then being repatriated to spread their influence further. Still more, there were slaves, upon whose backs so much of Roman society rested, captured in war and taken from subject peoples, used throughout the Empire on a very great scale indeed, so that in the fourth century Synesius bishop of Cyrene in North Africa could declare that there was 'scarcely a household of means without a Scythian as cook or house-servant, butler or steward'. But in the event the dual process of the Romanization of the Germans and the Germanization of the Romans was furthered more than any other means by the increasing use in the later Empire of *foederati*, *i.e.*

the use of federate or auxiliary troops, the large-scale recruit-
ment of Germanic tribes for employment by the Roman army.
A policy imposed by lack of manpower was made worse in its
effects by lack of money and the inability of the government to
stem the press of barbarian incursion in the north by force of
arms, so that whole tribes were allowed to settle on and within the
frontiers, and given lands to settle on in exchange for military
service. The *pax Romana* came to depend upon *foederati* and was
also threatened by them, and their leaders came inevitably to
play a part even on the central stage of Roman politics.

By these means by the fifth century the dual process of intermingling and mutual influence had gone very far indeed, and
while the barbarian tribes in their Germanic homelands were
progressively Romanized, within the Empire Rome itself was, as
it were, much diluted. Large numbers of barbarians were settled
there and living under their own laws, the Roman army was
largely composed of *foederati*, and high positions in the Roman
state were held by men of barbarian and Germanic origins.
Perhaps, indeed, nothing shows the extent of this dilution better
than to cite some well-known individual cases. Thus Stilicho,
the 'Roman' general who virtually ruled the Empire at the turn of
the fourth and fifth centuries, was in origin a Vandal. Odoacer
who in 476 deposed Romulus, the last real Roman Emperor in
the West, was similarly the barbarian general of a Roman army.
Theodoric, king of the Ostrogoths, who in his turn in 493 replaced Odoacer in Italy, had formerly been a hostage at Constantinople, and may serve as a classic instance of the Romanized
barbarian since he set himself to preserve Roman culture in his
new Italian kingdom which, indeed, he ruled nominally as the
deputy of the Roman Emperor now at Constantinople. The name
and example of Theodoric may also serve to remind us of figures
from the other side in the process of intermingling, of men like
Cassiodorus and Boethius who, *faute de mieux* in a disintegrating
world, served the new barbarian masters and sought to preserve
what they could of the past in so doing. Boethius we have met
before, who by his transcriptions and translations of classical

texts did much to preserve past learning for the future, and whose own book *On the Consolation of Philosophy* was itself to be a basic text of the Middle Ages (thus it was to be numbered among King Alfred's translations in England). He stands, like Cassiodorus, or Theodoric himself, as a visible, almost knowable link between the old world and the new, and of such men it has been well said that 'They were the first of the great medievals and began to build a new civilization in an attempt to restore the old.'[1]

The dual and gradual process of Germanization and Romanization which so diluted Rome, muted also the effects of the fifth-century invasions by Romanized barbarians when they came. But meanwhile in getting so far we have gone too fast, and there are two important factors yet to be inserted among the causes of the slow decline of Rome. The first is the Emperor Constantine, and the second, closely related, is Christianity. Constantine was sole Emperor of the whole Roman Empire from 324 to his death in 337, and he founded the city of Constantinople as the new capital of Empire, on the site of former Byzantium, in 325. In the circumstances of the time its establishment was a wise and even a necessary move. More convenient than Rome and then as now the meeting place of East and West, Constantinople was a strategic centre for the Empire, and more particularly for the defence of its richer, eastern half and of the frontiers on the Danube to the north and against the Persian Empire to the east. It was also a naval base whose unequalled harbour of the Golden Horn was no less valuable for trade. 'Into her harbours sailed expectantly the vessels of the world's trade, and the winds themselves conspired to bring merchandise to enrich her citizens'—thus Paul the Silentiary. But to us, endowed with the historian's gift (and curse) of hindsight, a principal importance of the foundation of Constantinople in 325 is that it shifted the centre of gravity within the Roman Empire from the declining west to the eastern and Greek half. The division whose beginnings are thus marked will, in the event, never again be healed, for in due course the western half of the once united Empire will fall away, fragmented

[1] R. H. C. Davis, *A History of Medieval Europe* (London, 1957), p. 53.

into barbarian kingdoms and successor states, and, increasingly under the spiritual leadership of Rome, the Eternal City, become the brave new world of Latin Christendom as opposed to Ortho- dox Byzantium. For every reason one should pause at the founda- tion of Constantinople as at one of the great moments in history, and not least because the city then established was also to stand for over a thousand years as the bastion of Christianity in the East against the Infidel. In this sense at least one can see why the fall of Constantinople to the Turks in 1453 could be taken by generations of historians as the end of the Middle Ages and the beginning of something else. One may add also that of all the renaming of ancient places which the modern period has endured in a fatuous attempt to eliminate the past none is more regrettable than the transformation of Constantine's Constantinople, 'the city of the world's desires', into present Istanbul.

The Emperor Constantine was also converted to Christianity, and as a result the new Christian religion became in due course the official religion of the Roman Empire. Perhaps none of the events related and to be related in this chapter are more important as marking the transition from the old world to the new, so that this might be taken in practice as the measure of our epochs rather than the birth of Christ itself (which we principally owe to Bede the Venerable, in seventh-century Northumbria in England). But meanwhile for our mainly secular purposes the adoption of Christianity must be counted amongst the causes of the decline of the Roman Empire, because in the beginning it proved a divisive force. It might be supposed that Christianity with its monopolistic claim to be the one true religion would therefore be cohesive for state and society alike, and so in general in the medie- val future it turned out to be, in spite of the potential friction between secular and ecclesiastical authority which, unknown in the ancient world, was to be realized more in the Latin West than in the Orthodox East. But disunity came first to make the times more out of joint, and, quite apart from the opposition of the old guard of pagan Rome, who saw the Christians as dangerous fanatics, drop-outs and radicals prone to put their tender consciences before social expediency and political necessity alike, the early Church itself was riven by dissensions. And here we must anticipate and look into the future. Of all the pullulating heresies of the early Christian Church, the most important in this respect, as also theologically, was Arianism. On the one hand by maintaining that God the Son is necessarily inferior to God the Father it seemed to attack the essential divinity of Christ, the central tenet of the Christian faith. ' "Great is the only begotten" declared the Catholics, and the Arians rejoined, "But greater is He that begot".'[1] On the other hand, though Arianism was suppressed within the Empire it was adopted by many of the barbarian tribes outside who, as part of the process of their Romanization, received Christianity, errors and all. And so it came about that of the barbarian tribes moving into the Roman Empire in the West in the fifth century, all save the still pagan Franks in Gaul and the Anglo-Saxons in England were not just Christians when they came but Arian heretics, to add one more disruptive element to a disintegrating world.

No narrative of these invasions by the barbarian, Germanic races, themselves pushed forward into the Empire by the Huns behind them, will be attempted here, nor of Attila the Hun, 'the scourge of God', nor of the reconquest attempted by the Emperor Justinian in the Indian summer of the seventh century, though some dates may toll the passing of antiquity, and the results go far to set the pattern of the future. In 378 there occurred the first great defeat of a Roman army by barbarians, in this case Visigoths, at Adrianople. In 410 Rome itself was taken and sacked for the first time by Alaric the Visigoth. In 429 the Vandals reached North Africa, and with it its corn supply to Rome. In about the year 450 the Angles, Saxons and Jutes began to enter Britain, long since evacuated by Roman troops. In 476 in Italy the barbarian Odoacer deposed Romulus Augustus, the last Roman Emperor in the West. By the end of the fifth century the Ostrogoths were settled in Italy, the Franks with the Burgundians

---

[1] Gregory of Nazianus in J. B. Firth, *Constantine the Great* (London, 1905), p. 206.

and the Visigoths in Gaul, the Visigoths also in the Iberian Peninsula, the Vandals in North Africa, the Angles, the Saxons and the Jutes in England. To this the efforts of Justinian in the next century made no difference in the end, save that in Italy, more devastated than ever by his wars, the Lombards replaced the Ostrogoths. Yet these events foretold the future in other ways than by the pattern of settlement. As, for example, the sack of Rome by Alaric the Goth in 410 was the inspiration of St. Augustine's *City of God*, one of the most influential of all books in the Middle Ages and thereafter, so the ruin of Italy and the physical destruction of so much of the past within it was the context alike of the Papacy of St. Gregory the Great and the monastic Rule of St. Benedict. And if all else failed, the impact of the Emperor Justinian upon Italy is still visible in Byzantine churches and the incomparable mosaics of S. Vitale at Ravenna.

To the pattern of settlement outlined above there were to be further changes, not least by the later incursions of the Vikings, the Magyars and the Moslem Arabs, and with the last of these we shall do best to deal now, for the Moslems not only wrested the Iberian Peninsula from the emergent West and seriously depleted the Eastern Empire of Byzantium so far untouched, but also in so doing set the medieval scene of a Latin Christendom and its two great neighbours, each for long infinitely more powerful, the Eastern Empire and the Moslem world. Any account of the origins of the latter, and of the great Moslem expansion of the seventh and eighth centuries which created it, must necessarily start with Mohammed and in Arabia—Arabia Deserta, the desert places between the Red Sea, the Persian Gulf and the Indian Ocean. A desolate region peopled by nomadic tribesmen ('I and my brother go against my cousin: I and my cousin go against the stranger'. And again, 'My enemy's enemy is my friend'), changed if at all only yesterday by the advent of Cadillacs and oil, then lying across the trade routes of the world, then therefore, as now, strategically important and subject to foreign influences, especially in the more settled north and south —which last account for the Jewish and Christian overtones in the religion which Mohammed founded. Mohammed himself, who was born about 570, was at first a man of no especial note, a trader and a native of the trading city of Mecca. The call to religion came to him only at about the age of forty, and in 622, his preaching having met with small success in Mecca, he moved to Medina. His success and the spread of his religion spring from this date and event, which the Moslems call *Hejirah*, and reckon their years from it as Christians from the birth of Christ. Eight years later Mohammed was able to return in triumph to Mecca as the acknowledged leader of a new religion, and he died in 632.

The religion which Mohammed founded is the faith of Islam, the word meaning in Arabic submission to the will of God. Those who follow it, the believers, are Moslems, literally those who submit themselves to the will of God. And the holy writ of Islam is the Koran, the Moslem bible, composed by Mohammed himself and containing all that could be found and remembered of his words and teaching after his death. Mohammed was and is the Prophet, not divine but one who under divine inspiration proclaims the truth and the will of God. ' "I awoke", said Mohammed, "from my sleep, and it was as if they had written a message in my heart. I went out of the cave, and while I was on the mountain I heard a voice saying: O Mohammed, thou art Allah's apostle and I am Gabriel".'[1] Hence the cry of the muezzin from the minarets to this day—'There is no God but Allah, and Mohammed is his Prophet'. Islam, like Christianity, is monotheistic, and the One God is Allah, the Jewish and the Christian God—which, together with innumerable lesser echoes of Christianity, helps to explain the mixture of fascination and repulsion with which Islam was regarded by the West throughout the Middle Ages and beyond.[2] But in Islam there was no Christ, or rather, no divinity of Christ, He being a prophet like any other, and therefore no Incarnation and no Trinity. Nor was

[1] Ibn Ishak (d. 768), in Tor Andrae, *Mohammed, the Man and his Faith* (London, 1936), p. 57.
[2] See R. W. Southern, *Western Views of Islam in the Middle Ages* (Harvard, 1962).

there any priesthood, all Believers being equally members of the Islamic faith and of Moslem society which made no distinction between Church and State. Mohammed and his successors the Caliphs (the deputies of the Prophet) wielded both secular and spiritual authority, and Islam was thus a theocracy. The West will come to be plagued by the text 'Render unto Caesar the things that are Caesar's, and unto God the things that are God's'. Not so in Islam: 'The Apostle of God said, Whoso obeys me, obeys God, and whoso rebels against me, rebels against God. Whoso obeys the ruler, obeys me: and whoso rebels against the ruler, rebels against me'.

Though Mohammed had preached, and the Koran proclaims, the necessity of holy war (*jihad*), and though he died in the preparation of a military expedition into Syria, the dramatic expansion of Islam far beyond the confines of Arabia, which, in other words, is the conquest of a vast Empire by the Arabs in the name of Allah, begins only after the Prophet's death. That event was followed by disputes about the succession to the leadership, the Caliphate, and by the falling away of some of the tribes previously converted, and it appears that it was the reconversion of the apostates by force of arms that led on inexorably to the overrunning of neighbouring territories, and then to an extraordinary sequence of conquests in every direction (Map 2). Though the spread of Christianity was not always peaceful, and though the Latin Church was later to adopt the concept of holy war, there has been nothing comparable to this in the annals of Christendom and the West. By 634, two years after Mohammed's death, the subjugation of Arabia itself was virtually complete. Six years later, by 640, the former Byzantine provinces of Syria and Palestine had been taken, while, even more remarkable, at the same time the conquest of the neighbouring Persian Empire was begun, to be completed by about 650. 'Believers! wage war against such of the infidels as are your neighbours, and let them find you rigorous'—thus the Koran; and from Persia the Sons of the Prophet swept on to Bokhara and Samarkand (which they reached in 712) and onwards into India. Meanwhile, to the south, Egypt, another province of Byzantium, was overrun (Cairo in 640), and from Egypt westward the whole of the North African littoral by the early eighth century. Thence, also in the early eighth century, they moved into the Iberian Peninsula, conquered in the main between 711 and 720, and were thus established in the emergent West. Before the initial impetus was spent they had raided deep into southern Gaul, now Frankia, to be stopped in this direction by Charles Martel in what proved to be the decisive battle of Poitiers, and at the other end of the Mediterranean, as a foretaste of the future, had twice besieged Constantinople, in 673 and 717, albeit unsuccessfully. As a postscript, the Moslems, by then a sea-power dominating the Mediterranean (once *mare nostrum* to the Romans) took Byzantine Sicily in the course of the ninth century, and thereafter moved up even into Italy, at one time threatening Rome herself and sacking St. Benedict's monastery of Monte Cassino.

The pace of the Arab, Moslem conquests is no less remarkable than their extent, and the whole achievement becomes more remarkable still when we reflect that it was made chiefly at the expense of the two greatest powers of the known world, the Byzantine and Persian Empires, and that the conquests included some of the most prosperous areas and principal centres of civilization—Ctesiphon, the Persian capital, Rakka and Rai, Jerusalem and Antioch, Damascus and Alexandria. And yet the most remarkable thing of all is that the Arab world thus created from the Pyrenees to Persia and far beyond has lasted, and that, with the exception of Sicily, Spain and Portugal, the conquests of the Sons of the Prophet made principally in the seventh and eighth centuries remain Arabian to this day. To explain this phenomenon, as to explain the initial conquests and expansion, would require another book than this which is a history of the West, but one prime factor must be emphasized since it was itself to have an immense influence upon Latin Christendom. That factor is the brilliant civilization which the Arabs made and, with it, their faculty of Islamization. 'It was the Arabization of the conquered provinces', writes Bernard Lewis, 'rather than their

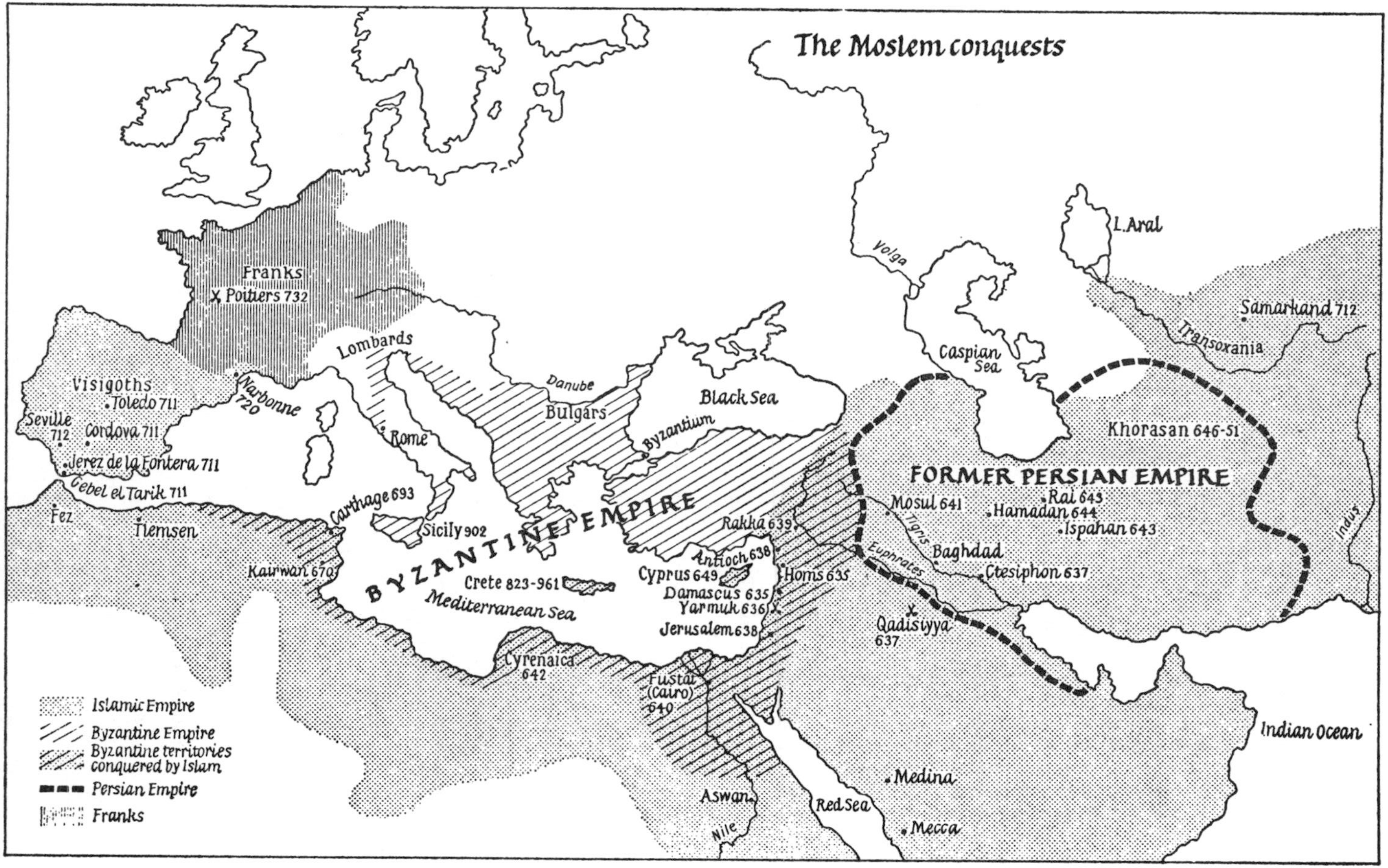

The Moslem conquests

Samarkand 712

Transoxania

L. Aral

Khorasan 646-51

Amu

Caspian Sea

FORMER PERSIAN EMPIRE

Mosul 641
Hamadan 644
Rai 643
Ispahan 643
Baghdad
Ctesiphon 637
Tigris
Euphrates

Volga

Indian Ocean

Medina.
Mecca.
Red Sea
Qadisiyya 637

Black Sea

Byzantium

Rakka 639
Aleppo 639
Homs 635
Damascus 635
Cyprus 649
Yarmuk 636
Jerusalem 638
Fustat (Cairo) 640
Aswan
Nile

Bulgars

BYZANTINE EMPIRE

Danube

Crete 823-961
Mediterranean Sea
Cyrenaica 642

Lombards

Rome

Sicily 902

Carthage 693

Kairwan 670

Franks
X Poitiers 732

Narbonne 720

Visigoths
Toledo 711
Cordova 711
Seville 712
Jerez de la Frontera 711
Gebel et-Tarik 711
Fez
Tlemcen

▒▒ Islamic Empire
/// Byzantine Empire
╱╱ Byzantine territories conquered by Islam
▬▬ Persian Empire
░▒░ Franks

MAP 2

military conquest that is the true wonder of the Arab expansion'.[1]
The contrast between the overrunning of the classical East and
West is often pointed by historians. In the West the barbarians
came part-Romanized and eager to be fully so, adopting the
language and religion of Rome and whatever they could of a
classical culture they admired. Not so the Arabs, who came as
outright conquerors in the name of Allah, retaining their faith
and their language to create, with copious borrowings from Greek
learning which they themselves developed, an advanced and
glittering civilization of their own and to make an Islamic
world. What we in the West owe to that Arabian civilization can
scarcely be calculated, though it will be touched on at a later
stage,[2] but meanwhile it seduced the subject peoples. Bearing
in mind that in so far as the Arabs occupied some of the most
developed and advanced areas of the ancient world, so also they
occupied some of the main centres of the early Church—the
bishoprics of Antioch, Jerusalem and Alexandria rivalling Rome
in pre-eminence: North Africa whence came the desert fathers—
and that those areas became and have remained ever since
predominantly Moslem, we may listen with both sympathy and
understanding to the outraged voice of a Christian lamenting
in Spanish and Moslem Cordova in the mid-ninth century:
'Many of my co-religionists read the poetry and tales of the
Arabs, study the writings of Muhammadan theologians and
philosophers, not in order to refute them, but to learn how to
express themselves in Arabic with greater correctness and ele-
gance. Where can one find today a layman who reads the Latin
commentaries on the Holy Scriptures? Who among them studies
the Gospels, the Prophets, the Apostles? All the young Christians
noted for their gifts know only the language and literature of
the Arabs, read and study with zeal Arabic books, building up
great libraries of them at enormous cost and loudly proclaiming
everywhere that this literature is worthy of admiration. Among
thousands of us there is hardly one who can write a passable

---

[1] *The Arabs in History* (London, 1958 edition), p. 132.
[2] *See* Chapter XI.

Latin letter to a friend, but innumerable are those who can express themselves in Arabic and compose poetry in that language with greater art than the Arabs themselves.'[1]

In this chapter we have seen the settlement of the barbarian, Germanic tribes in the western Roman Empire, the survival of that Empire in the East, though much reduced by Moslem conquest, and the establishment of a new Islamic world. In so doing we have dealt, from the Western point of view, mainly with negative factors, with decline and destruction. The positive achievements, quick and real even in these earliest centuries of the emergent West, have yet to be inserted. Yet even so we have begun to witness at least the beginnings of the transition from the old world to the new, the origins of the 'Middle Ages' in the West, and therefore of modern western society. Exactly where the dividing line comes must be a matter for debate, if indeed it can be drawn, for only in England does there seem to be a clean break between Roman Britain and the future. But at this point we must already refer to the thesis of the late Belgian scholar, Henri Pirenne, even though to judge its validity requires a knowledge of future events, of what happens next, as well as an appreciation of those early medieval achievements just mentioned but not yet discussed. For Pirenne the climacteric in the West was not the Germanic invasions themselves, the 'decline and fall of Rome' in the conventional sense, but the expansion of Islam. 'It was the end of the classic tradition. It was the beginning of the Middle Ages.'[2] Setting down his conclusions at the end of his book, *Mohammed and Charlemagne*, which he finished in 1935, and just before his death, he wrote:[3] '(1) The Germanic invasions destroyed neither the Mediterranean unity of the ancient world, nor what may be regarded as the truly essential features of the Roman culture as it still existed in the 5th century, at a

[1] Quoted by Bernard Lewis, *op. cit.*, p. 123.
[2] Henri Pirenne, *Mohammed and Charlemagne* (trans. B. Miall, London, 1939), p. 164.
[3] As above, pp. 284–5.

time when there was no longer an Emperor in the West . . . The Orient was the fertilizing factor: Constantinople, the centre of the world. In 600 the physiognomy of the world was not different in quality from that which it had revealed in 400. (2) The cause of the break with the tradition of antiquity was the rapid and unexpected advance of Islam. The result of this advance was the final separation of East from West and the end of Mediterranean unity . . . The Western Mediterranean, having become a Musulman lake, was no longer the thoroughfare of commerce and of thought which it had always been . . . The West was blockaded and forced to live upon its own resources. For the first time in history the axis of life was shifted northwards from the Mediterranean . . . The development was completed in 800 by the constitution of the new Empire [*i.e.* that of Charlemagne] . . . the manifest proof that it had broken with the old Empire which continued to exist in Constantinople.'

Pirenne's book must be read in its own right, but it is probable that most historians would nowadays subscribe to his insistence upon continuity in the fifth and sixth centuries and be reluctant to proclaim an absolute end to the Roman Empire in the West as the immediate result of the barbarian invasions. There is less agreement with his substitution of a clean break in the eighth century as the result of the Moslem conquests which for him, through the loss of the Western Mediterranean and with it trade and contact with the East, turned the West in upon itself, moved the centre of gravity from the commercial and Romanized south to the new Germanic north, and caused the emergence of a new, feudal society based upon land, under the leadership of a new Frankish, Carolingian dynasty. Meanwhile the Papacy, unrivalled now through the fall of Antioch, Jerusalem and Alexandria, and despairing of help from Constantinople against Lombards and Moslems in Italy, threw in its lot with the West and sought help from the Carolingians and Charlemagne. Grand patterns such as this are suspect to lesser men, and are also, perhaps rightly, out of fashion now if only because history, like life itself, tends to be untidy. But certainly the society of

Charlemagne's kingdom of the Franks in former Roman Gaul, to which we must next turn, though still straining with some success after the classical past to which it saw itself the heir, was very different from anything that had gone before.

CHAPTER II

The Franks and Charlemagne's Empire

The context of the future having thus been set, we turn to the Franks to whom much of that future will belong. For though in the annals of Western European civilization the Franks may have been somewhat slow starters by the standards of the Angles, the Saxons and the Jutes in England, they were to make of France (whose name, via Frankia, is derived from them), and northern France especially, the cultural centre of the medieval world, while more immediately they will produce both the Empire of the Franks and the person of Charlemagne. Like the Anglo-Saxons, they were in origin of West Germanic stock, and had already achieved some form of settled agricultural society when they entered the Roman Empire, unlike their East Germanic kinsmen, the Goths and Vandals, Burgundians and Lombards, who were still nomadic when they came. Like the new English also, and unlike the East German tribes who were Christians but Arian heretics, the Franks were pagan on arrival, and for over a century afterwards, and thereby hangs a tale.

They entered the Roman province of Gaul from the north, settling first in the fourth century in modern Belgium and along the middle Rhine. Thence they conquered and expanded southward until within a century they were the masters of all Gaul, their progress being marked by their great and final victory over the Visigoths in 507 and by the collapse of the Burgundian kingdom in 534. The kings of this earliest stage of Frankish history are known as Merovingians, from Merovius, the name of one of them, and the Merovingian period extends to 751. By far the most important Merovingian to emerge, quite literally from the mists of time, is Clovis, who reigned from 481 to 511. Though to speak of France as yet is seriously to anticipate, it has been said of Clovis that without him 'Gaul would not have become France',[1] and in this respect even his name is important. In his own language it meant 'battle of glory', which marks the man and his times, but from its Latin form, Chlodovechus, the French form, Louis, is derived, and though it is too late now, by long-established habit, to call him anything but Clovis, he is in a real sense the first of the long line of French kings Louis. Clovis 'lived and died a Frankish chieftain, a warrior of the Heroic Age, a man of blood and a seeker after gold',[2] yet the most important event of his reign, notwithstanding the bloodshed and the wars, was his conversion to Christianity, and Christianity in its Catholic, orthodox and Roman form. This event, which took place in 496 and was followed by the conversion of his kingdom (or rather of his pagan Frankish followers, since Roman Gaul had long since been Christian), is another of the great moments in history, but it may seem entirely characteristic of this marvellously personal age that it was the direct result of a vow taken in a hard-pressed moment on the battlefield and of the persistent persuasion of his wife Clothild, a Catholic, Burgundian princess. The ceremony took place and the sacrament was conferred at Rheims by St. Remigius the bishop. 'The streets were over-shadowed with coloured hangings, the churches adorned with white hangings, the baptistry was set in order, the smoke of incense spread in clouds, perfumed tapers gleamed, the whole church about the place of baptism was filled with the divine fragrance.... Like a new Constantine,[3] he [Clovis] moved forward to the water, to blot out the former leprosy, to wash away in this new stream the foul stains borne from old days. As he entered to be baptized the saint of God spoke these words with eloquent lips: "Meekly bow thy proud head, Sicamber; adore

---

[1] Ferdinand Lot, *La Naissance de la France*, Paris, 1948, p. 44.
[2] J. H. Wallace-Hadrill, *The Barbarian West 400–1000* (London, 1952), p. 75.
[3] NB. the deliberate invocation of the historical parallel.

that which thou hast burned, burn that which thou hast adored".
. . .'¹ Thus Gregory of Tours, the prime source for Merovingian
Gaul, though writing about a century later, and we may share
some of his enthusiasm whether or not we share his faith.
The reception of Clovis and his Franks into the Catholic and
Roman Church points the direction of the future and is doubled
in importance because of the future pre-eminence of the Franks.
Immediately it welded Clovis' dominions into something more
resembling a unity, for in a world not only overrun by uncouth
barbarians but also threatened by Arian heretics, it gave him the
support of the surviving Gallo-Romans, his hitherto reluctant
subjects, clinging to their faith as a symbol of vanishing
'*Romanitas*', as it gave him the support also of the Gallic bishops.
When in 507 Clovis marched against the Arian Alaric II, king
of the Visigoths, he did so with the blessing of the Church and
under the protection of St. Martin of Tours, which he himself
had sought. And Clovis had the victory, slaying Alaric in the
fight by his own hand. 'Thou hast girded me, O Lord, with
strength unto the battle; Thou hast subdued under me those
that rose up against me. Thou hast also made mine enemies turn
their backs upon me, and thou hast destroyed them that hate me'.²

When he died in 511 at the age of forty-five, Clovis by his
victories against the Visigoths and Burgundians had more or less
subdued all Gaul: he had thus founded the kingdom of the
Franks; and he had made it Christian. We may go so far, but we
may scarcely go further. The territory with which we are dealing
is the former Roman province of Gaul, not yet France, comprising
not only modern France but also the Low Countries, part of
Switzerland and part of Germany (Map 3). The Germans thus,
as well as the French, can claim to be the heirs of the Franks, so
that Charlemagne's capital is Aachen to the one and Aix-la-
Chapelle to the other. In every direction we have a very long
way to go. The Merovingian 'kingdom' was so in little more

¹ Gregory of Tours, *History of the Franks*, trans. O. M. Dalton (Oxford,
1927) ii, 69.
² *Ibid.*, p. 76 (Ps. xvii, 40–1).

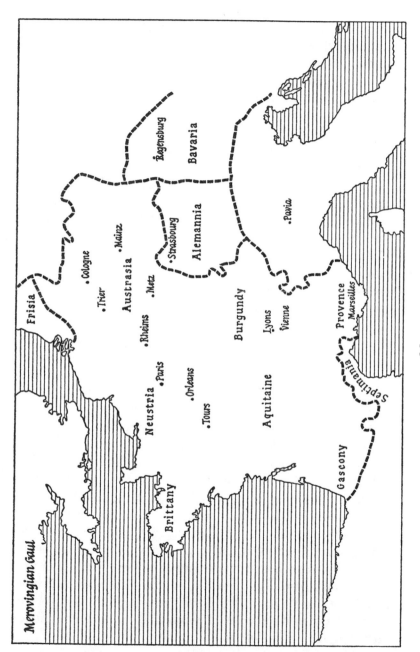

Merovingian Gaul

Frisia

Cologne
Trier
Austrasia
Rheims
Mainz
Metz
Strasbourg
Alemannia
Regensburg
Bavaria

Neustria
Paris
Orleans
Tours

Burgundy
Lyons
Vienne
Pavia

Brittany

Aquitaine

Provence
Marseilles

Septimania

Gascony

MAP 3

than name. All the Roman apparatus of the state had gone save for those scattered fragments preserved and utilized by the bishops seated as survivors of the past in metropolis and city. There was no civil service, no royal officials, even, worth the name, no standing army, no one unifying law, no central public law courts, no system of taxation. Taxes indeed were regarded as immoral by the Franks: in early Germanic society the king, like any other lord but more so, was regarded as a giver rather than a taker by his followers, and the largesse he distributed should come from his own substance and the tribute and loot exacted from his enemies—from which we may see that the doctrine that the king should live of his own is not the invention of English seventeenth-century Parliamentarians but has a very ancient lineage indeed, though seldom practical in the Middle Ages when taxes to the king are one of the earliest symptoms of the reviving state. The kingship of the Merovingians, even at their strongest, was personal not territorial, a lordship, as yet little developed, over persons rather than land, derived from a tribal past and from the fundamental German institution of the war-band (*comitatus*), the aristocratic company of the war-leader and his companions (*comites*), described by Tacitus in his *Germania* in the first century A.D. and prominent in all heroic literature, fighting together on the battlefield and roistering in the hall. This is the world of Beowulf and the Nibelungs. Crude, coarse and irresponsible, largely the creation of the monarch's strong right arm and those of his warrior retainers, early Germanic kingship yet had, even before and even after the advent of Christianity, an element of mysticism, a lasting touch of pagan divinity, symbolized in the case of the Merovingians by their long fair hair, the sign of their regality, and transmitted by inheritance by kin-right and royal blood. Nothing shows the strength of this real yet supernatural element better than that the Merovingian kings remained on the throne of the Franks until 751, long after they had become ineffective and effete, with all their power in practice wielded by their chief functionaries, the Mayors of the Palace.

Christianity, when it came to the Franks and their Merovingian kings after the baptism of Clovis, may seem for long to have sat lightly upon them, or, rather, they moulded it to their own desires and needs, seeking the God of Battles rather than the God of Love. Thus Wallace-Hadrill writes: 'The Franks had no hesitation in bringing their thank-offerings to the shrines of miracle-working Gaulish saints such as St. Martin [of Tours], under whom they had won their battles and amassed their treasures; and no sense of moral obloquy or incongruity pursued them when they left the shrines to cut the throats of unloved kinsmen.'[1] In the end the Catholic Church, though often debased by them, will be the principal agent in the civilizing of these rude warriors now lording it over Gaul, as it was also a principal agent in the reconciliation of the Gallo-Romans to the despised lordship of the Franks until the two by mutual influence and intermingling become indistinguishable. But both processes took time, and the contempt of the Gallo-Romans needed, and rightly needed, more than Clovis' conversion to overcome it. Sidonius Apollinaris, a gentleman of the old school who wrote in the fifth century, has nothing but disdain, whenever he can bring himself to mention it, for the uncouth barbarian, who smelt as the result of smearing rancid butter in his hair and other disagreeable habits. 'I am fain to call your eyes and ears happy,' he wrote to a friend more fortunately placed without barbarian neighbours, 'happy too your nose, for you don't have a reek of garlic and foul onions discharged upon you at early morning from ten breakfasts'.[2] More than a century later, the most striking feature of Merovingian society to emerge from the pages of Gregory of Tours is its duality, the almost complete dichotomy between the surviving Gallo-Romans on the one hand, degenerate no doubt, but still tenaciously clinging to 'Romanitas' and going through the motions of civilized Roman living, and, on the other, the Frankish kings and warlords, casually doing each other to

[1] *Op. cit.*, p. 78.
[2] Sidonius Apollinaris, Poems and Letters, trans. W. B. Anderson, (London, 1936), i, 213.

death in a barbaric manner lacking all finesse. The textbooks rightly tell us that a new society and a new civilization will emerge out of the blend of Rome and Germany: by reading the sources of this period one can see the process happening before one's eyes in terms of persons and social habits, blunderings and misconceptions, torments and anguish. Bede in England has the splendid story of King Sigeberht of Essex who was slain by his own kinsmen because, under the influence of new-found Christianity, he took to forgiving his enemies in flagrant contravention of the barbarian's code. 'When they were asked why they did it, they could make no reply except that they were angry with the king and hated him because he was too ready to pardon his enemies, calmly forgiving them for the wrongs they had done him, as soon as they asked his pardon. Such was the crime for which he met his death, that he had devoutly observed the gospel precepts'.[1] A writer in seventh-century Gaul, the Pseudo-Fredegar who continued the history of Gregory of Tours, seems to place innocently and nicely, side by side in one passing sentence, surviving Roman hygiene and barbarian morals: 'On the same day when [king] Dagobert was preparing to leave Losne for the council at Chalon, before dawn, as he entered the bath, he ordered the assassination of Bradulf, the uncle of his brother Charibert'.[2]

Frankia after the death of Clovis was torn by civil wars, for the kingship, being personal, was divided among the sons or descendants of the dead king like any other Frankish property. Though the later Merovingians produced one great figure in the person of Dagobert (629–639) who happened to succeed to the whole inheritance, anarchy again followed him, with the kingdom threatening to fall apart into the provinces and arbitrary divisions of Austrasia, Neustria and Burgundy, while Aquitaine in the south-west was already in practice independent, and the

---

[1] Bede, *Ecclesiastical History of the English People*, ed. B. Colgrave and R. A. B. Mynors (Oxford Medieval Texts, 1969), p. 285.
[2] Quoted by Robert Latouche, *Caesar to Charlemagne* (trans. J. Nicholson, London, 1968), p. 264.

kings themselves were increasingly *rois fainéants*, ineffective puppets manœuvred by rival noble factions and their power in the hands of their chief official, the Mayor of the Palace (*major domus*). In this violent world of high but personal politics, where the stakes were death by assassination or wealth beyond the dreams of avarice, there emerged to pre-eminence the house and family of the Arnulfings, the descendants of St. Arnulf, bishop of Metz (d. 641), as mayors of the palace in Austrasia, one of whom, Pepin of Herstal or Pepin the Young, managed to gather the government of all Neustria and Burgundy as well as Austrasia into his hand. When he died in 714 his son, Charles Martel or Charles the Hammer, albeit illegitimate (by a concubine called Alpais), was able to succeed him as the effective ruler of the kingdom, and he it was who in 732 near Poitiers defeated a Moslem army invading southern Gaul from Spain. And here we pause, for this, with hindsight, is generally regarded as the decisive battle which stopped in the West the hitherto invincible advance of Islam, and the victory was won by Charles Martel, the leader of the Franks and the founder of the Carolingian dynasty which takes its name from him.

But Charles Martel was not yet King of the Franks when he died in 741. That fateful elevation was achieved by his son and successor in the mayoralty, Pepin III, the Short, who, having first obtained the opinion of Pope Zacharias 'that it was better that he who wielded the power should be called king than he who remained without royal power;'[1] was crowned thus with Papal approval and by the hands of St. Boniface in 751 at Soissons, the last Merovingian king, Childeric III, being deposed and sent to a monastery, the tonsure removing his royal locks. 'Samuel had anointed David king in the place of Saul, and so the Church, aware of the parallel, anointed Pepin and his successors. The Franks were the Chosen of the Lord and their armies the columns of Israel'[2]. Indeed the occasion and the method employed by

---

[1] *Annales Regni Francorum*, ed. F. Kurze (Hannover, 1895), p. 8; quoted by Latouche, *Caesar to Charlemagne*, p. 323.

[2] Wallace-Hadrill, *The Barbarian West*, p. 97.

Pepin to carry out his *coup d'état* of 751 fairly bristle with significance. To depose the Merovingians, however effete, and to deprive them of their blood-right, was a serious matter, and to raise up himself and his house in their stead required some element of legitimacy and divinity to replace that which was broken. That element Pepin obtained from the Church, who, in the person of St. Boniface, not only crowned but anointed him as king in 751, while three years later the new Pope, Stephen II, further anointed and consecrated him king, together with his two sons Charles and Carloman—'Stephen the Pope . . . consecrated him in the honour of the royal dignity by a sacred anointing, and with him his two sons'[1]. Though there were then special circumstances and though there will afterwards be further developments, it is on this double occasion of 751 and 754 that the sacring of kings begins, to be carried over also to other nations, and with it the nature of kingship changes from the comparatively irresponsible Germanic lordship of a war-leader wielding a personal regality over his followers to the responsible concept of Christian kingship. King by the Grace of God (*Rex Dei Gratia*), anointed with holy oil and consecrated in the sacrament of his coronation as a bishop was consecrated, the monarch will henceforth be part priest as well as king, *rex et sacerdos*, the defender of the Church and of the Faith, as much responsible for the soul's health of his subjects as for their material well-being and his own. And though the radically reforming Papacy of the eleventh and twelfth centuries will come to regret and deny the sacerdotal element in kingship, it will remain—

> Not all the water in the rough, rude sea
> Can wash the balm from an anointed king

The voice of Shakespeare speaks for the 'modern' period, the England of the Tudors and the Stuarts, the France of Louis XIV and beyond.

There are other implications of the events of 751 and 754, and

[1] *Annales Regni Francorum*, p. 13; Latouche, *op. cit.*, p. 324.

we may reach some of them by quoting Shakespeare again through
the mouth of Richard II—

> ... no hand of blood and bone
> Can grip the sacred handle of our sceptre,
> Unless he do profane, steal or usurp.

By unction and by blessing the Church and the Papacy legiti-
mized the usurpation of the Carolingians, and greatly strengthened
—indeed, virtually created—their claim to the kingship thereby.
Thus Pope Stephen II in 754, blessing in their turn the sons of
Pepin 'with the grace of the Holy Spirit', bound the Franks 'by
an interdiction and the threat of excommunication that they
should never in future presume to choose a king sprung from the
loins of any save those whom the divine piety has deigned to
exalt and has purposed to confirm and consecrate'[1]—*i.e.* the
Carolingians. So too, more generally, the power and status of
kingship were greatly increased by the monarch's new sacerdotal
role as a vicar of God on earth, and his authority raised thereby
to the level of theocracy. Yet also, to follow another train of
thought, a limit has been set to that authority, since the responsibilities of Christian Kingship bring standards to be judged by,
and the Christian King must be subject to Divine Law of
which the Church is the custodian. Similarly, a third element,
that of the Church, has been brought into the making, which
involves the selection of kings, hitherto created only by blood-
right and that recognition of the most suitable member of the
royal kin which is the 'elective' element in early kingship.
Finally, if within the kingdom of the Franks Church and State,
regnum and *sacerdotium*, were henceforth to be brought ever
closer to the point of being almost indistinguishable, the events
of 751 and 754 have a further significance of great moment as
marking the beginning of a lasting alliance between the Papacy
and the Franks which will bring about, amongst other things,

[1] *Monumenta Germ. hist. scripta rerum Merov.*, i, ed. W. Arndt (Hannover,
1884), pp. 464–5; quoted Latouche, p. 325.

the Empire of Charlemagne. It was a very real alliance, of this world as well as the next, signalized as when in 755 and again in 756, to carry out his part of the bargain of 751 and 754, King Pepin marched into Italy to defend the Pope against the Lombards, and made over to him the government of what will be the Papal States. And the further significance of these events is that the Papacy, threatened in Italy and despairing of help from Constantinople and the surviving Roman Empire of Byzantium, is perforce turning more and more towards the new, barbarian West, dominated by the Franks but of which it could claim the leadership through the apocryphal 'Donation of Constantine'.[1] Add the close and special relationship of the Papacy with new Christian and Catholic England, add the papally orientated reform of the Frankish Church now put in hand by the Carolingians, and one begins to see the emergence of a Latin Christendom whose distinctive qualities also mean a widening break between East and West.

The next phase of Western European history in every sense, and the consummation of the Carolingian succession in 751, is the age of Charlemagne, *i.e.* Charles, and subsequently Charles the Great, eldest son of Pepin III. In his reign (768–814) the concept of Christian Kingship was both enhanced and put into practice at a new level of endeavour, all Latin Christendom save Britain was both brought under his rule and greatly enlarged in extent (Map 4), the whole was ruled with a new degree of efficiency in administration and military techniques a world away from the 'despotism tempered by assassination' of Merovingian Gaul with which this chapter began, and the whole was crowned, on Christmas Day 800, with the imperial diadem, and acclaimed, in a sense we shall have to discuss, as 'the revival of the Roman Empire' in the West. One of the most recent and distinguished historians of this period is the author of a short, sharp paper entitled 'Charlemagne's Failure', but he has also written, in the preface to the volume of English translations of his work which contains it, that 'What the Carolingians, above all

[1] See below, p. 72.

The Empire of Charlemagne

Slavonic Peoples

Serbs

Bohemians

Avars

Wiltzi

Sorabi

Carinthia

Saxony

Paderborn

Fritzlar

Thuringia

Fulda

Regensburg

Bavaria

Aquileia

Cologne

Mainz

Milan

Venice

Frisia

Utrecht

Maestricht

Aachen

Alemannia

Kingdom of

Perugia

Strasbourg

Pavia

the Lombards

Rome

Austrasia

Rheims

Burgundy

Neustria

Paris

Lyons

Vienne

Orleans

Provence

Tours

Aquitaine

Bourges

Gothia

Brittany

Vasconia

Spanish

March

MAP 4

Charlemagne, attempted and for a time achieved is of fundamental importance. Without a serious knowledge of the Carolingian era there can be no proper understanding of the Western Middle Ages, or even of the centuries habitually grouped together under the title "the modern period".[1]

Any account of Charlemagne should probably begin, as he himself, a true Frank, would probably have wished, with his conquests. They begin in Italy where, like Pepin III before him, he was requested by the Papacy to intervene against the Lombards, in this case by Pope Hadrian I in 773. But Charlemagne went further than his father and, not content with victory, annexed the Lombardic kingdom and proclaimed himself King of the Lombards as well as King of the Franks. In this it is impossible not to see the start of a chain of events which continues to the nineteenth century. Charlemagne's greatest military achievement, the conquest of Saxony, occupied altogether over thirty years from 772, when the outcome was probably not envisaged, to 804. 'No war undertaken by the Franks', wrote Einhard, Charlemagne's contemporary biographer, 'was so protracted or so fierce, and so full of toil and hardship.'[2] The result was not only the huge extension of the Kingdom of the Franks eastwards into Germany from the Low Countries to the Elbe, but an equal extension of Christendom, for the heathen Saxons were forcibly converted in a devastating exercise in militant Christianity. Since this is an aspect of Christian kingship unlikely to commend itself to the modern reader, it should be noted that there were those contemporaries who protested also. Alcuin of York, scholar and intellectual, a principal adviser of Charlemagne, head of his palace school and one who devoted his life to the conversion of the heathen Germans, dared to criticize the methods of his master. 'One ought ... to recognize', he wrote, 'that faith comes of free-will, not of compulsion. How can

[1] F. L. Ganshof, *The Carolingians and the Frankish Monarchy: Studies in Carolingian History* (translated by Janet Sondheimer, London, 1971). The essay in question, first published in 1947, is at pp. 256–60.

[2] Einhard, *Life of the Emperor Karl the Great* (trans. William Glaister, London, 1877), p. 39.

a man be compelled to believe what he does not believe? You may force a man to the font, but not to the Faith'.[1] Noble, and, one may add, timeless words, but Charlemagne had the alternative answer which worked not a wit less successfully than that other but contrasting notable extension of Christianity, into Anglo-Saxon England, carried out in peace and with marked humanity two centuries earlier.

Eastwards in what will be Germany Charlemagne also annexed the duchy of Bavaria in 788 and in the next decade pushed further along the Danube, driving out the Avars and sending Christian missionaries and Bavarian colonists among the subject Slavs. The eastern 'march' or frontier district of Bavaria then established will be the future Austria, and the south-eastern expansion of Germany begins at this time with obvious effects upon the future. Yet Charlemagne's most lastingly famous wars, albeit the least successful, were waged southwards into Moslem Spain. Here the campaign of 778 was a failure and ended in disaster when the rearguard of the retreating Frankish army, crossing the Pyrenees, was ambushed and decimated by the Christian Basques in the pass of Roncevaux. Amongst those slain, Einhard informs us, was Roland, Count of the Breton March, and here, then, is the germ of the later epic of the 'Song of Roland', destined to echo with the sound of his horn down through the Middle Ages. But in the event, Charlemagne was able to establish, south of the Pyrenees, his Spanish March, the future county of Barcelona, and though in this direction his effort, like others of his achievements, may seem premature, it is not entirely fanciful to see in it the beginnings of a Western recovery against Islam, the beginnings of the Christian reconquest of Moslem Spain, and a foretaste of the Crusade, of Holy War against the Infidel.

If Charlemagne's conquests and campaign against the Infidel are one manifestation of his concept of Christian Kingship, the Carolingian Renaissance, the revival of ancient learning, which

[1] Quoted by H. St. L. B. Moss, *The Birth of the Middle Ages* (Oxford, 1935), p. 227.

began in his reign and under his inspiration, is another, with no less important or less lasting results. The two, indeed, are intimately connected, for if the Franks were a chosen people, 'the Christian people' (*populus Christianus*) and 'the people of God' (*populus Dei*), as in official and intellectual phraseology they were increasingly becoming, and their righteousness vindicated in victorious wars against the heathen, so must they be educated or, more especially, educated in the faith, both to be worthy of their role and to fulfil it. For this, above all, an educated clergy was required. Thus Charlemagne's Renaissance was, like the man himself, severely practical as well as inspired: it was Christian-orientated; and it was also, so to speak, state-directed, through the necessary agency of the Church, of whose own Carolingian reformation it was also an integral part.[1] And though it is tempting to feel a satisfying sense of inevitability about a rebirth of learning and a revival of culture coinciding with the re-established political stability of the Carolingian age, the Carolingian Renaissance was artificial rather than spontaneous in the sense that the required scholars simply did not then exist within the Kingdom of the Franks, and had to be imported. Thus Peter of Pisa, the grammarian, and Paul the deacon were brought from subject Lombardy, Theodulf the Visigoth from Spain, and, the most important figure of them all, Alcuin from York in England, to add lustre to, and work at, Charlemagne's palace school at Aachen, which was to be a second Rome, even a new Athens. This is not to say that the individual scholars, and perhaps even Charlemagne himself (of whom it was said by his biographer that he practised writing when he could not sleep), did not also work in the glow of that divine light which sees

[1] 'The Renaissance with which Charlemagne was primarily concerned, aimed at a rebirth, a regeneration of the whole Frankish people ... For the first time, at least so far as Western Europe is concerned, we are here confronted by the conscious effort to shape the character of a society in consonance with the axioms of a particular doctrine, here the Christian norms'— W. Ullman, *The Carolingian Renaissance and the Idea of Kingship* (London, 1969), pp. 6–7. See especially Chapter I for an emphatic enunciation of the thesis that the Renaissance was an integral part of Carolingian kingship, directed to the end of moulding society.

knowledge as an end in itself, and certainly the results of their labours transcended their immediate aims, however grandiose. The emphasis of the Carolingian Renaissance was literary, the editing and copying of the basic sources of wisdom, and not only of the Bible and the Fathers—Cyprian, Jerome, Augustine, Gregory the Great—but also Boethius and, behind him, Vergil and other classical authors. The consequence was that they preserved much of ancient learning for the future, and to them we still owe much of our knowledge of the classics as well as purely Christian tradition. The story has often been repeated, yet manifestly needs still wider broadcasting to traduce the popular view of the Middle Ages as the Dark Ages ended only by the Dawn of the fifteenth-century Renaissance, that when the scholars of that age hunted for classical manuscripts, what they found were Carolingian, though in their arrogant ignorance (which is amongst their principal bequests to our modern age) they mistook them for the real thing, and the beautiful 'Carolingian miniscule' in which they were written to be the *scriptura Romana* and the one, true, classical hand.

The most famous event in the reign of Charlemagne took place on Christmas Day, 800, when in the church of St. Peter at Rome Pope Leo III crowned him Emperor. 'On the most holy day of the Nativity of the Lord, as the king rose from prayer before the *confessio* of St. Peter to hear mass, Pope Leo placed a crown on his head, and he was acclaimed by all the people of the Romans: "To Charles Augustus, crowned by God, great and pacific emperor of the Romans, life and victory!" And after these acclamations he was adored by the Pope in the manner of the princes of old, and the title of patrician was discarded and he was called Emperor and Augustus.'[1] About the significance, even the importance, of this occasion historians had long debated, and still do.[2] Was this the revival of the Roman Empire in the West,

---

[1] *Annales Regni Francorum*, ed. F. Kurze; quoted by Latouche, pp. 352–3.

[2] For a useful anthology of much of the literature, see *The Coronation of Charlemagne*, ed. R. E. Sullivan ('Problems of European Civilization', Boston, U.S.A., 1959). See also F. L. Ganshof, *The Carolingians and the*

and also, and thereby, the foundation of that Holy Roman
Empire which survived until 1806 and which, during the Middle
Ages at least, was (in the words of Lord Bryce) a 'universal
monarchy' embodying the 'loftiest ideal of human government'?
And was the imperial coronation of Charlemagne therefore (to
quote Bryce again) 'not only the central event of the Middle
Ages, [but] also one of those very few events of which . . . it may
be said that if they had not happened the history of the world
would have been different'?[1] Or was it, as the French historian
Ferdinand Lot once described it, 'a comedy improvised by a
handful of antiquarian-minded ecclesiastics'?[2] It always seems
dull to say that the truth lies between two extremes, though
indeed it often does, and does so here. Assuredly the coronation
of Charlemagne was no joke nor meant to be, but, on the other
hand, the enthusiasm of Lord Bryce requires amendment. On a
golden *bulla* or seal attributed to Charlemagne as Emperor there
is engraved the legend '*Renovatio Romani imperii*', *i.e.* 'The
revival of the Roman Empire'; but obviously in no strict sense
was Charlemagne's Empire, differing even in territorial extent, a
revival of the Roman Empire, which in any case, legally, historically and visibly, still existed at Constantinople—though in
saying this we must also remember that the Roman Empire in
the West had never officially or definitely ended or been abolished,
and far from forgetting it, contemporaries were more prone to
idealize what was regarded as a lost universality of good order,
sound learning and true religion. Again, as a matter of historical
fact, Charlemagne's Empire did not long outlive him, and when
the concept of empire in the West was revived again by Otto I
of Germany in 962 and in a form which did last, however changed

---

Frankish Monarchy (London, 1971), and W. Ullman, *The Carolingian
Renaissance and the Idea of Kingship* (London, 1969), whose views, which
seem to me correct, have greatly influenced what follows.

[1] Extracts from James Bryce, whose book, *The Holy Roman Empire*, was
first published in 1864 as the expanded version of an Oxford prize essay of
1863, are given in Sullivan's, *The Coronation of Charlemagne*.

[2] F. Lot, *Le fin du monde antique et le début du moyen âge* (Paris, 1927),
p. 296.

and enfeebled, until 1806, that, as a matter of historical fact, was
something different again. What then did those involved in the
ceremony of Christmas Day 800 think that they were doing?
There seems no doubt that the initiative in the matter came from
the intellectuals of Charlemagne's entourage, Alcuin especially
(in this sense, therefore, the imperial coronation was the result
of the Carolingian Renaissance), who succeeded in winning
over to their views a half-reluctant, half-comprehending king—
for Charlemagne, in spite of all efforts, was no intellectual, and
there were high issues of state involved, since the court at
Constantinople was unlikely to take kindly to any imperial
usurpation in the West. A letter of Alcuin to the king, written in
June, 799, if placed, moreover, in the immediate contemporary
context which so worried him (a damaging scandal at Rome
weakening the Pope's position, and a vacancy and worse at
Constantinople where the Emperor, Constantine VI, was deposed to be replaced by a woman), lifts the veil drawn by centuries of change and legend and controversy between us and
these events, to show them in the clear perspective of the living
past: 'Until now there have been three men of the highest rank
in the world. That is, the apostolic sublimity, governing from
the throne of the blessed Peter, prince of the apostles, as his
vicar; what has been done to him who sat in that throne [*i.e.*
Leo III] you have in your kindness advised me. Another is the
imperial dignity and secular power of the second Rome [*i.e.*
Constantinople]; it is rumoured abroad far and wide how the
ruler of that empire [*i.e.* Constantine VI] has been impiously
deposed not by aliens but by his own people and fellow citizens.
The third is the royal dignity which by the dispensation of our
Lord Jesus Christ is conferred on you as governor of the Christian
people [*rector populi christiani*], and this is more excellent than
the other dignities in power, more shining in wisdom, more
sublime in rank. Now on you alone rests the tottering safety of
the churches of Christ.'[1] There is a logical compulsion about that

[1] Alcuin, letter no. 174, in *Monumenta Germaniae Historica, Epistolae*, iv
(1895), p. 288. Cf. Latouche, *Caesar to Charlemagne*, p. 351.

passage which leads straight to the Christmas ceremony at St. Peter's in Rome.

The times are out of joint, the body needs a head (and used to have one), the Church and the Faith above all need protection, Charlemagne, by the sheer facts of his position, king of the Franks and of the Lombards and the ruler of all Latin Christendom save only Britain, towers above any other figure in the West (or even East), seemingly ordained by God. The empire conceived by Alcuin and realized, so far as the dreams of men can ever be realized, on Christmas Day 800, was the empire of the Christian people, an empire of the faithful, the empire, in short, of Latin Christendom now coming to be identified as Europe.[1] As such it was, in a real but new sense to fit the times, the Roman Empire, since it comprised all those peoples on the mainland of Europe who were members of the Roman Church and for whom Rome was the spiritual capital and something more, and for whom (as indeed for us) it was difficult any longer to think of the surviving Roman Empire in the East as in any real sense 'Roman' at all. Thus 'his [Charlemagne's] Roman empire was to represent the rebirth of the ancient pagan Roman empire in the guise and shape of a new Latin-Christian one which was for all practical purposes identical with the notion of Europe'.[2] The concept was fundamentally religious as well as, or more than, political, though in the prevailing near-theocracy of the age the distinction is scarcely relevant.

To us seeking especially to show the relevance of medieval history to the future and the present, the principal importance of the coronation of Charlemagne on Christmas Day 800 and the 'revival of the Roman Empire' in the West is as a manifestation of the growing self-awareness of the West, of Latin Christendom, as an entity. It is thus also another step, and a big one, in the widening separation of East and West, for Charle-

---

[1] For the growing concept of Europe and its identification with Latin Christendom, see W. Ullman, *The Carolingian Renaissance and the Idea of Kingship*, pp. 135–9.

[2] Ullman, *op. cit.*, p. 135.

magne's Empire towards the east coincided, as it were by definition, with the limits of the Catholic Church of Rome, and those
beyond the pale who subscribed to the Greek Orthodox Church
of Constantinople were not members of it, and not 'Roman'.
The pattern of the future thus comes more sharply into focus,
and what had once been the single world of imperial Rome is
now formally two, with Islam a third world *de facto*. Moreover,
though Charlemagne, like Otto and his German successors after
him, was lord of much of Italy, the political centre of gravity in
the empire of the West has shifted from the Mediterranean to the
Germanic north beyond the Alps. There is, too, one other feature
of Christmas Day 800 which will be a controlling factor in the
future—and the imperial coronation of Charlemagne, like many
great historical events (*e.g.* Magna Carta on the smaller stage of
English history), can be argued to have a greater future than
contemporary importance. The Pope, Leo III (who himself in
these events took a big step into Europe), crowned Charlemagne.
This was evidently his initiative, unforeseen, unplanned and undesirable to the Franks, and this was evidently the cause of the
king-emperor's annoyance and his off-repeated remark, recorded
in Einhard's biography, that if he had known what the Pope
would do he would never have entered the church, Christmas or
not. Certainly when the time came, in 813, to designate his successor, he himself placed the crown on the head of his son Louis,
and in his own palace church at Aachen, not at Rome. To
Charlemagne, the Christian King and Emperor, the Lord's
anointed, who bestrode his world like a colossus, the Pope tended
to be only the first of his bishops whose prime duty was to pray
for his success. But Leo's coronation of Charlemagne could be
construed as the conferment of the imperial dignity upon him by
the Papacy, and will be so in future when a revived Papacy meets
another Empire in conflict for dominion in the West.

CHAPTER III

The Church and the Papacy
to the time of Charlemagne

There is more to the history of religion than just religion, simply because in all periods at least of Western history, with the possible exception of our own, religion has been so integral a part of society that you cannot study the one without the other. So far as medieval history is concerned, so much must already be apparent from the pages written above, wherein, though we sought for convenience to separate secular political history from ecclesiastical history and to deal with the former first, Christianity emerges as fundamental to any analysis of the situation at any given time, and the landmarks in any such narration inevitably include the conversion of Constantine, the baptism of Clovis, St. Augustine's mission to England, and the apotheosis of the Carolingian concept of Christian Kingship in the imperial coronation of Charlemagne. Students of the present generation, it may be suggested, labour under a serious disability from the increasing lack of any inbred knowledge of religion, or worse, from a disinterest in, or worse still, a positive hostility to, ecclesiastical and religious history; for religion simply cannot be left out of history (which is a contradiction in terms) without sacrificing all hope of understanding the society and the period under study. Nor, it must be said at once, since there are undoubtedly those among the young who shun medieval history as being especially 'religious', is this peculiarly, still less exclusively, true of the so-called Middle Ages. To some extent this doubly mistaken attitude is the fault of those who teach and write, for while it has been well said that 'The habit of separating ecclesiastical history from secular history has tended to make

everything ecclesiastical appear more rarified than it really is'[1]
(the antidote to this is that splendid remark to the effect that the
chief weakness of the Church has ever been that it has only the
laity to recruit from), the medieval historian should always be on
guard against the fact that, since the medieval Church had a near-
monopoly of literacy, a distorting amount of the evidence surviving is ecclesiastical in provenance, and, by remembering this,
keep a due sense of proportion. In my youth, I remember, it
was reported that a very eminent medieval historian used to go
through the streets of Oxford inveighing against 'those [*blank*]
holy men!'. I was shocked then but see what he meant now, as I
experience how easy it is for predominantly ecclesiastical historians to equate medieval history with ecclesiastical history,
the exclusive province of the Papacy, the religious orders and the
canon law, seen through a stained-glass window darkly. 'Christ!
that I were back in my bed, And my love in my arms again!'
(Anon.)—'Thy command brought me, not the love of God, to
the habit of religion' (Heloïse to Abelard)—and the battle cries
of 'God help us' by the Normans on the field of Hastings, where
Odo, bishop of Bayeux, fought beside the duke, his brother—
such fragments and straws in the wind seem to me a truer indica-
tion of that integration of medieval religion and society as it
really happened amongst imperfect men and women. And certainly all this is scarcely left behind after 1485. The Reformation
and the Tudors and Stuarts, all now all the rage, can scarcely
be studied without religion, nor, for that matter, can Mr.
Gladstone be, any more than William the Conqueror. And if the
Reformation shattered the medieval concept of a united and
conformist Latin Christendom, it did no more than shatter it into
fragments. The idea of the Christian society remained in the
belief that the fragments, the nation states, must be united
religiously no less than politically, and in this respect *cujus
regio ejus religio* was a bad exchange for the plenitude of
papal power, since the national prince was far more effective

[1] R. W. Southern, *Western Society and the Church in the Middle Ages*,
p. 360.

in enforcing uniformity than ever the medieval Papacy had been.

There is, too, in the study of medieval history, a disability under which many English-speaking people labour arising from the mere fact of living in Protestant countries, thus to be steeped, perhaps quite unconsciously, in Protestant traditions or, it may be, Protestant prejudices. This operates at many levels, and always as a bar to understanding. It can be a confused feeling that the Church of England was somehow always in being and England never quite a part of Latin Christendom and therefore Western Europe; or a feeling that the Reformation was so obviously right as to have been most curiously delayed; or an instinctive disapproval of the Papacy; or a total lack of comprehension of monasticism; or a faint awareness of the importance of the sermon accompanied by no awareness at all of the importance of confession as a means of spiritual guidance. But here at least the remedy is obvious, and effective if applied in time, for it is the sovereign virtue of history that it inculcates a sympathetic understanding of beliefs and standards other than one's own. 'A plague on both your houses' will not do for the historian, who must appreciate each.

In this chapter, then, we shall be concerned with the early history of the Church especially in the West down to the time of Charlemagne, and therefore, once again, with origins and foundations. In so doing we shall inevitably traverse something of the same ground covered in previous chapters, but shall look at it from a different point of view, for our concern is now the development of organized religion, the development of the Latin, Roman Church in the West, and therefore and especially with the origins and development of the Papacy, that unique medieval creation which becomes not merely the chief religious institution, but in every sense the central and dominant institution of medieval Latin Christendom and that which gives it its essence and its unity.

To do so we begin, as before, in the Roman Empire, and obviously the conversion of the Emperor Constantine to Christianity in *c*.312, and the subsequent establishment of Christianity as the official religion of the Empire by the Emperor Theodosius I in 391, are landmarks and climacteric events in the story. But also for Christianity to become effectively the established religion of Rome required more in practice than the *fiat* of Emperors: it was necessary, if the Outsiders were to become Insiders, for the Christians and their embryonic Church to come to terms with what had been pagan Roman society, and also with what was still pagan classical culture and learning. The early Christians, in their hatred of Roman society, fanned by persecution, had been anti-intellectual, and it was their arrogant ignorance as well as their refusal to conform to the urbane standards of a civilized society that won for them in turn the contempt of the Roman establishment and Tacitus' accusation that they stood for 'a hatred of the human race', an *odium generis humani*. Thus Tertullian of Carthage could write as late as the late second century: 'Stand forth O Soul and give thy witness. But I call thee not as when, fashioned in schools, trained in libraries, fed in Attic academies and porticoes, thou belchest forth thy wisdom. I address thee simple and rude and unlettered and untaught, such as they have thee who have thee only, that very thing, pure and entire, of the road, the street and the workshop'. But for Christianity to win the élite as well as the unlettered, and to sway governments, such an attitude could not endure. Knowledge as well as wisdom was necessary for the survival and vindication of the true Faith long before any desire for knowledge for its own sake, though the one will ever overflow into the other. And so the Church entered upon what was to be not the least of its achievements, the absorption and transmutation into a Christian mould of the whole of ancient learning, and, in terms of the history of the West, soon to be overrun by the barbarians, entered also into its textbook role of the hander-on of classical civilization to the future.

Which brings us to the next point. Not only was Christianity itself in origin an eastern religion, but also the Christian Church of these early centuries, like the Empire of which it formed a part, and even before the coming of the barbarians, was increasingly eastern orientated, the principal centres of intellectual activity and theology being in the east, at Antioch and Alexandria especially. This imbalance, of course, became even more marked when the West was overrun by the barbarians in the fifth and sixth centuries, and in this respect at least Rome herself was in no way pre-eminent in the beginning. What we have to trace out and understand, therefore, is the dual process whereby not only does the new Germanic West become increasingly divided from the surviving Roman Empire in the East, but also Rome, the city, bishopric and Church of Rome, becomes the capital of the emergent West. This latter process was, as we may see, anything but inevitable, though thus expressed it may also seem as con-temporaries saw it, a simple and obvious matter of the survival and continuation into the present and future of Rome the capital of Empire and the Eternal City.

We may begin to approach the phenomenon of the pre-eminence and eventual supremacy of Rome as the centre in the West of what will be Latin Christendom through some considera-tion of the organization of the early Church, if only because any religious (or other) movement is likely to contain as part and parcel of it a compulsion towards uniformity to be achieved through centralized administration and control—the possession of the Truth being accompanied by a natural and sincere desire both to propagate it and defend it against error and schism. In the earliest days Christian organization appears to have been as shadowy, minimal and elementary as one would expect, and that which for convenience we may call 'the Church' consisting in reality of a loose congeries of individual churches, some originally founded by the itinerant apostles themselves and all simply small, fluid and clandestine Christian communities or congrega-tions, their resident leaders called indifferently 'bishops' or 'presbyters' and assisted by deacons and deaconesses. Bishops in, as it were, historically recognizable form scarcely appear to our knowledge before the second century, but when they do we can begin to see also the organization of the Church inevitably following the pattern of Roman civil organization. In the West, not the least of the 'non-religious' contributions of the Church to the future will be the preservation of something of the fabric, and much of the concept, of classical Roman government and administration—as, for example, in England the first written laws appear (in Kent) at the time of St. Augustine's mission, and the first charters, the written records of the conveyance of property, from the time of archbishop Theodore. Thus early ecclesiastical organization, like Roman society and administration, was essentially urban, a bishop residing in a city and presiding over the Christian community within it, and presiding also over the wide surrounding and dependent countryside of the city, which will become his diocese. The majority of early Christians being townsfolk, and the countryfolk outside the towns being backward in respect of religion, the Latin word for countryman, *paganus*, became synonymous with unbeliever, and hence the word 'pagan', replete like so many words with history. In function the early bishop should be regarded as the priest or vicar of an extremely large parish (as, indeed, he was to remain perhaps until the eleventh century when bureaucracy overtook him), having himself the ministry and the cure of souls —though he might from an early date have assistant clergy, as the bishop of Rome is known to have had forty-six presbyters and seven deacons already by 251. In the early days moreover all bishops could be regarded as equal, and thus St. Jerome (*d.* 420) said that they were all equally successors of the apostles. But also from an early date some were more equal than others, and a special pre-eminence attached to certain bishops. As Pope Boniface I (418–422) was to put it, though all bishops might hold 'one and the same episcopal office', they should yet 'recognize those to whom for the sake of ecclesiastical discipline they ought to be subject'.

That hierarchy which is amongst the most familiar and fundamental features of what will be the medieval Church evolved in two ways but for one fundamental reason—to maintain unity, uniformity and the purity of the Faith against the danger of deviation, division, separatism and schism. One way, and in the event of great importance especially at the very highest level, was the inevitable following out a stage further of the pattern of Roman civil administration. Thus when, as was necessary, conferences, councils or synods were called to discuss ecclesiastical affairs, it was natural and convenient that they should assemble at the principal city, the capital or *metropolis* of an existing Roman province, and thus a certain pre-eminence accrued to the bishop of that city, who will in due course become the metropolitan, *i.e.* the archbishop. And though there was some ecclesiastical distaste for this secular train of thought and evolution, immense prestige in fact attached to the bishops of Rome and Constantinople, the old capital of the whole Empire and the new. Indeed Constantinople had no other claim than this to the pre-eminence and supremacy she will come to exercise over the Church in the East, while even at Rome, whose official claims to primacy were to be based on other and more spiritual arguments, the sheer prestige of the Eternal City remains a factor of inestimable value in the development of Papal supremacy in the barbarian West.

This, however, is to anticipate. The other basic factor in the evolution of an episcopal hierarchy and the pre-eminence of Rome was a logical extension of the doctrine of the apostolic succession. It must be emphasized that in the early Church the bishops were not only the successors of the apostles in a doctrinal sense, as they still are, but also in a real, immediate and practical sense, and as a matter of necessity, for, at a time when there was no canon of accepted scripture nor body of defined belief, the veracity of the Faith depended upon an oral tradition handed down. But if, nevertheless, there should be disagreements and sectarianism, as there were, then surely one must look to the living and continuing tradition of those churches actually founded by the apostles themselves to find the truth, for there lay authority. Thus Ireneus, who became bishop of Lyons in 178, and thus after him Tertullian who, writing about 198, argued that what Christ revealed to his apostles, which is the Christian religion, 'can only be proved by the same churches which those apostles founded. Was anything hidden from Peter, who was called the rock on which the Church would be built, who received the keys of the Kingdom of Heaven, and the power of loosing and binding in heaven and upon earth? Was anything hidden from John, the most beloved of the Lord, who leaned upon his breast, and to whom alone the Lord foretold the treachery of Judas?'[1]

To us, armed as we are with hindsight, there is already implicit in this the argument for the primacy, and hence supremacy, of Rome as the Church founded by St. Peter, Prince of the Apostles. But though Tertullian, like Ireneus, stressed the particular pre-eminence of Rome, and though he also laid stress upon the special position of Peter among the apostles, his argument was for the authority of apostolic churches in general, and there were many such, including others—Antioch and Alexandria— which could claim foundation by St. Peter. Nor is it of itself a derogation of the theory of the primacy of Rome based upon the unique authority of St. Peter as its founder, to say that it was evolved and developed over a long period, notably in the fourth and fifth centuries, and often in response to external events, to explain, justify or assert an undoubted pre-eminence in fact. Thus Pope Damasus I (366–84) was stung into the outright assertion of the Petrine authority of his church in 382 by a decree of the ecumenical Council of Constantinople (to which he had not been invited) in the previous year, whereby it was declared that 'the bishop of Constantinople shall have primacy of honour after the bishop of Rome, because this town is the new Rome'— and shared, therefore, some of the dignity of the church of Rome. To this the response of Damasus and his Roman council was that the 'primacy' of Rome owed nothing to any 'synodal decisions' but resulted from the powers conferred by Christ on Peter. Pope Boniface I (418–22), again reacting against the pretensions of Constantinople, declared that the church of Rome stood in

[1] Quoted by G. Barraclough, *The Medieval Papacy* (London, 1968), pp. 14–15.

relation to the other churches of the world 'as the head is to its members', and it was Pope Leo I, the Great (440–61), who, in an Empire rent by barbarians in the west and controversy in the east, brought the doctrine of the Petrine authority of Rome to its consummation in authoritative and lasting form: 'For the solidity of that faith which was praised in the chief of the Apostles is perpetual: and as that remains which Peter believed in Christ, so that remains which Christ instituted in Peter. For when, as has been read in the Gospel lesson, the Lord had asked the disciples whom they believed Him to be amid the various opinions that were held, and the blessed Peter had replied, saying, "Thou art the Christ, the Son of the living God", the Lord says, "Blessed art thou, Simon Bar-Jona, because flesh and blood hath not revealed it to thee, but My Father, which is in heaven. And I say to thee, that thou art Peter, and upon this rock I will build My church, and the gates of Hell shall not prevail against it. And I will give unto thee the keys of the kingdom of heaven. And whatsoever thou shalt bind on earth, shall be bound in heaven; and whatsoever thou shalt loose on earth, shall be loosed also in heaven".'[1]

It has been said of Leo I that he 'carried the Papacy as far theocratically as it could go',[2] and certainly we have reached here in theory the ultimate papal position, 'To deny the Pope is to deny Peter: to deny Peter is to deny Christ'. St. Peter, to whom these powers had been given, had founded the Roman church where his body lay, and the bishops of Rome were his successors. No doubts or scholarly qualifications of the historical premises marred for contemporaries the logical deductions— 'Peter has spoken through Leo!' Yet though we have come so far in theory we shall have much further to go in practice for the translation of that theory into facts—and indeed in any period of the Middle Ages, and beyond, the reality of papal primacy and supremacy will vary not only according to what is possible

[1] Quoted from *The Medieval World 300–1200*, ed. N. F. Cantor (New York and London, 1968), pp. 95–6.
[2] Barraclough, *Medieval Papacy*, p. 27.

but also according to what is deemed appropriate at the time. Certainly there were obstacles in the mid-fifth century. There were, so to speak, the rival bishoprics, of Antioch and Alexandria especially, but also of Constantinople with its *de facto* eminence, and all of them save Rome set in the flourishing eastern half of the Empire while the western half declined. There was the alternative concept, to be revived in the later Middle Ages in the West, that ultimate authority in the Church should lie in ecumenical councils. There was also the threat of imperial control, to be manifested not least under the theocracy of Justinian. What might have happened otherwise we cannot tell, but in the event it was a series of external events which produced the medieval pattern of the supremacy of Rome, at one and the same time accepted in but confined to the West—*i.e.* the formation of Latin Christendom under the hegemony of Rome. The barbarian invasions of the fifth and sixth centuries, as we have seen, greatly accentuated the growing division between the western and eastern halves of Empire, and geographically Rome stood in the former. The Moslem invasions of the seventh century obliterated for all practical purposes the great Christian sees of Antioch, Jerusalem and Alexandria, so that henceforth in a shrinking Christendom Rome and Constantinople alone remained as rivals in pre-eminence. And yet what we know is going to happen was anything but obvious to contemporaries. We know, but they did not, that the last visit of a Roman Emperor to Rome took place in 663, and that the last Pope to visit Constantinople was Constantine I in 710. For centuries the Popes (who began to appropriate the title *papa*, pope, once applicable to any bishop, only from the sixth century) inevitably and naturally looked to Constantinople as the seat of government, and to the surviving Empire in the east as the civilized world of which they were a part. The imperial government, especially after Justinian's reconquest in the mid-sixth century, retained territories in Italy with a capital at Ravenna, and many of the Popes were 'Greek'. It is, or should be, an antidote to hindsight and the insularity of English history to note that in 668 it was a Greek-speaking monk

from Tarsus whom Pope Vitalian sent to England as archbishop
of Canterbury in the person of Theodore. 'No one could better
have exemplified the unity of the Greco-Roman world. Born in a
Byzantine city, educated at Athens, a refugee in Rome from the
invading armies of Islam, chosen by the Pope to lead the newest
and most westerly province in Christendom, Theodore stood for
the unity of the whole Christian world'.[1] It is true that with
Theodore the Pope sent abbot Hadrian (from Naples but an
African in origin) to see that the former 'introduced no Greek
customs contrary to the true Faith into England', which is a
straw in the wind, but we are still almost a century from the time
when it can be said that the Papacy has broken its links with the
East and cast in its lot with the West. That eventuality will
require the stimulus of an internal, ecclesiastical dispute in the
form of the Iconoclast controversy, and the pressure of external
political developments which occur in the threat of the Lombards
in Italy, the incapacity of Byzantium to help, and the growing
power of the Franks as potentially more effective allies.

Meanwhile in the West, where there were both souls and a
civilization to be saved, positive developments, as well as the
negative facts of barbarian incursion, were taking place which
would confer upon the bishops of Rome an unquestioning
obedience of a kind unlikely to be found in the sophisticated
sectarianism of the imperial East. For the surviving 'Roman'
population in the West—though with a difference among the
Celts in Britain who, being literally cut off, become increasingly
different—the Christian faith in general and the Roman Church
in particular, stood as the one stable and wholly desirable element
in a disintegrating world. For the barbarians, who came, it will
be remembered, not to destroy but to enjoy, the sheer prestige
of Rome and therefore the Roman religion was scarcely less.
While the conversion of the pagan Franks and Anglo-Saxons
cannot have been quite so smoothly easy as it sometimes appears
in the pages of text-books (and one is reminded again of Bede's

[1] R. W. Southern, *Western Society and the Church in the Middle Ages*,
p. 56.

story of the converted pagan king who was slain because he took
to forgiving his enemies), in its accomplishment sheer prestige
is a factor scarcely less important than the obvious superiority
of the Christian faith to the heathen beliefs it displaced—and the
same is true, *mutatis mutandis,* of the in some ways more difficult
task of eradicating the Arian heresy of others of the invaders.
Prestige came to the Church also from its material as well as
from its spiritual labours. As the fabric of the Roman state
collapsed and civil government ceased, whatever local administration, justice, public order or public works there were devolved
upon the bishop, who undertook them *faute de mieux* as the one
surviving public figure capable and concerned. 'You are the
salvation of your country', wrote Venantius Fortunatus in
Merovingian Gaul to Felix, bishop of Nantes, who amongst
other good works altered the course of the river Loire for the
benefit of his diocese, 'you who give to the lands what justice
requires and restore to them the joys of the past . . . Voice of the
principal citizens, light of the nobility, defender of the people, you
are the port in which shipwreck can be escaped'. And in Italy
and in Rome and its countryside the bishop of Rome perforce
took on responsibilities of the same kind but on an even greater
scale, and acted, so to speak, upon a world stage—as when Pope
Leo I in 452 persuaded Attila the Hun to withdraw from Italy,
or when Pope Gregory I undertook the defence of the city against
the Lombards.

In the spontaneous growth of papal supremacy within the
emergent West itself, the result of desire and demand from below
far more than of any imposition from above, the pontificate
(590–604) of Gregory I, Gregory the Great, and also St. Gregory,
stands out. Often hailed as 'the first of the medieval popes', if
there is any justification for the appellation it is only because his
pontificate seems now full of significance for the future, and not
because he himself foresaw the Papacy of Gregory VII or
Innocent III and followed a conscious policy to achieve it. He
did what he did as a matter of necessity, duty and Christian
charity: it seems very right that the proud humility of the papal

title, 'servant of the servants of God' (*servus servorum Dei*), was adopted in his time; and he had above all the vision and compassion to turn to the barbarian West, not in order to extend the hegemony of Rome, nor to gain emancipation from the Empire of which he loyally saw himself as the first bishop, but to save souls. The times were out of joint. 'Succeeding to the papacy at a time when all Italy was in utter confusion and despair, he found himself at the head of the only stable institution in a changing world'.[1] Italy was devastated by the wars of Justinian's attempted re-conquest and now by the invading Lombards. Thus Gregory, like other bishops elsewhere, did what he could to administer and protect his city and its countryside. It is said that if a beggar died in the streets of Rome he held himself responsible and abstained from his priestly functions as a penance. In this local government and in Gregory's equally careful administration of the lands belonging to his church, the 'patrimony of St. Peter', all over Italy, historians have seen the origins of the Papal States, and through both the Roman bishop, like other bishops, is becoming, of necessity, a temporal power. 'Head of a strong central organization, unquestioned arbiter of justice, armed with the Keys of Peter and the old majesty of Rome, he [Gregory] is an almost superhuman figure, beside whom, in the eyes of the suffering population of Italy, the Emperor is but a far-off potentate, and the Exarch [*i.e.* the imperial vice-regent at Ravenna] merely an ineffectual general or an unjust governor'.[2]

But Gregory, as befitted the first bishop of the Empire, and the only apostolic bishop in the West, operated also on a wider front. He sought to establish relations, in the interest of reform, with the Visigothic churches in Spain now abandoning Arianism, and with the Frankish churches in Gaul, though in both spheres he met with little success. He also undertook, and was to be largely responsible for, the conversion of the Arian and thus heretic Lombards in Italy. And he also dispatched, in 597, a mission under St. Augustine to convert the heathen English, in what

---

[1] H. St. L. B. Moss, *The Birth of the Middle Ages* (Oxford, 1935), p. 135.
[2] Moss, *op. cit.*, p. 133.

had been the most westerly province of the Roman Empire, on the edge of the known world. It is not insular to say that the occasion is momentous, on a level with the baptism of Clovis a century before,[1] and, as always, there is more to it than religion and the propagation of the Christian faith. From the beginning St. Augustine's mission to England was a Roman undertaking, personally conceived, guided and controlled by Gregory through his personal representative, and it established at once that close and special relationship between England and the Papacy which is a fact of medieval history. Further, and in a wider context, such a relationship between the Church of Rome and a distant province of Christendom was new, and, further still, it was institutionalized and given expression in the organization of the new English Church in accordance with Gregory's directions. There were to be two specifically metropolitan archbishops, each with suffragan bishops under him, and each receiving the *pallium*, as the sign and symbol of his authority, from Rome.[2] St. Jerome had said that all bishops were equally the successors of the apostles, but Bede was to say that Theodore of Canterbury was the first archbishop whom all the English Church obeyed. In this way, therefore, what will become the familiar hierarchy of the Roman Church—Pope, archbishop, bishop—is established for the first time and in England. Nor is this all, but only the beginning of a train of events set in motion by St. Gregory in 597. When a century later, as part and parcel of that extraordinary flowering both of Christianity and culture (the two ever going together) which then took place in England, especially in the north, the English missionaries went out to convert the heathen

[1] See p. 35 above.

[2] Gregory's original plan, of two equal metropolitan archbishops at London and York (a clear extension of former Roman civil government in Britain) each with twelve suffragans, was never fully realized. In particular, Canterbury, as the church first founded by Augustine, has ever since remained the southern metropolitan see, and York, making a late start, never succeeded in achieving parity with Canterbury in spite of the later efforts of its medieval archbishops. The *pallium*, a band of white wool, is from this time forward the symbol of what henceforward is the particular authority of an archbishop.

of the Continent in the Low Countries and in Germany, they did so willingly in the name and with the authority of the Pope, the *pallium*, so to speak, in their knapsacks. St. Willibrord and St. Boniface each established a metropolitan archbishopric, at Utrecht and at Mainz respectively, and each obtained his *pallium* from Rome. And so, too, when the time came for the much needed reform of the Church in Frankia under the new Carolingian dynasty, it was achieved largely through the agency of the same St. Boniface, and upon the new model. On the need of that reform we may let St. Boniface speak: 'Religion', he wrote, 'is trodden under foot. Benefices are given to greedy laymen or unchaste and publican clerics. All their crimes do not prevent their attaining the priesthood; at last, rising in rank as they increase in sin, they become bishops ... ' With this we may contrast the Declaration of the Frankish bishops made in 747, and in so doing lift any veil we may have of lingering Protestant prejudice by remembering that what is being done is done with passionate conviction as the necessary means to the end of conversion, reform and salvation. Thus they publicly declared that they would 'maintain the Catholic faith and unity and subjection to the Roman Church until the end of their lives ... be subjects of St. Peter and his Vicar [*i.e.* the Pope], hold a synod every year, and that the metropolitans would ask for their *pallia* from that see ... '

With the eighth-century reform of the Frankish Church under Pepin III, Carloman and St. Boniface, we approach also another momentous event in the form of the alliance between the Papacy and the Carolingians. We must therefore retrace our steps for a moment to note that the conversion of the heathen Anglo-Saxons had been achieved as much by the old British or Celtic churches as by St. Gregory's Roman mission, by Irish monks from Lindisfarne and Iona as much as by St. Augustine and his followers at Canterbury. But yet the Roman Church was to prevail, and when the moment of confrontation came, at Whitby, in 663, and it fell to King Oswiu of Northumbria to choose (as it would happen, once and for all, for all England) between Roman and Celtic practices, we may see the doctrine of Petrine authority working at its simplest but not least effective level. Bede is our informant. 'First King Oswiu began by declaring that it was fitting that those who served one God should observe one rule of life and not differ in the celebration of the heavenly sacraments, seeing that they all hoped for one kingdom in heaven; they ought therefore to inquire as to which was the truer tradition and then all follow it together.' In the ensuing debate, the chief spokesman for the Celtic party was bishop Colman from Iona, and for the Roman, Wilfrid of Ripon. Colman cited the authority of St. John ('the disciple whom the Lord specially loved'), Anatolius, and St. Columba: Wilfrid cited principally that of Peter. Colman spoke first, and Wilfrid ended: 'For though your fathers were holy men, do you think that a handful of people in one corner of the remotest of islands is to be preferred to the universal Church of Christ which is spread throughout the world? And even if that Columba of yours—yes, and ours too, if he belonged to Christ—was a holy man of mighty words, is he to be preferred to the most blessed chief of the apostles, to whom the Lord said, "Thou art Peter, and upon this rock I will build my Church and the gates of hell shall not prevail against it, and I will give unto thee the keys of the kingdom of heaven"?' In Bede's words the king and council then reached their decision: 'When Wilfrid had ended, the king said, "Is it true, Colman, that the Lord said these words to Peter?" Colman answered, "It is true, O King". Then the king went on, "Have you anything to show that an equal authority was given to your Columba?" Colman answered, "Nothing". Again the king said, "Do you both agree, without any dispute, that these words were addressed primarily to Peter and that the Lord gave him the keys of the kingdom of heaven?" They both answered, "Yes". Thereupon the king concluded, "Then, I tell you, since he is the doorkeeper I will not contradict him; but I intend to obey his commands in everything to the best of my knowledge and ability, otherwise when I come to the gates of the kingdom of heaven, there may be no one to open them because the one who on your own showing holds the keys has turned his back on me." ' [1]

While one of the earliest and most important lessons for the historian to learn is not to regard the past as inferior, and while nothing of the kind is intended here in view of the materialistic crudities of our own age, it would be foolish to deny that the men of the new barbarian kingdoms in the West tended to bring their religion down to earth and make it tangible, not least with relics and the bones of saints. The Church spoke of the living God, and in this sense the saints were living too. The fact, as all believed, that St. Peter was physically present in his tomb at Rome, still speaking and still working through his Vicar, the Pope, was an aspect of the doctrine of Petrine authority that all could grasp and was not the least of the factors which drew men to Rome.[2] 'Peter's Pence', it will be remembered, was what the English paid throughout the Middle Ages, and not, as later reformers would have it, some unjustified tribute to the bishop of Rome. Certainly something like the compulsion of public opinion should be included in any analysis of the reasons which led the Papacy to commit itself, as it happened irrevocably, to the West, and therefore to the leadership thereof, in the mid-eighth century. The ground was both fertile and prepared: England, Germany, France, these were 'the only places where papal influence could be strong because it was strongly desired'. And men like Wilfrid, enthusiastic exponents of the papal cause, journeying to Rome—in Wilfrid's case on the occasion of the first appeal to Rome in English history—were discomfited on arrival to find a cosmopolitan Graeco-Roman court with a Greek Pope speaking to his councillors in a language they could not understand. They distrusted the East and wanted to possess Rome and St. Peter exclusively for themselves.[3]

Nevertheless, what we may see, though contemporaries did not, as the irrevocable commitment of Rome to the West, and

[1] Quoted from Bede's *Ecclesiastical History of the English People*, ed. B. Colgrave and R. B. Mynors, Oxford Medieval Texts (Oxford, 1969), pp. 299–307.

[2] Cf. Southern, *op. cit.*, pp. 30, 94.

[3] Cf. Southern, *op. cit.*, pp. 57–8.

the breaking of its ties with Constantinople and the East, in the
second half of the eighth century, still required the pressure of
events to cause them. There was the iconoclastic controversy
instigated by the Emperor Leo III in 726 as an attack upon the
worship of images. When the Pope would not conform, the
estates of St. Peter in southern Italy and Sicily were confiscated
and, worse, archbishoprics and provinces hitherto under the
jurisdiction of the Roman bishop in Greece and again in southern
Italy and Sicily were withdrawn, and placed under the patriarch
of Constantinople. By these means, Rome in effect 'was cut off
from the imperial church, of which it had hitherto regarded
itself as the head',[1] and in effect also was ejected from the 'Roman'
Empire. In addition to these traumatic experiences there was a
renewal of Lombard advance in Italy itself, which bade fair
to bring the whole peninsula under their control. The threat
was dual, both to the position of the Papacy and to its protector,
the Eastern Emperor. In fact the Byzantine government was driven
from Ravenna and north Italy by the victorious Lombards in 751,
and the Papacy, despairing of help from Constantinople, turned
to the West and to the Franks. As Gregory III had unsuccessfully
appealed to Charles Martel, so Stephen II appealed to the newly
crowned King Pepin, and on his knees before him, in 754, obtained his aid. Thus the alliance of the Papacy and the Franks
was made, and set in train a momentous series of developments
and events, of which the most immediate were the intervention
of both Pepin and Charlemagne after him in north Italy as the
protectors of St. Peter, the papal anointing of Pepin and his
sons, and the papal coronation of Charlemagne as Emperor on
Christmas Day 800.[2]

For us now, in this chapter as before, the principal significance
of these events must be the emergence of Latin Christendom.
But also Latin Christendom is synonymous with the Roman
Church, increasingly separate and distinct from the eastern,
Greek Church of Constantinople, and within this community

[1] Barraclough, *Medieval Papacy*, p. 35.
[2] Above pp. 41–4, 49.

of the West there will henceforth be no question of the spiritual hegemony of Rome, the apostolic see, endowed with the keys of Heaven. In addition, the Papacy emerges for the first time as a temporal power in its own right, no longer just *de facto* or as the agent of the Eastern Empire. Pepin as the result of his intervention against the Lombards at the Pope's behest conferred upon St. Peter the territory which becomes the Papal States, carved out of the former Byzantine exarchate of Ravenna, and the Papal States, confirmed though reduced by Charlemagne, last until the nineteenth century, with profound but not altogether desirable effects upon papal policy and papal history. Yet even this is by no means all, at least in theory if not in fact, for it is difficult not to set in the context of these events (or vice versa) one of the most famous of medieval documents—albeit a forgery—the Donation of Constantine. This translated into legal form upon parchment the long-current legend that the Emperor Constantine at the time of his conversion and baptism, transferring the seat of his empire to Constantinople and the east, conferred upon Pope Silvester I not only the Lateran Palace at Rome (correct) but also the city of Rome and dominion over 'all the provinces, districts and cities of Italy, and the western regions'.

Some other word than 'forgery' should be coined for the compilation of spurious documents in the early Middle Ages, for in a world which had almost lost but was beginning to seek again the authority of the written record as opposed to oral tradition, they carry little or none of the ugly immoral associations of forgeries in later periods. Many persons and institutions possessed in righteousness property and privileges without any title deeds, and as the demand for such things increased so they were supplied to meet it, without any doubt of the veracity of the claims thus enshrined in writing. A well-known instance in English history involves the documents produced in the late eleventh century to show and prove the supremacy of Canterbury over York, without any necessary attempt to defraud—and so it is, on a more majestic scale, with the Donation of Constantine, the date and exact purpose of which nevertheless remain unknown. An 'extraordinary perversion of history' it undoubtedly is, and a 'dream-world of Roman theocracy'[1] it may be said to embody, but it also embodies beliefs, ideas and ideals, current, most would agree, in the late eighth century, of the claims of the Pope to a universal temporal authority in the West as the visible successor in Rome to the Caesars, and it is at least probable that the imperial coronation of Charlemagne on Christmas Day, 800, was intended to put the concept into practice as the delegation of such temporal authority. Most would also agree that the assertion of temporal authority by the Papacy over the West, as indeed in Italy itself, was a mistake, though if we try to follow contemporaries by thinking in terms of theocracy and by making little distinction between spiritual and temporal power we may the more easily see how it came about. Meanwhile, in this chapter as in the last, we have come a long way from the beginning. More pieces of the pattern of the future have been set, and these include not only the potential Papacy of Gregory VII, Innocent III and Boniface VIII, but also the potential rivalry of the two powers now raised up, the Empire and the Papacy. Much of medieval European history is written in that theme, even to the point of tedium; yet rightly so, for out of it emerges a triumphant Papacy which makes the Reformation possible, and a broken Germany whose weakness, first, and subsequent reuniting, dominates the history of the 'modern' period.

---

[1] Moss, *Birth of the Middle Ages*, p. 219.

CHAPTER IV

Monasticism and the Religious Orders

'Listen, my son, to the precepts of your Master, and incline unto them the ear of your heart ... To you, therefore, whoever you are, my words are directed, who, renouncing your own will, takes up the strong and excellent arms of obedience to fight for the true King, Christ our Lord' (The Rule of St. Benedict, Prologue).

While the Papacy is, quite obviously, one central and fundamental institution of the medieval Latin Church and of medieval Latin Christendom, monasticism is another scarcely less so, although perhaps less obviously at first sight. Not only would it be impossible to write any account of the medieval Church without monks, but also to write any account of medieval society, of medieval history, or of the development, therefore, of the modern West. In a very real sense these men as much as any men made us what we are, and their contribution to Western civilization is immense. Even at this rarified level of spiritual endeavour, and indeed perhaps especially at this level, there is thus much more to the history of religion than religion, and, furthermore, monasticism, like so many other medieval institutions, is with us still. Clearly, then, we can go no further without saying something on this subject, though in so doing it seems best to transcend the chronological limit of A.D. 800 we have so far reached in other chapters, and to deal with monasticism as a whole, together also with the very different Religious Orders of the friars with which our entire period ends.

To understand the contribution of monasticism to Western society may seem at first difficult enough since the achievement is largely paradoxical (for how could those who renounced the World contribute so much to it?), but to understand monasticism itself, to grasp, that is, its attraction and compulsion so that for long centuries almost anyone who was Anyone was a monk, requires especially the exercise of those virtues which it is the particular benefit of medieval history to bestow, *i.e.* the humanity and humility and compassion necessary to appreciate standards and ideals other than one's own. Although historically in the West monasticism is a medieval institution, it is not in fact confined to the West, nor to what we call the medieval period, nor even to the Christian religion, and it may be best therefore to seek understanding through the realization that it is a timeless impulse and also, given certain circumstances (chiefly a belief in a God or at least in some non-materialistic standard of perfection), even a universal one. For monasticism is based upon asceticism, and an ascetic is one who practises severe self-discipline. There can be few of us who have not, at some time or another, for this purpose or that, practised at least a mild form of asceticism, of self-denial—cutting down, it may be, on food, or drink, or cigarettes, going to bed early, getting up early, and this in order to slim, or economize, or keep fit, or to work harder, or whatever—and there can be few of us also who have not felt a satisfying sense of virtue and achievement as a result of such modest exercises in self-discipline. Further, the satisfaction resulting is likely to increase with the amount of renunciation and with the degree of self-discipline exercised, and in this way we may begin to see the appeal of asceticism to some people irrespective of period and place. We may also add another element and suggest that this appeal is likely to be all the stronger if associated with service, if the self-denial and renunciation are undertaken for the sake of some person or thing—by parents for their children, for example, or by a man or woman for a cause—and that it will increase in direct proportion to the worthiness of the end thus served. If all this is so, then by it we come close to both the appeal and the logic of monasticism, to grasp which we have only to add or insert religion and the love of God, together with the belief in salvation and a desire to obtain it. The monk, the religious ascetic, will renounce the world by withdrawing from it, will take the three basic monastic vows of Poverty, Chastity and Obedience (the last of which, obedience, involving the renunciation of self-will), and practise far greater self-discipline than this, for the love and the service of God (religious 'service' is a phrase we still all use whether comprehending it or not), and by thus perfecting himself in this life attain salvation in the next. So John Cassian, a fifth-century monk of Marseilles, by whom St. Benedict himself was to be influenced: 'The end of our profession indeed is the . . . Kingdom of Heaven; but the immediate aim or goal is purity of heart, without which no one can gain that end . . . Whatever can help to guide us to this object, *i.e.* purity of heart, we must follow with all our might, but whatever hinders us from it we must shun as a dangerous and hurtful thing. For . . . this we do and endure all things, for this we make light of our kinsfolk, our country, honours, riches, the delights of this world, and all kinds of pleasures; namely that we may retain a lasting purity of heart . . . For this we must seek for solitude, for this we know that we ought to submit to fastings, vigils, toils, bodily nakedness, reading, and all other virtues, that through them we may be enabled to prepare our heart and to keep it unharmed by all evil passions, and resting on these steps to mount to the perfection of charity . . .'[1] From here it is but a short step to St. Benedict's Rule, that 'persevering in God's teaching until death in the monastery, we may by patience share in the sufferings of Christ'. And for these things there is, of course, as there had to be, New Testament authority, for did not Our Lord say, 'If anyone wish to come after Me, let him deny himself'? Of course monasticism, like all forms of religion, reflects the society which practises it, answering its needs and ideals and changing also as that society

[1] Quoted by Dom Cuthbert Butler, *Benedictine Monachism* (2nd. edition London, 1924), pp. 48–9.

changes,[1] but also we have so far met in it nothing which is exclusively medieval (nor even exclusive to what, in modern terminology, is now the Roman Catholic Church). The Venerable Bede was a monk, and so is Dom David Knowles, until recently Regius Professor of Modern History at Cambridge—nor is it, as we shall see, without significance that both are scholars.

Religious asceticism appears early in the Christian Church and, like much else, was first developed in the East. The way of life chosen was eremitical, that is to say its practitioners were hermits, solitaries and individualists, waging their spiritual battles alone in desert places. Their asceticism was severe, extreme because the more extreme the better, reaching by the fifth century heights which may seem absurd. 'Athletes of God' was a phrase for these men and athletes indeed they were as they vied with each other in penitential abstinences which are feats of sheer physical endurance, preaching the while and praying for lesser men. The case of St. Simeon Stylites who remained, on a platform too small to enable him to lie down, perched on his pillar for thirty-three years, is well known. His record was broken by three months by his disciple St. Daniel, and was to be broken again in the sixth century by St. Simeon Stylites the Younger, who is said to have done penance on his pillar for sixty years together. Such examples must of necessity be rare, and one should not too easily either smile or condemn, but there were obvious spiritual as well as physical dangers in the competitive practice of extreme asceticism, including, it may be supposed, those of pride and its neighbour envy. Thus it was said of St. Macarius of Alexandria that 'if he ever heard of anyone having performed a work of asceticism he was all on fire to do the same'. Nevertheless the first monasteries to be established, like those of St. Anthony in Egypt (traditionally the first and in A.D. 305) and St. Pachomius, were simply communities of hermits, and it was this eastern form of monasticism, based

---

[1] A particular and illuminating emphasis upon the integration of society and the Religious Orders will be found in Southern, *Western Society and the Church in the Middle Ages.*

upon the eremitical life and extreme asceticism, that was first introduced into the West. Hence, amongst other manifestations, those Irish and Celtic monks whose itinerant life and impressive asceticism made of them the perfect instrument of evangelization, and who made so great a contribution to the conversion of the heathen English. The very word 'monk', though it now means 'one leading a religious or ascetic life in a community', is derived from the Greek *monakhos* meaning 'solitary', and even in the West the individualistic and extreme life of the hermit never disappeared as an alternative form of religious asceticism to that provided by the stable, and comparatively moderate, corporate communities of the Benedictines and the later Monastic Orders of the Middle Ages.

Yet to all intents and purposes the founder of Western monasticism, medieval and modern, is St. Benedict, St. Benedict of Nursia, born of an ancient and noble 'Roman' family, near Spoleto in central Italy, about the year 480, and dying in *c*.543. St. Benedict turned his back upon the eremitical way of life and put in its place the concept of a religious community, living in all things a communal life, and bound together by obedience and stability. He founded such communities of his own at Subiaco and elsewhere, and subsequently on the lofty site at Monte Cassino. It was there that he drew up his 'Rule' for his monks. The Rule of St. Benedict was to become perhaps the most influential single document of the Middle Ages, and the Abbey of Monte Cassino, the cradle and nursery of all Benedictine monasticism and thus of all Western monasticism, is still there on its rock, recently rebuilt after its destruction (by us) in the last war. We reach therefore another great and founding moment in the history of the West, commemorated thus by the English historian of the Benedictine Order—'And this was the community and these the men, destined by God to play so great a part in repairing the ruin, religious, social and material, in which Europe was lying, and in converting, christianising and educating the new nations that were to make the great Christian Commonwealth.'[1]

[1] Cuthbert Butler, *Benedictine Monachism*, p. 33.

In substituting for the individualism of the eremitical life an ordered religious community bound by a common Rule with all things held in common, St. Benedict turned his monks also away from the possible excesses and attendant spiritual dangers of extreme asceticism. His Rule, he wrote, was 'a little rule for beginners', and in his 'school of the Lord's service, in which we hope we have laid down nothing harsh or burdensome', he asked for no more, he believed, than ordinary men, through faith and perseverance, might achieve. The main elements of the asceticism he required were obedience and humility: obedience unquestioning and immediate to the word of God and the dictates of true Christian living, but as uttered through the mouth and precepts of the abbot, the absolute head of the community (though elected by it), the father of the religious family of the monastery, and God's vicar to his monks: obedience, therefore, which comprised humility in the denial of self-will. With obedience and humility went stability, the necessity to remain and persevere until death in that monastery where one had made one's profession—'persevering in God's teaching until death in the monastery, we may by patience share in the sufferings of Christ'. The monastic life itself, the daily round, was to consist of three components. First there was the *Opus Dei*, the work of God, over which, says the Rule, nothing is to take precedence. This was the communal worship, prayer and services in the monastic church, which daily round, built upon the two biblical precepts, 'at midnight will I rise to give thanks unto thee' and 'seven times a day do I praise thee', consisted of a long night office and seven regular offices throughout the day (Matins or Lauds, Prime, Terce, Sext, Nones, Vespers and Compline). Interspersed with the *Opus Dei* were the two other components of Benedictine living, the *Opus Manuum* or manual labour, and the *Lectio Divina* or time set aside for the reading of devotional works and meditation.

It now seems virtually certain that St. Benedict derived much of his Rule from an earlier rule of an anonymous 'Master', *i.e.* 'The Rule of the Master', but the changes and amendments he

made are the measure of his genius, transforming an unremark-
able compilation into one of the most influential of all medieval
works. It is difficult to summarize the reasons for its immense
success, but its combination of asceticism with compassionate
humanity, its worldly (in the best sense) as well as unworldly
wisdom, its precise instructions combined with sufficient
flexibility for changes to evolve over the centuries while the
spirit remains intact, all this and much more have ensured its
survival as an attractive and satisfying way of religious life over
nearly fifteen hundred years from St. Benedict's day to our own
—which is to say throughout the entire history of the West so
far. This is impressive enough, but its initial success in the early
medieval centuries is even more so. St. Benedict composed his
Rule for his own monks and did not see himself as the founder of
a universal order. It is now known, indeed, that his rule did not
spread out from Monte Cassino with quite such immediate
speed as was formerly naïvely supposed (so that, for example,
it is very unlikely that either Pope Gregory I or his agent St.
Augustine were Benedictines though they were certainly monks),
but already by Charlemagne's time the King and Emperor could
inquire whether there was any other form of monasticism than
the Benedictine. From about 800 until about 1100 the Rule of
St. Benedict was universal in the West and all the innumerable
monks in Latin Christendom lived by it,[1] and even when the new
monastic orders came in the early twelfth century they were either
influenced by the Rule or sought, as like Cistercians, to return
to its original purity rather than to strike out in new directions. Obviously a movement achieving such success must
have provided what the times required, and it is not easy, now
those times have gone, to capture and put in words, without
experience, the core of timeless excellence which Benedictinism
can provide for those who seek a strictly religious life. It seems
entirely characteristic of Benedictine monachism that the genius
of a 'modern' writer, Cardinal Newman, may come closest to

[1] For the Cluniac variation of original Benedictinism in the tenth century,
and thereafter, see pp. 131–6 below.

interpreting it to us: ' "The monastic institute", says the biographer of St. Maurus, "demands *Summa Quies*, the most perfect
quietness"; and where was quietness to be found, if not in revert-
ing to the original condition of men as far as the changed circumstances of our race admitted; in having no wants of which
the supply was not close at hand; in the *nil admirari*; in having
neither hope nor fear of anything below; in daily prayer, daily
bread, and daily work, one day being just like another, except
that it was one step nearer than the day just gone to that great
Day which would swallow up all days, the day of everlasting
rest.'[1]

'Come unto me all ye that labour and are heavy laden, and I
will give you rest.' If we have got anywhere near explaining the
attraction of monasticism and of Benedictine monasticism in
particular to the individuals who made their profession, their
number, however great, always remained a minority, and they
cannot alone account for the overwhelming success of the movement. What then were the motivations of those innumerable
founders and benefactors who cover the entire spectrum of
medieval society, from kings and magnates with their lordly
foundations to the proverbial widow with her mite, and who in
the 'Benedictine centuries' from 800 to 1100 especially gave of
their substance to support Benedictine monks (as later, *mutatis
mutandis*, they will give to the later religious orders)? Given
faith and more especially the Catholic faith, given the belief in
salvation and the desire to obtain it, given also the concepts and
doctrines of penitence and the remission of sins,[2] of the benefits
of good works and intercession, then the process of foundation
and benefaction appears so obvious as to be seen as the answer to
a social need. For the founders, and their descendants who were
the patrons, the monasteries were like the later medieval chantries

---

[1] J. H. Newman, 'The Mission of St. Benedict' (*Historical Sketches*,
London, 1896, ii, 377); quoted by Butler, *Benedictine Monachism*, p. 34.

[2] Thus John de Chesney, so we are told by the cartulary of the house, had
vowed to found Sibton Abbey in Suffolk, in the mid-twelfth century, 'on
account of the many evils he had done' both in time of peace as sheriff of
Suffolk and in time of war (Pipe Roll Society, New Series 36, p. 65).

but on a more grandiose scale as befits a more heroic age, praying
and interceding ceaselessly for the safety of their souls, while
warding off evil in this world as well. 'For the salvation of my
soul and of the souls of my family, ancestors and successors' is
the almost invariable type of the phraseology of early charters
recording gifts to religious houses, and in lesser degree lesser
benefactors than the founders themselves expected, and indeed
contracted for, like benefits. When Ordericus Vitalis tells us that
in mid-eleventh century Normandy the magnates, following the
example of their duke, vied with each other in the foundation of
monasteries, we may also suspect, without undue cynicism, an
element of status symbol in some cases, for there are fashions in
religion as in other human activities. Certainly there were other
and more worldly benefits for the founders and patrons of
religious houses arising from their position, including the ability
to place in a fitting station and a suitable career any landless
younger sons and spinster daughters. In a world dominated
by secular lordship as well as by organized religion it is not
surprising that the monasteries (rather like English public
schools in the modern period) become aristocratic or upper-
class institutions, but meanwhile it also follows from this exercise
of patronage combined with the system of oblates, whereby
children were dedicated to religion at an early age by their
parents, that not all inmates of a monastery were there entirely
as the result of vocation. We live in an imperfect world, and
always have done, even in the monastic centuries, and even for
individual aspirants to the monastic profession there might be
other motivations than religious fervour or parental pressure and
decision. It should perhaps be remembered more often than it is
that there were few careers for men in the Middle Ages, even
fewer for nobles, and none at all for women. Those seeking
scholarship and the intellectual life were certain to become
clerks and almost bound to become monks before about 1200,
and for the rest, if gentlemen, the choice was little more than the
profession of arms or the Church. Square pegs in round holes
are not uncommon in the Middle Ages, especially in the earlier

centuries, and we should have compassion for them whether they are militant clerics like Odo, bishop of Bayeux, or warriors against their inclination like Stephen, count of Blois.[1]

Though there was room in the Rule of St. Benedict for service beyond the confines of the monastery (*e.g.* through charity and the care of the sick), the original and fundamental ideal of Benedictine monasticism was the salvation of the soul of the individual monk by withdrawal from the world. How then did it come about that Benedictine monasticism made so great a contribution to the civilization of the West and to the development, even material, of the world which in concept it shunned, and of what kind was that contribution? Most if not all of the answer involves paradox and even tragedy, and leads us into the great paradox of monasticism as indeed of most religious movements, that success itself is often the cause of failure or at least of the loss of original intentions and even ideals. If one is to attempt a catalogue of Benedictine benefits, one can at every point begin with the obvious and then observe an inevitable and inexorable overflowing beyond the monastic community itself and beyond the intentions of St. Benedict. Thus buildings, ever more elaborate for the glory of God (or the founder) and to house expanding numbers, produce great architecture and have a central place in the architectural history of the Middle Ages, while the fine arts of sculpture, painting, iron-work and glazing are also integral to medieval building. The regular round of services and offices in the *Opus Dei*, also becoming more elaborate, has not only left the monastic imprint upon the liturgy of churches until the present day, but also required books and the copying of manuscripts whose illumination is a basic element in the development of medieval art, as it also came to require music, and at all times accurate time-keeping, which leads to mathematics, horology and chronology and so to mechanical weight-driven clocks on the one hand (thirteenth century) and Bede on the other (eighth century), to whom we owe the universal custom in the West of dating our

[1] For whose career, crowned in the end with glory, see Steven Runciman, *A History of the Crusades*, vol. i (Cambridge, 1953).

epochs from the Birth of Christ. I write these words in 1971 because of Bede. The religious life and education of necessity went together. 'Of what use is a man who is ignorant of letters and of the commandments of God?'—thus the self-educated abbot Herluin at Bec in mid-eleventh-century Normandy, encouraging his monks in their studies.[1] Novices had to be educated, not least the increasing numbers of child oblates, and hence the monastic schools, which in numerous cases were thrown open to the community. Ordericus Vitalis, a monk of St. Evroul writing in the earlier twelfth century, who has also left us a picture of his own abbot urging his monks to study harder, says of Bec (exceptional in excellence, not in type) in Lanfranc's time that 'his reputation for learning spread throughout all Europe, and many hastened to receive lessons from him out of France, Gascony, Brittany and Flanders', and of the monks there under the teaching of first Lanfranc and then Anselm that 'they are thus become so devoted to literary pursuits, and so exercised in raising and solving difficult questions of divinity, that they seem to be almost all philosophers'.[2] And here, of course, we reach one of the greatest single contributions of monasticism to the civilization of the West in the preservation and enlargement of learning. The Benedictines were never an out-and-out learned order such as the later Dominican friars were to be, but a measure of learning was a necessity of their life, and as the years passed the *Lectio Divina* and the *Opus Manuum* of their Rule were devoted, or could be devoted, more and more to intellectual pursuits and scholarly labours, so that in their age of monastic monopoly and in the centuries of their supremacy—in Bede's Northumbria, or Charlemagne's Frankia, or all over Latin Christendom in the great days of the tenth and eleventh centuries—they were the intellectual as well as the spiritual centres of their world. Bede was a Benedictine monk

[1] *Vita Herluini* in J. Armitage Robinson, *Gilbert Crispin abbot of Westminster* (Cambridge, 1911), p. 104.
[2] *The Ecclesiastical History of Orderic Vitalis,* ed. Marjorie Chibnall (Oxford Medieval Texts, 1969), ii, 50, 250, 296.

and so was Anselm, 'the most luminous and penetrating intellect between Augustine and Aquinas'[1] (and of those two the latter was a friar), and the books and manuscripts produced by the monasteries were not only devotional works, nor accurate texts (*i.e.* new editions) of the Bible, the Fathers and the Ancients, but also creative works of theology, philosophy and law, grammar, science and mathematics.

Institutions such as these whose development in fact we are discussing attracted the most ardent and many of the most intellectual and intelligent spirits of the age. But the world could not spare them nor could they be deaf to the world's needs. Hence the monastic and the Benedictine centuries were largely dominated by Benedictine monks who were the confidants and counsellors of kings and princes. Hence the numerous monastic bishops, seeking to reform the Church and the world with it. In English history alone in the tenth and eleventh centuries, amongst many other possible examples, St. Dunstan, Lanfranc and St. Anselm are each of them Benedictine monks and each of them archbishops of Canterbury. The abbots of Cluny in the same age were public figures in Western Europe of a stature and influence to which there is no modern analogy save possibly the Secretary of the United Nations in a vintage year. By this route, then, we reach the great paradox of monasticism, as we do by others. Prestige, too, works the same way in general as well as in such eminent particular instances as a Lanfranc or an Anselm. Monks were, by common consent, the spiritual élite; at any time before *c.*1200 monasticism was held to be the most perfect form of Christian life, and at any time between *c.*800 and *c.*1100 Benedictine monasticism was the only form known in the West. From the beginning the monasteries shone like good deeds in a bad world, and their influence for good even as a silent witness in the Dark Ages of barbarian Europe cannot be calculated as it cannot be measured. But they did not remain only a silent witness, and in practice their direct contribution to the conversion,

[1] David Knowles, *The Monastic Order in England* (2nd. edition, Cambridge, 1963), p. 96.

christianization and civilization of the heathen was immense. Missionaries planted monasteries like castles of God where they went and garrisoned them with the soldiers of Christ. The religious communities thus founded served not only as the active centres of spiritual regeneration, but also and of necessity developed the land upon which they were settled, and taught the inhabitants not only Christianity but also economy, rather like Western firms in underdeveloped areas today. Nor have we yet mentioned the most rewarding penalty of prestige and success. The universal veneration in which monasticism came to be held in the monastic centuries, and the social needs and aspirations which, as we have seen, it answered, brought wealth and worldly position to those who in theory turned their backs on both. The self-sufficient community of St. Benedict's Rule needed endowment to function, but wide estates in this age especially brought not only wealth but also great and secular responsibilities. As the feudal concept of the fief, of service in return for land, took hold, many lands of many monasteries were obliged, as is well known, to render military knight-service as well as the service of prayer, and in any case that lordship which went with land involved the duties of local government. Further the literacy and particular skills of monks, like those of other clergy, plus the solid establishment of their houses which might seem like the pillars of society as well as of heaven, plus, it may be, the attitudes and assumptions of the theocratic government of the age, made abbeys and abbots seem especially suitable to take on that delegation of authority whereby kings and princes sought to administer their territories at a distance and exercise functions beyond their own capacity. It might seem irreverent in any case to meddle in the affairs of the living saint to whom a monastery might be dedicated and whose relics it might house, while abbots, like other lords, were glad to avoid such intermeddling. Thus it came about that all over Latin Christendom great Benedictine abbeys became the heads of great liberties or franchises from which the officials of secular government were excluded and which their abbots administered through their own officials on behalf of the king or prince and in the name of the saint. To this day (*i.e.* as I write, before the impertinent reformers of local government move in) as one instance, the whole of West Suffolk is administered from Bury St. Edmunds, separately from East Suffolk based upon Ipswich, as the eight and a half hundreds of the former liberty of St. Edmund.

By the eleventh century, therefore, no longer in practice withdrawn from the world, the Benedictine monasteries were an integral part of society which had made them what they were, and which they had come to serve. They were, for good or ill, as we might say, part of the Establishment. They had come a long way from the far-off days of St. Benedict at Monte Cassino, and not all the developments they had undergone, though always meant for the best and never with ill-intent, were within the spirit, or even the letter, of their Rule. It was partly for this reason, as a conscious reaction and desire for renewal, that new monastic movements developed from a welter of individual experiments and searchings in the late eleventh and early twelfth centuries, though the historian, with his broader vision, can also see the new variety of the new orders, which broke the time-honoured monopoly of the Benedictines, as a reflection of the new variety of the more sophisticated and rapidly developing society of the age. All these movements which lasted became religious 'orders' in the strict sense, now accepted but then new, of organizations with central direction, as opposed to the ancient autonomy of Benedictine houses each merely following the same Rule. Cluny[1] and her daughter houses had been a step in this direction as from the tenth century, but the organization of the new orders was of a different kind and typical of an organizing age, and in the end even the Benedictines had to succumb to it and become an 'order'. All the new orders, too, were inevitably deeply influenced by, or directly derived from, Benedictine monasticism which thus remains in the West the parent stock, though they reacted against its current practice and sought, like most religious movements, to return to an original simplicity

[1] See below, pp. 131–6.

now lost. They sought what they saw as the timeless core of monasticism and asceticism now overlaid by later accumulations and irrelevancies or worse, and in so doing they attracted to themselves many of the most ardent spirits of the age. The Carthusians, sprung from the Grande Chartreuse in southern France, went back, like many of the individual seekers of this time, beyond St. Benedict to the older eastern traditions of the eremitical life and a more severe, austere asceticism, though they successfully combined both with the cenobitic habit of living in community. In many ways the chosen few, they never became a numerous order like the Benedictines or the Cistercians or the Augustinians, and perhaps for this reason they never were to be, and have never been, bent by the pressures of society from their original concept and ideal. *Nunquam reformata quia nunquam deformata,* never in need of reform, they stand to this day upon the ancient ways, a shining and hopeful exception, whatever one's views, to the otherwise pervasive paradox of monasticism.

Not so the Cistercians, sprung from Citeaux, again in France, at once the most successful and the most impressive of the new orders, whose lofty and high vaunting ideals make the paradox the more strident. Unlike the Carthusians, they sought perfection and their heart's desire not by going beyond St. Benedict to a remoter past and earlier traditions but by a return to the Rule, entire, complete and undefiled. Not for them the splendours of established Benedictinism, the long development and evolution of St. Benedict's Rule in practice from its original simplicity, the opulent liturgies added to the offices by the tenth-century Cluniac reformers, the easy, lordly integration with society, the fine buildings, or even the scholarship. They would live literally by the Rule and by the Gospel in the imitation of Christ, and they would in reality shun the world. 'Whatever St. Benedict ordained was altogether established by the Providence of the Holy Spirit, so that nothing can be imagined that is more profitable, more holy, or more blessed. Indeed the Rule of St. Benedict is an exposition of the whole Gospel, not allegorically but in

terms of simple experience and visible works.'[1] They were the
Puritans of the twelfth century. And what happened? Their
effective idealism brought them prestige, prestige brought
success, and success brought wealth. They fled the world for the
waste lands, the forests and the empty places, and it turned out
that these were the development areas of an expanding society.
In England they put their barren lands to grass and sheep, and,
as it happened, wool was the growth point of the economy.
Their very Puritanism made them richer, for they would not
spend upon ostentation as the world did, and therefore their
money grew. They could not avoid success nor, since they had a
message, could they wish to. In 1118 there were seven Cistercian
abbeys and less than fifty years later, by 1152, there were three
hundred and twenty-eight. St. Bernard of Clairvaux became, as
it were, the public conscience of Europe as the abbot of Cluny
had been before him. They attracted the patronage of kings and
princes. One English instance must suffice to demonstrate the
near-inevitability of the world's slow stain and the failure that is
latent in success. When in the 1270s Edward I undertook a
religious foundation in the furtherance of a vow, he chose the
Cistercian Order and planted it at Vale Royal. The abbey church
he and his masons planned there in the event was never finished,
too expensive to complete (castles in Wales drained supplies),
but if it had been finished it would have been the largest, grandest
Cistercian church in England and the second in all Europe—for
the founder was Edward I, King of England and Duke of Aquitaine, the most potent prince in Christendom.[2] Edward's Vale
Royal has vanished now but Fountains, which it should have
excelled, still stands as the negation of the Cistercian prohibition
of fine buildings. Yet which of us would have it otherwise?

Far less impressive and less powerful, and in that sense less
important, than the Cistercians were to become, and intentionally

[1] *Memorials of Fountains Abbey*, ed. J. R. Wolbran, Surtees Society, 42,
1863, i, 15. Quoted by Southern, *Western Society and the Church in the
Middle Ages*, p. 251.

[2] For Vale Royal, see *The History of the King's Works*, ed. H. M. Colvin
(London, H.M.S.O., 1963), i, 248–57.

far less austere than the Carthusians, the Augustinian Canons are in some ways the most interesting and significant of the new religious orders of the late eleventh and early twelfth centuries. They were monks with a difference, residential canons, and like the Carthusians they too went back beyond St. Benedict, but in a different direction, to an earlier concept of an apostolic life of service to the community instead of withdrawal from it. They thus played Martha to the contemplative's Mary. Their Rule was simple, imprecise, fluid and informal by current monastic standards, derived from a letter of St. Augustine laying down principles but not detailed instructions for a communal religious life. They thus represent a break with the past characteristic of the age, and, in their success and the growth of their order, a break in the hitherto dominant monastic ideal of withdrawal from the world and of the contemplative life. It has recently been said of the early Cistercians that 'They were the last generation of medieval men to believe that it was good for all men to be monks',[1] and the Augustinians thus look to the future and the age of the friars. That age was the thirteenth century, during which all over Latin Christendom the friars achieved their first pre-eminence and near-universal reverence and popularity, before the nemesis of success overtook them also in their turn. With the thirteenth century this book ends in any case for other reasons, though also, as it happens, there were to be no other major religious orders founded before the shock of the Reformation. The friars therefore come at the end of the line, yet also—though anticipated by the Augustinians, from whom the Dominicans are derived, and though the Franciscans can be seen as the spiritual heirs of the Cistercians—the orders of the friars are something new. They mark the end of the monastic centuries, that is to say, four centuries and more dominated by the concept of monasticism which, nevertheless, continues on its way. Whereas the monastic ideal was one of withdrawal from the world, and of the enclosed contemplative life whose main object was the salvation of the individual monk, so that all the great

[1] Southern, *ut supra*, p. 257.

services which the monasteries had come to render to society were in fact secondary, though contemporaries, especially critics (what do they *do* for all that property?), were coming to put them first, the friars were out and out evangelists and missionaries. To go out among the multitude and bring salvation to the many was their purpose, and in fulfilling it they both reflected the now outward-looking attitude of the official Church and met the new needs of a rapidly developing society. Preaching and teaching and the confessional were their methods and in their itinerant life they recalled the wandering monks of old, but not the stability of the Benedictines and their successors. While the whole world was their province and their cloister, they concentrated especially upon the towns and cities and the expanding urban population of the times, ill-served otherwise by a Church already ancient and long-since territorial. They concentrated also upon the Universities, the new feature of the age, the product of the twelfth-century renaissance,[1] and the new centres of intellectual and influential opinion. The realistic Dominicans, the Order of Preachers, born in the context of heresy to be overcome, were a learned order from the start. The Franciscans, like the Cistercians, in their seeking after simplicity, began by eschewing learning together with all other worldly possessions and accomplishments, but soon came to see that learning was indispensable, if not for one's own salvation then certainly for the salvation of others.

[1] See Chapter XI.

CHAPTER V

Vikings, Magyars and Moslems

It is time now to return to the main outline of secular affairs (in so far, as always, as the distinction can be made), and to return also to the beginning of the ninth century where we last left them. We may do so with the summary remark that by about the year 800 a great deal had been achieved, and much of the foundation of the future firmly laid. The medieval, and therefore the modern, world had begun to emerge from the painful fusion of classical and Germanic elements, the new arising phoenix-like from the ashes of the old. The great kingdom of the Franks had been established, and this, under the responsible Christian kingship of Charles the Great, in whose honour the concept of Empire had been revived, had come to comprise the whole of a greatly enlarged Latin Christendom with the single exception of the British Isles. Moreover, Latin Christendom itself, if not entirely co-extensive with the Christian Empire of Charlemagne, was yet no less (perhaps more) an entity under the now undoubted spiritual hegemony of the Papacy, the apostolic see, and to the centripetal eminence of Rome there was added, so to speak, the devotional inspiration and the driving force of a common Benedictine monasticism. By all these means Western Europe, which was Latin Christendom, distinct now from the Eastern Empire and the Greek Church, had discovered its identity. And to this end no less important was the remarkable revival of learning which the eighth century had witnessed, beginning first and going furthest in England, and culminating in the continental Carolingian Renaissance in which the English Alcuin of York played a leading part. As with the Carolingian Empire, so with the

Carolingian Renaissance, it was both a revival and also something new, Latin, Christian and European.

'Present promise', therefore, 'and wealth of the future beyond the eyes' scope', and the present securely grounded on the past of which it seemed a mere continuation or recension. One might have supposed that the emergent West would now be left free to develop along the lines laid down, expanding further to the east and striking back against the Moslems to the south hemming it in from the Mediterranean, as Charlemagne had carried fire, sword and Christianity into Germany and had established his Spanish March across the Pyrenees. But it was not to be, or rather, not yet to be. These things will happen, but not yet; meanwhile in the ninth century and the early tenth Latin Christendom was subjected to a new wave of barbarian invasions and to a triple onslaught from outside and all directions by Vikings, by Magyars and by Moslems. The fact that the West survived, as it were, bloody but unbowed, is tribute to the firmness of the foundations already laid, but afterwards nothing will be the same again, and this testing time is thus a watershed in history second only to the first barbarian invasions of the fifth and sixth centuries. It is worth reflecting that the origins of Europe were thus hammered out on the anvil of war, which accounts, for example, for the military ethos of feudal society, for the dominance far into the modern period of a warrior aristocracy, and for such manifestations of militant Christianity as the Crusades and Holy War.

With the Moslem threat in the south, which is in fact the last wave of the great expansion of Islam beginning in the seventh century, we have already dealt,[1] and it suffices now to remember and focus upon the fact that it was in the ninth century that the Arabs (under the powerful Aghlabid dynasty from north Africa) raided and devastated deep into southern France up the Rhone valley (in which context, therefore, Poitiers in 732[2] appears a decisive battle to us armed with hindsight rather than to contemporaries), and also into Italy. They conquered Sicily in the

[1] Above, pp. 25–33.
[2] Above, p. 28.

decades following their initial assault in 827, established themselves upon the mainland, and swept on, to sack, for example,
Monte Cassino and attack Rome itself. Sicily they took from
Byzantium and not from Latin Christendom, but they were to
retain it until the coming of the Normans in the eleventh century, with profound effects upon the island and through it upon
the West. The new learning which was the stuff of the Twelfth-
Century Renaissance came to the West mainly through the two
Arabic sources of Moslem Spain and Moslem Sicily.[1] Further,
the fact that in the outcome the rest of the Moslem onslaughts in
the ninth century were abortive should not obscure their importance at the time nor their potential to affect the future. A recent
writer has put the huge question of what might have happened
had Rome fallen—'the whole history of the middle ages in the
west might have been different.'[2] The Papacy was able to survive
migration from St. Peter's to Avignon in the fourteenth century,
but whether it could have survived the loss of Rome in the
ninth century is quite another question.

The Magyars or Hungarians came from the east only late in
the century, though it is convenient to deal with them now.
They were a Finno-Ugrian race of nomads from the steppes of
Asia, driven west by other nomadic tribes behind them, to
appear on the frontiers of the kingdom of the East Franks (the
Frankish kingdom being now divided) in 862 and to enter the
future Hungary in 895. From that time forward for sixty years
they struck terror throughout a disunited West, raiding the length
of Italy from Lombardy to Apulia, across the kingdom of the
West Franks, the future France, as far as the Spanish frontier,
and especially devastating the East Frankish kingdom which will
be Germany and which lay more immediately to hand. They were
intrepid and superb horsemen and their extreme mobility and
fluid mounted tactics were evidently the military reasons for their
far-flung success. Effective resistance, it was learnt, came from
fortified places which they would not attack, and Henry 'the

[1] Below, Chapter XI.
[2] Maurice Keen, *A History of Medieval Europe* (London, 1967), p. 25.

Fowler', Duke of Saxony and King of the East Franks, built fortresses against them as Alfred and his successors built 'boroughs' against the Danes in England. Henry himself had a great victory over them at the Unstrut in 933, but their final defeat came at the hands of his son and successor, Otto I, at the Lechfeld in 955, in a battle as decisive as any in history. For three days, we are told, the pursuit and the slaughter continued. The age of the great raids was thereafter over and the Magyars henceforward settled in Hungary as mere troublesome neighbours of the German kingdom and empire. At the end of the century their ruler, St. Stephen I (997–1038), was baptized into the Christian and Catholic Church and began the forceful conversion of his country, to be crowned in the year 1000 as the first and 'apostolic' King of Hungary by Pope Silvester II.

Although the results of the Magyar invasions, therefore, were the extension of Latin Christendom through their conversion and the establishment of their new kingdom, and although Otto I's great victory at the Lechfeld in 955 (bearing the Holy Lance of the Emperor Constantine in his hand) set him in the role of the saviour of Christendom from the heathen, greatly strengthened his position in the German kingship, and led to his coronation as Emperor by the Pope in 962, these, as it were, are sequences of events rather than the products of Magyar creativeness, and it cannot otherwise be said that they had any great constructive influence upon the West. Not so the Vikings who throughout the ninth century and on into the tenth plundered and havocked at will over much of Europe, for though the Western sources at the receiving end naturally speak exclusively of terror and destruction and rapine—'From the fury of the Norsemen, O Lord deliver us!'—land settlement and trade as well as plunder and martial fame were the objectives of these sea-rovers and warrior bands, and the saga of their deeds includes extraordinary achievements some of which last to mould the future.

Viking, meaning sea-rover, is a contemporary name given to the Germanic peoples then inhabiting Scandinavia, Denmark, Norway and Sweden. Ethnically therefore these peoples now

irrupting into Latin Christendom were related to the original
Germanic races who had overrun the Roman Empire in the
West four hundred years before. In a real sense the Viking
incursions can thus be seen as part of the larger whole of Germanic migration, though thereafter it is more illuminating to
focus upon them in their own right as the Viking Movement and
Viking Age, extending in all through four hundred years from
the late eighth to the late eleventh century. Since during this
time Viking penetration by raid or trade or settlement ranged
over almost the whole known world and also far beyond, from
Frisia and the Baltic and the Faroes in the north to Italy in the
south, from Kiev, Novgorod and Constantinople in the east to
the shores of North America via Iceland and Greenland in the
West, that canvas may indeed seem broad enough.

The reasons and causes of the Viking Movement still remain
something of a mystery, though they certainly include an expanding population combined with centrifugal political pressures at
home, the relatively crabbed and confined life in the homelands
combined with a desire for a place in the sun and a share, if only
by plunder, in the opulence of the more developed regions;
and, above all, the technical accomplishments which made it
possible, the requisite navigational skills and the ability to build
and sail swift, seaworthy and ocean-going ships. The Vikings
were heathen and barbarian when they came, but they were far
from being primitive savages, and their skills included metal-
work and weapon-making as well as carpentry and boat-build-
ing. The reasons for their outrageous success include their
sovereign mobility (like that of the Magyars, but in their case
based upon the waters, though they soon took to horses for over-
land speed), the defencelessness of the lands they attacked, and
their own supreme self-confidence. No doubt the Viking ethic
can easily be romanticized, as it is in the Norse sagas, and seemed
anything but glamorous to those they slaughtered, maimed or
overcame, but it must be placed in any survey of the motivations
which drove them on.

—[1]A man must be imperturbable, wise, and ready for battle; cheerful and active until death.

—A coward seeks to escape death by avoiding his enemies, but old age no man escapes even if he survives the spears.

—A man should never be parted one step from his weapon; neither on the road nor on his field he never knows ... when he will need his sword.

—Young I was long ago, I was wandering alone and lost my way, but I found wealth in a companion. In man is man's delight.

—Do not trust a woman's words, be she single or married; their hearts run on wheels, they are a prey to moods.

—Cattle die, kinsmen die, I myself shall die. I know what does not die: the judgement of a dead man's life.

Theirs was predominantly a man's world of the heroic virtues, and of the loyalties and companionship of long voyages and long campaigns, fame as well as wealth the spur, with the ultimate rewards of a warrior's Valhalla, feasting and roistering for ever in the hall.

While in the age of their greatness the Vikings voyaged north, south, east and west, and there is no part of Western Europe especially which completely escaped their depredations, there are four principal areas of their activity of particular importance for the future; in the east and what will be Russia, in Gaul or West Frankia, in Britain and more especially England, and in the North Atlantic. In the east the Vikings, in this case chiefly Swedes, can claim to be the founders of the Russian state, or, at the least, prominent among its founding factors. In this direction, from the Baltic, they worked their way during the ninth century, in search of trade and more, down the trade routes and the rivers Dnieper and Volga which traverse the Russian landmass, and so to the Caspian and the Black Sea. From here they were in touch

[1] The following extracts are taken from the later Norse 'The High One's Words' (*i.e.* Odin's), as quoted by Johannes Brondsted, *The Vikings* (Penguin, Harmondsworth, 1960), pp. 233–5.

with Constantinople and also the Moslem east. Few things are more surprising than to meet these barbarian traders from the frozen north in the pages of sophisticated Arabian and Byzantine writers, and we would not expect their record to be entirely flattering. 'I saw', wrote Ibn Fadlan in the tenth century, 'the Rus folk [*i.e.* Norsemen] when they arrived on their trading-mission and settled at the river Volga. Never had I seen people of more perfect physique. They are tall as date-palms, and reddish in colour . . . No one is ever parted from his axe, sword and knife . . . They are the filthiest of God's creatures. They do not wash after discharging their natural functions, neither do they wash their hands after meals. They are as lousy as donkeys.'[1] Here in the south the Vikings, known to the Byzantines as the *Rus* and/or Varangians,[2] traded with Constantinople, unsuccessfully attacked the city on several occasions, and left their name by taking service with the Emperor to form the future Varangian Guard, the *corps d'élite* of imperial armies. But their most important role in history was further north, in Russia, which takes its name from them. Along their route they founded trading stations and settlements, including Kiev and Novgorod. Oleg, traditionally the son of the legendary Rurik, prince of Novgorod, took possession of Kiev as well, and out of the two a rudimentary principality was made. A century later, Vladimir, Great Prince of Kiev (980–1015), beginning life as a doughty heathen and ending it as a saint, was baptized into the Greek Orthodox Church and enforced conversion upon his nobles. At what point the Viking core of Novgorod and Kiev is swallowed up by the Slav peoples surrounding it, to be further altered beyond recognition by Greek Christian religion and Byzantine civilization, is anybody's guess and a matter of debate, but the origins of modern Russia are to be found in the fusion of these elements, and events are set in train which lead to 'Holy Russia' and the claim of Moscow to be, via Constantinople, the 'Third Rome'.

[1] Quoted by Brøndsted, *The Vikings*, p. 247.
[2] On these names, see the long and valuable note (2) to p. 246 of Gwyn Jones, *A History of the Vikings* (Oxford, 1968).

With the Viking settlements of Kiev and Novgorod we have thus passed beyond the confines of Latin Christendom, but if we turn next to the realm of the Franks we return to its heartlands. Few if any regions suffered more from Viking depredations in the ninth century than Gaul, the western Frankish kingdom and the future France. The list of sackings seems endless, beginning at the monastic and commercial centre of Noirmoutier at the mouth of the Loire in 835. In 841 the target was Rouen. In 842 there occurred a particularly well-recorded and therefore particularly horrific raid upon Nantes on the Feast of St. John the Baptist, the 24th of June. 'They slew in the streets, they slew in the houses, they slew bishop and congregation in the church. They did their will till nightfall, and the ships they rowed down river were deep-laden with plunder and prisoners'.[1] In 845 Paris was sacked, on Easter Sunday. In 847 it was the turn of Bordeaux, in 853 of Tours, in 854 of Blois, and 856 Orleans. In 857 Paris was attacked for the second time, though the famous year-long siege of the future capital was to be reserved until 885–6. The chronicler Ermentarius of Noirmoutier, writing in the 860s, could see no hope as things seemed to grow yearly worse. 'The number of ships increases, the endless flood of vikings never ceases to grow bigger. Everywhere Christ's people are the victims of massacre, burning, and plunder. The vikings overrun all that lies before them, and no one can withstand them. They seize Bordeaux, Périgueux, Limoges, Angoulême, Toulouse; Angers, Tours and Orleans are made deserts. Ships past counting voyage up the Seine, and throughout the entire region evil grows strong. Rouen is laid waste, looted and burnt: Paris, Beauvais, Meaux are taken, Melun's stronghold is razed to the ground, Chartres occupied, Evreux and Bayeux looted, and every town invested.'[2] But in these indiscriminate devastations, of which we have cited only some as illustrations, there was a pattern imposed by the rivers of France which the Vikings used for their passage, and amongst them the Seine and the Loire were the entries to espe-

[1] Gwyn Jones, *History of the Vikings*, p. 211.
[2] Quoted by Gwyn Jones, *op. cit.*, p. 215.

cially favoured areas of operation. And it was the Seine Vikings
who were to be the cause and the instrument of one constructive
event in the midst of so much destruction. To them under their
leader Rollo, in 911 at St. Clair-sur-Epte (when in fact, as we can
see but men at the time could not, the fury of the Norsemen
was beginning to die down), the Frankish king, Charles the
Simple, granted territories about the Seine, in an effort to contain
them and win them to his side. These territories bounded by the
rivers Bresle, Epte, Avre and Dives, comprising the modern
departments of Seine Inférieure, Eure, Calvados, Manche and
part of Orne, are the modern Upper or eastern Normandy, and
out of this combined with the further grants of Lower Normandy
in 924 and 933 the future Norman duchy was born. Within a
hundred and fifty years from its foundation it will emerge as the
most potent feudal principality in France, and from it the
Normans, *i.e.* the Norsemen of Normandy, will ride and sail out
to conquer England, southern Italy, Sicily and Antioch. In so
doing they alone will alter the whole history of the West, and to
them we shall return.[1]

Meanwhile England suffered scarcely less than Gaul from the
depredations of the Vikings, principally Danes, whose raids and
expeditions here were closely interconnected with those on the
other side of the Channel and North Sea, being often part of the
same voyages and campaigns carried out by the same Viking
fleets and armies. The first recorded raids in the West were in
fact those of *c.*789 on the south coast of Wessex and the far worse
sacking of Lindisfarne in Northumbria in 793. The first must
have seemed at the time an isolated event of no great meaning,
a cloud no bigger than a man's hand. We are told by the Anglo-
Saxon Chronicle and Æthelweard's recension, how the local
royal reeve rode out of Dorchester to the harbour with only a
handful of men, assuming the visitors to be traders—'for he did
not know what they were; and they slew him'.[2] The second was

[1] Below, Chapter X.
[2] *Anglo-Saxon Chronicle*, ed. D. Whitelock and others (London, 1965),
p. 35 and note.

a portent—'In this year dire portents appeared over Northumbria and sorely frightened the people. They consisted of immense whirlwinds and flashes of lightning, and fiery dragons were seen flying in the air. A great famine immediately followed those signs, and a little after that in the same year, on 8 June, the ravages of heathen men miserably destroyed God's church on Lindisfarne, with plunder and slaughter.'[1] To Alcuin at Charlemagne's court the news of the destruction of the holy place of Lindisfarne was shattering, and the event attributable only to God's wrath visited upon the sins of the people. He quoted Jeremiah—'Then the Lord said unto me, Out of the north an evil shall break forth upon all the inhabitants of the land'—and his own comment is a fitting introduction to the Viking age now dawning: 'It is some 350 years that we and our forefathers here inhabited this lovely land, and never before in Britain has such a terror appeared as this we have now suffered at the hands of the heathen. Nor was it thought possible that such an inroad from the sea could be made.'[2] The longboats of the Vikings made such visitations all too possible, and the defenceless wealth of churches will be their favourite prey.

In the next decades, however, Norse attentions (principally Norwegian) were focused upon Ireland, and it was not until the 840s that the full fury of the Norsemen was launched upon England as upon Gaul. Thereafter things could only get worse before they could get better. In 850, at Thanet, the Danes wintered in England for the first time (as they had previously done at Noirmoutier in Gaul in 843—'As if they meant to stay for ever', wrote the chronicler), and did so again in Sheppey in 855, all too obviously merely resting and waiting for a thus inevitable renewal of devastation in the spring. In 865 a new and worse phase opened with the arrival of the 'great army', under Ivar the Boneless, Ubbi and Halfdan, ready to campaign for years, not just for loot now but to conquer and retain whole kingdoms. What happened in the outcome is sufficiently well

---

[1] *Ibid.*, p. 36.
[2] Quoted by Gwyn Jones, *History of the Vikings*, pp. 194–5.

known—the conquest of all England save for Wessex and part of Mercia, the martyrdom of St. Edmund, last King of East Anglia, the heroic resistance and hard-won victory of Alfred alone in the west, and Alfred and Guthrum's treaty of 878 at Wedmore, whereby the latter withdrew from Wessex and accepted the Christian faith.

What matters to us here especially is the result of these events. In fact, setting aside even the obvious social and ethnic effects upon the English of the Danish settlement and their occupation of the Danelaw, *i.e.* more than half of England lying north and east of a line drawn from the mouth of the Thames to Chester, and setting aside also the subsequent influence of the Danes so settled upon English trade and agriculture, law, language and arts, nothing could be more important in terms of sheer political history and the development of the English state than the Viking incursions of the ninth century.[1] At this high level the overall result is the paradoxical one of the achievement of political unity for the first time since the days of Roman Britain. All the English kingdoms save only Wessex under Alfred, and a part of Mercia, fell to be incorporated in the Danelaw, but the next phase of English history is the slow reconquest of the Danelaw by Alfred and his successors, until in the mid-tenth century the point was reached where the kingdom of Wessex became the kingdom of England. In consequence, and notwithstanding the conquest of all England by the Danish Cnut in 1016, here ancient monarchy, together with much of the old Germanic world, survived and continued, and something like a nation state emerged. In this outcome lies, amongst other things, the fundamental explanation of the absence of feudalism, and the survival of an older and pre-feudal society, in tenth and eleventh-century England down to 1066. And this outcome also, as we shall see,[2] is the direct opposite of what happened in France, where the incursions of the Vikings, with the Magyars and the Moslems, in the ninth and early tenth centuries brought about the collapse

[1] For England, see also Chapter X.
[2] Below p. 211 and Chapters VI and IX.

of central, monarchical authority and the consequential establishment of feudal society. Meanwhile, the mention of 1066 and the Norman Conquest of England, itself among the results of the Viking Age, serves as a reminder that the Danes brought weakness as well as strength to England. If there was political unity at one level there was disunity at another, for the Danelaw remained at least until the later eleventh century as a deep division within the realm, and fostered in the north especially a dangerous element of separatism.

The British Isles may lead us, as they led the Vikings, via the Orkneys, the Shetlands and the Faroes, on into the great spaces of the North Atlantic, which are the fourth main area of Viking activity to require particular attention, and in many ways the most remarkable of all. They had reached the Faroes by about the year 800, and sailed on to find the rumoured land of Iceland further west somewhere about 860 to 870. Iceland they vigorously colonized and remain there to this day. By about 930 that colonization was complete, and the questing Viking prows skimmed and butted further west, to Greenland. Here also settlements were made, beginning in 986, and it was from Greenland that North America was discovered by the Vikings about the year 1000, half a millennium before Columbus. Of this, to us at least the most exciting of all Norse feats, there is no longer any doubt, the long-known but hitherto suspect evidence of the sagas being now confirmed by maps and archaeological discoveries in Canada. They called their landfalls Markland and Vinland, but the settlements they made there were in the event abortive and were probably abandoned by about 1020, shown to be impracticable by the over-extended lines of hazardous communication, the lack of sufficient manpower to follow up, and the hostility of the natives who were, presumably, Red Indians. But when they withdrew they did not lose contact nor did they forget, and the knowledge in the West of a land beyond the Atlantic lingers on as a tenuous yet vital link between the voyages of Bjarni Herjolfsson and Leif Erikson and those of John Cabot and Christopher Columbus.

The identification of Markland and especially Vinland has
proved almost as hazardous as their discovery. It now seems very
likely that the former is Labrador and probable that the latter is
Newfoundland, with both therefore in Canada, though the
insistence of the sagas on the wine and gentle climate of Vinland
leads the imagination further south and enables the healthy longing for antiquity in the United States to argue for almost any
coastal territory between New England and Florida. With the
Vikings all things were possible by sea, and time and archaeology
may tell. Meanwhile no reader would expect a book like this to
refrain from claiming the discovery of North America as one
more in the long list of medieval achievements, though not the
most important. It remains the great non-starter of medieval
history, attempted perhaps too late as well as too early. For it
came towards the end of the saga of the Viking Age: the world was
changing and the Vikings with it; their day was nearly done,
together with the circumstances that had made it possible.
The American landfalls were not exploited, and even Greenland
came to be too far away. That colony, as we now know, was
doomed. 'Wise after the event, we can now see that everything
about the Greenland settlements was temporary and marginal.
Sailing the fjords or walking the pastures there today two things
are immediately intelligible: how certain it was that men from
Iceland would be attracted by the green and grassy oases of the
south-west, make their homes and lodge their destinies there—
and when events turned against them how certain it was that they
could not survive.'[1] They were in any case, as Pope Alexander VI
expressed it, 'at the world's end', and events did turn against
them, to make a tragic epilogue to the Viking Age come to pass
long centuries later. Steadily after about 1200 the climate wor-
sened and grew colder: the Eskimos returned in consequence:
the sea-passage became more dangerous and less attempted: the
changing pattern of European trade took away the profit motive
in keeping communications open. By the fourteenth century it
was thought in the West that the Greenlanders had abandoned

[1] Gwyn Jones, *History of the Vikings*, p. 307.

the Christian faith—untrue but symptomatic of a lack of contact. The last bishop to visit them did so in 1377. The last ship making the regular Greenland run sank in 1369. Slowly, inexorably, the Norse colony in Greenland vanishes from recorded history, and the fading signals cease. By about 1500, it is thought, the last, the eastern, settlement died—and, as it happened, at the very time when new voyages of discovery were heading west from Europe.

In dealing so far separately with the impact of the Saracens, the Magyars and the Vikings in the ninth century and on into the tenth we have already seen something of the results of each. From the Saracens in the south comes the fact of Moslem Sicily until the eleventh century. From the Magyars and Otto's success against them follow the greatly increased powers of kingship in Germany and the acquisition of the imperial title and dignity. The results of the Viking incursions include the parallel increase of royal power in England to the point of the achievement of political unity, and the foundation of the duchy of Normandy, while beyond the confines of Western Europe the Rus were a potent element in the origins of Russia. Yet all this is not enough. For Henri Pirenne, as we saw before,[1] the impact of the Moslems alone brought about the real break between ancient and modern, classical and medieval, and caused the formation of Latin Christendom and the West. Though few would now go with him all the way in this, most or all are agreed on the lingering continuity of the fifth and sixth centuries and beyond, and the absence of any datable cataclysmic 'fall of the Roman Empire in the West'. If then we bring all the dramatic factors of the ninth and earlier tenth centuries together, and examine their joint impact as a whole, we may well conclude that the combined effects upon the West of Saracen and Magyar and Viking are at least as great as those of the first barbarian invaders four centuries before, and this period scarcely less a turning point than that. Huge changes came about in Western Europe at this time and in all of them the impact of the invaders was at least a

[1] Above, p. 31.

contributing if not always a primary factor. In the first place, the Carolingian Empire collapsed in fact if not in theory, in spite of the high-flown concept of a Christian empire, whose ideal unity should override mere race and local custom, held by Charlemagne's son and successor, Louis the Pious (814–840), and his clerical and monastic confidants and counsellors ('All are one in Christ'). It collapsed principally, one may say, because its reach had exceeded its grasp, and its unity depended over-much on the driving force and genius of one man's personality. It disintegrated also because of the (to the modern mind) fatal principle, still held among the Franks in spite of Louis' efforts, that the kingdom like any inheritance must be divided among the sons on the death of the father. Louis himself had succeeded to the undivided whole of Charlemagne's dominions only through the chance of sole survival, and during his reign and after his death elaborate plans were made, and fratricidal wars were waged, for the partition of his realm. The most famous of these agreements and the most lasting in its effects was the Treaty of Verdun in 843 (Map 5), whereby of his sons Charles the Bald was to have a western kingdom, Louis the German an eastern and the eldest son, Lothar, the title of Emperor and the so-called 'Middle Kingdom', extending north to south from the Low Countries to Italy inclusive and thus containing both imperial capitals, at Aachen and at Rome. The pattern of the future emerges here with clarity, for the Middle Kingdom will not survive but be nibbled and swallowed by the other two, while they, West Frankia and East Frankia, differing already in language in 843, will become France and Germany respectively. But the disintegration of Charlemagne's Empire does not stop here, nor with the ensuing dismemberment of the Middle Kingdom. Verdun coincides in time with the full fury of the Norsemen directed principally against the future France and England. While in the German Kingdom, spared the traumatic experience of the Vikings, the monarchy survives and waxes by its later success against the Magyars, and while in England, as we have seen, the paradoxical result of the Danish onslaught was

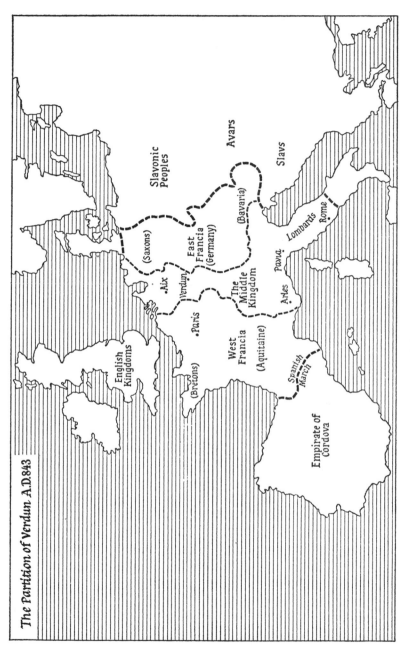

The Partition of Verdun A.D. 843

English Kingdoms

Slavonic Peoples

(Saxons)

Avars

.Aix

East Francia (Germany)

Verdun.

(Bavaria)

Slavs

.Paris

The Middle Kingdom

Lombards

Rome.

(Bretons)

West Francia (Aquitaine)

Arles.

Pavia.

Spanish March

Empirate of Cordova

MAP 5

also the expansion of monarchy and the achievement of political unity, in France it was otherwise. The sheer size of the kingdom of the West Franks and of their commitments proved altogether too much for the latter-day Carolingian kings, faced with the extreme mobility of endless Viking depredations combined with the raids of Moslems in the south and, later, of Magyars from the east. What happens in consequence is the progressive decline of an overworked and ineffective central and monarchical authority, and its replacement in practice by an effective local lordship on the spot. The needs of defence were paramount: remote authority, albeit sanctified, could not provide it. Men turned to those who could, and those who could took over. 'It was agreed that it was God's will that His people should unite, but when the Vikings, the Moslems, and the Hungarians were abroad, the urgent necessity was a safe stronghold and a lord whose protection would be at hand.'[1] In these circumstances we see, if not the origins of feudalism, then certainly the origins of feudal society, and this in France. From France the new feudal concepts will radiate in all directions in the future, to permeate all Latin Christendom. Here, then, is a change to conjure with in the whole nature of society in the West, and one brought about in the ninth and tenth centuries. It is impossible to think of the so-called Middle Ages without feudalism, and thus in the broadest sense 'feudal' and 'medieval' are terms used synonymously by historians. Nor is it to be expected that concepts so potent and inbred, and the institutions to which they gave birth, would vanish without trace at whatever date one declares 'The Middle Ages' to have ended. In reality, feudalism, no less, let us say, than the Christian and Catholic Church, or the classical and Germanic inheritances combined, is one of the basic formative influences which have made the modern West.

Nor is this all if we seek to summarize the effects in general of the holocaust of the ninth and early tenth centuries, for it was followed as a natural reaction by a great revival in the West in almost every sphere of human activity—politically in the growth

[1] R. H. C. Davis, *History of Medieval Europe*, p. 173.

and formation of states; economically in the expansion of trade and industry, wealth, settlement and population; socially in feudalism and the effects of those developments already listed; culturally in the so-called Twelfth-Century Renaissance which begins in the eleventh; religiously in the great monastic reform movements emanating from Cluny and elsewhere, and culminating in that reform movement in the whole Church, revolutionary in its implications and going by the name 'Gregorian'. Revival, indeed, is not the word for this and more, which is development and therefore change. We move at least, after the watershed of the ninth and early tenth centuries, in conventional terminology from the Early to the High Middle Ages, and it is difficult not to feel that the latter are the true Middle Ages with all the characteristic features that the term 'the medieval period' brings to mind, and that we have, in short, passed a turning point in history.

CHAPTER VI

Feudal Society

Anyone seeking to write a book designed to show the importance and 'relevance' of the so-called Middle Ages to the future and the modern West, as the age of origins and foundations and therefore lasting influences, has no shortage of good cards to play: the only problem lies in what order to play them. Arrived as we now are on the brink of perhaps the most important period of all—from, let us say, *c.* 950 to *c.* 1250—in the pace and wide range of its developments, we shall do best to begin with some discussion and appreciation of certain basic factors and motive forces in society, before attempting any account of political history or narrative of what happened. In this chapter, therefore, we shall deal with feudalism, as the very mould in which society was cast, and, in the next, once more with the Church, especially with the great ecclesiastical revival of the late tenth to early twelfth centuries—remembering, however, and making due allowance for, the artificiality of thus separating things secular and things ecclesiastical, which in reality, at the time, were inextricably entwined.

Few words, and no historical terms, are more abused and misunderstood at the present time than 'feudal' and its derivatives. Feudalism having come to be regarded as a Bad Thing as from 1789 and the French Revolution, and an even worse thing through the workings of Marxist dialectic, the adjective 'feudal' is now used outside academic circles, mainly as an epithet even more insulting than 'medieval', though those who so use it chiefly reveal their own profound ignorance and lack of education. Yet even for historians of the medieval centuries the words

evidently have attendant difficulties, arising out of imprecision.
It is not that 'feudal' and 'feudalism' are any less capable of
being meaningful than other portmanteau terms, like democratic,
socialist or capitalist, used to describe types of society, but that
they are in practice even more loosely used than those analogies.
Possibly this owes something to the fact that our terms were
coined after the event to describe a state of affairs already past
or passing: in the English language, for example, 'feudal' does
not appear until the seventeenth century, nor 'feudal system'
until the eighteenth, while 'feudalism' only begins in 1839. Since
contemporaries thus had never heard of feudalism, historians
are the more free to make of it what they will. However this may
be, there is a danger that the word will, or has, come to mean,
first and foremost, different things to different historians according to their particular approach and interest—social, economic,
legal, political or military—the one stressing one feature and the
next another. There is also the certainty in practice of the dual
use of 'feudal': precisely, as an adjective to be attached only to
those characteristics and features of society which are peculiar
and unique to feudalism, and which alone justify our use of that
descriptive noun; and loosely, via a concept of a feudal period,
to be applied to all or any features of a society and a time which
for certain precise reasons only is properly called feudal. In the
second and loose usage the word becomes little more than a
synonym for 'medieval'. Thus a well-known and distinguished
book by the American J. W. Thompson is entitled *Feudal
Germany*,[1] but in reality is a history of Germany in the feudal
period,[2] which is rather different, and the reader will not in fact
find as much as might be expected about German feudalism in it.
Again, the greatest of all books on the subject of feudalism, Marc
Bloch's *Feudal Society*,[3] discusses under that title aspects of
society within the feudal period, such as the difficulties of

[1] New York, 1928; republished, 1962.
[2] See *e.g.*, p. vii.
[3] *La Société féodale*, 2 vols., Paris, 1939–40. English edition (to which
references are here given), translated L. A. Manyon, London, 1961.

transport or the age at which men died,[1] in no sense strictly 'feudal' (as, of course, the author knew). Maitland, whose own work on feudalism remains fundamental, nevertheless once smiled at 'feudalists of the straiter sort',[2] but we must all be of that sort in order to understand.

We must begin therefore with fundamentals. Feudalism closely analysed and strictly defined is fundamentally a secular and upper-class affair. The fundamental members, so to speak, of feudal society, those who make it feudal, are the knights, the heavily armed and specialist cavalrymen, who, at first a military élite, became almost at once and of necessity a social élite also. The fundamental bond of that society, without which it cannot be called feudal, is vassalage, an aristocratic tie binding two free men together, with reciprocal obligations, as lord and vassal, lord and man, created by the ceremony of vassalic commendation, comprising homage, fealty and (usually) investiture with the fief. The fundamental institution of feudalism is the fee or fief, from which indeed (Latin *feudum*) the word itself is derived. The purely personal relations of lord and man established by commendation early became rooted in the soil: the lord owed maintenance to his vassal, the vassal owed service (especially expensive military and mounted service as a knight) to his lord, and both were made possible by an endowment, usually of land, bestowed by the lord on his vassal, and held by the vassal as a tenant of the lord. Hence the benefice or fief with which, after he has done homage and sworn fealty to his lord, the vassal is invested in the full ceremony of vassalic commendation. Further, to these three fundamentals of feudalism—knights, vassalic commendation and the fief—castles, the fortified residences of lords, may be added as a fourth, as we shall later see. Next, feudalism thus described finds its origins in West Frankia, in northern France especially, in the area bounded to the east by the Rhine and to the south by the Loire. From that area it spreads, sometimes more or less naturally, as into southern

---

[1] Pp. 61–2, 72–3.
[2] *Domesday Book and Beyond* (Fontana, paperback edition), p. 198.

France, Germany east of the Rhine, and northern Italy, sometimes by conquest, as in the case of England, southern Italy and
Sicily, and the crusading states of Outremer, until it comes to
comprise more or less all Latin Christendom. But as in the beginning, so later elsewhere, feudalism develops in response to
particular circumstances and particular needs, and therefore
at different times and with different details in different places
(which is why the phrase 'the feudal system', implying uniformity,
is frowned upon), though always with those fundamental
features just described.

Just as feudalism spread outwards from northern France, so
also feudal concepts spread from the upper ranks of a military
and militant secular society which was their source into other
social orders and other social spheres. Thus the Church became
heavily feudalized from the tenth and eleventh centuries, so that
bishops and abbots became also vassals rendering military knight
service for their lands, though more pertinent here is that in the
ecclesiastical sphere the feudal concept of service in return for
land could also be expressed in more purely spiritual terms, so
that a church might also hold lands by the feudal tenure of
frankalmoign, *i.e.* in free alms, by which was meant free of all
earthly service but in return for the service of prayer. So, too,
towns and cities, which fitted ill into this essentially territorial
society, were and had to be treated as corporate vassals owing
corporate services. And so too the peasant, the serf, the villein,
owing, as everyone knows, agricultural services to the lord of the
manor in return for his share of the manorial land. Which brings
us to a prominent instance of the loose usage of the word 'feudal',
causing perhaps more confusion through loose thinking than
any other. Neither the manor nor a subject peasantry tied both
to the land and the lord thereof are amongst the fundamentals of
feudal society as unique and generic to it. It is true that they
exist concurrently with it (as do many other things—the sun,
the moon, the stars), but they can and do also exist outside it,
in periods and places which are not feudal because they lack
those fundamentals which really are unique to feudalism (thus

Sardinia in the Middle Ages; England before 1066. And was nineteenth-century Russia really 'feudal'?). So, too, the ties that bound the villein to the land may have had a remote common origin with those superior ties that bound the warrior vassal to his lord, but they developed very differently and for a different purpose. Feudalism, it needs to be insisted once again, was an upper-class affair of knights and castles, lords and vassals who were also lords (or would-be lords). This glittering superstructure may have rested upon the broad backs of a subject peasantry, but was by no means unique among types of society in so doing. For that matter it also rested, more moderately but increasingly as the centuries passed, upon the labours of the townsmen, the bourgeoisie, yet no one would think of making them a fundamental element of feudalism, essential to its definition. Nor, since we have touched upon the medieval feature of a subject peasantry, is it to be used as a stick to beat the Middle Ages with —part of the myth of a brutal Dark Ages beyond all liberal comprehension, such as those unhappy many who in England began their history in 1485 are taught to scorn. It is a crude and uncomprehending over-simplification to talk of medieval society too much in terms of exploiters and exploited. It contained this human factor no more, and quite likely less, than the societies of other more 'enlightened' periods. Even if we make no reference to the real social Dark Ages of the English Industrial Revolution, we may yet suggest that the medieval serf or villein was in some respects better off than his modern counterpart, and much better off, for example, than the English agricultural labourer of the hard times between the wars. If Hod was a villein and legally unfree, he was no wage slave. He had his land; he had security; he was a member of a community such as few of us now are. He benefited also, one may further venture to suggest, from that paternalism which only the insanely inverted standards of today's bogus liberalism has turned into a dirty word, while shrugging off the responsibilities involved upon the impersonal state.

Feudal society was not born overnight and in its evolution we must not expect firm dates. As we have seen, it may be said to have first established itself in northern France in the course of the ninth and tenth centuries. In this development there were three basic and crucial factors. Immediately, as it were, and contemporaneously, the collapse of central authority and its ineffectiveness against the triple menace of Viking and Magyar and Moslem, the disintegration, that is to say, of the Carolingian state, caused society painfully to reform itself on the foundations of local lordship. This transmutation itself, of course, was slow and gradual, but the other two factors in it began earlier and were to that extent more long-term in their operation. One was a change in the nature of warfare, evidently concentrated in the course of the eighth century, and the other was the inexorable decline of trade and commerce, beginning in late Roman times and cumulative in its effects until the point was reached where land had become almost the sole form of wealth and the sole basis of power and status. In the prevailing shortage of money, therefore, men rendered their obligations and their rents either in kind, or, more frequently, in services. But if the origins of feudal society are to be found in the ninth and tenth centuries in the sense that it then became established and recognizably in existence, the origins of some of those elements which, fused together, make feudalism, lie much further back, so that historians following this train of thought can speak of the origins of feudalism, if not of feudal society, in the seventh and eighth centuries, in early Carolingian or even Merovingian Gaul. We must return, therefore, to our fundamentals, because by tracing their development we shall the better understand that feudalism which they formed and which, once established, like most social systems long outlived the immediate circumstances and conditions which gave it birth.[1]

We shall understand the better if we begin with knights and with that change in the nature of warfare as waged by the Franks already mentioned as one of the basic factors in the formation of feudal society. This crucial aspect of our subject also stands

[1] What follows draws heavily on the present writer's *Origins of English Feudalism* (London, 1972).

as a classic instance of the influence of warfare upon society, indeed of the complete integration of the two, and an awful warning against the folly of ignoring military history (which means much more than battles), especially in the Middle Ages, yet as medieval historians especially do. Feudal society, it is often said, is society organized for war, and though it is not unique in that respect, the dictum does suggest that war was important to it. What, after all, is the feudal period if not one dominated by a military and a militant aristocracy, living for the most part in castles, their feats of arms echoing endlessly through the literature of the age, representing themselves upon their tombs and on their seals alike as knights armed *cap-à-pie*? One may even digress at this point to suggest that those historians who, hypnotized by the Church, concentrate almost exclusively upon the Papacy and the Religious Orders to give the impression that medieval history is ecclesiastical history, do both the period and their pupils some disservice in an age when, in any case, the Church soon made its peace with war, the Papacy dreamt— and sometimes realized the dream—of harnessing the knightly chivalry of Latin Christendom to the cause of Holy War against the Infidel, and when, in a favoured metaphor, monks were the knights of Christ manning the castles of God. But to resume, while in this matter as in others we must avoid the sharp contrast of black and white, it is clear that, whereas in both classical and early medieval times cavalry had played at most a secondary role in war, and the Franks in particular had traditionally fought on foot (hence their characteristic weapon, the *francisca* or battle axe), by about the middle of the eighth century, and for reasons still obscure, they had developed heavy cavalry to be their dominant arm. The date generally taken to mark the point of effective change is 755, when king Pepin altered the annual assembly of the Frankish magnates from March to May, *i.e.* the season of first forage for the horses. And out of this military development a new social and ruling class in due course will arise, built up, as it were, by the Carolingians as mayors of the palace, kings and emperors, and establishing itself in the dis-

integration of the Carolingian state in the ninth and tenth centuries. For the vital point is that the association of knighthood
and gentility began early, and inevitably so since the former is
both expensive and exclusive. No doubt the hand-picked warrior-
retainer of earlier Germanic society was also released from and
raised above the sordid necessity of tilling the soil in order to
serve and fight the better in the warband, and grew rich upon
loot and the lord's munificence. Yet in the last resort the warfare
which he waged did not differ in kind from that waged by those
free peasants beneath him who might be summoned to the same
campaign. The development of heavy cavalry to dominate the
field of battle changed this affinity, for it became inevitably a
corps d'élite, and the advent of the war-horse to pre-eminence
elevated the status of the warrior who bestrode it. His business
is not just to ride, though that in itself is expensive, but to fight
on horseback, which is doubly expensive and becomes yet more
expensive as standards rise. You needed not only a horse, but
one specially trained and specially bred. You needed more than
one such mount, as you nowadays need more than one pony to
play polo. You needed the means to feed them, and you needed
servants or attendants to look after them, and also to furbish your
increasingly costly and elaborate gear—not least the hauberk,
the long coat of mail, which became so much the sign of knighthood that in Normandy the knight's fee was the *fief de haubert*.
You needed also time, which is freedom from other occupations,
to devote to the necessary long training and constant exercises
which, also, had to begin in early youth. 'You can make a horse-
man of a lad at puberty; later than that, never'—thus an early
Carolingian proverb, echoed by a later German poet: 'He who
has stayed at school till the age of twelve and never ridden a
horse, is only fit to be a priest.'[1] Hence the long apprenticeship
of the young men, esquires, *tirones,* in eleventh-century Normandy before the arms of knighthood were conferred upon them,
and the full-time, residential service in the court and household
of a lord, glimpsed in the pages of eleventh- and twelfth-century

---

[1] Quoted by Bloch, *Feudal Society,* pp. 152, 293-4.

chronicles. Hence the professionalism, for these men became as professional as the age could make them. Hence the dedication to, and love of, war, the glorying in feats of arms mirrored in the secular epics and *chansons de gestes* composed to be read to knightly audiences. Hence, too, the cult of knighthood, the cult of chivalry, and the cult of violence also. 'I love the gay Eastertide, which brings forth leaves and flowers; and I love the joyous songs of the birds, re-echoing through the copse. But also I love to see, amidst the meadows, tents and pavilions spread; and it gives me great joy to see, drawn up on the field, knights and horses in battle array ... Maces, swords, helms, of different hues, shields that will be riven and shattered as soon as the fight begins; and many vassals struck down together; and the horses of the dead and wounded roving at random. And when battle is joined, let all men of good lineage think of naught but the breaking of heads and arms; for it is better to die than to be vanquished and live.'[1]

Knighthood, then, early became an upper-class affair, and so remained. Of course at no time were all knights great men, but from an early date all great men were knights (in mid-eleventh-century Normandy all from the duke downwards), which ensured the social distinction of the institution even though each generation will produce its landless knights and (comparatively) poor knights to the extent that it produces younger sons, young men on the make, and failures in the rat race of the times. Meanwhile this military élite, worth now much more in war than the cheap soldiers who are thus their inferiors, become also a social élite. There is much history in words, and by the late tenth and early eleventh centuries in Normandy and northern France the word *miles*, in classical Latin meaning simply 'soldier', has come to mean exclusively 'knight'—*i.e.* the heavily armed specialist in cavalry warfare, in his own eyes and those of most of his contemporaries monopolizing the best military virtues—and in consequence is found attached to men's names in charters and formal writings as a mark of some distinction, a title of some

---

[1] Twelfth-century troubadour, probably Bertrand de Born, quoted by Bloch, *op. cit.*, p. 293.

honour. And so the knights were launched on their long career, at once an officer class and a ruling class, and the *force de frappe* of medieval armies, capable, of course, of fighting on foot, and doing so as the occasion demanded, but mounted warfare their *raison d'être* and their charge the ultimate weapon. As they became still more exclusive as the centuries passed, other inferior horsemen had to be added to them to maintain the numerical strength of the cavalry arm, and hence the horsed 'sergeants' of the twelfth century and the troopers of later times, but the knights' own eminence had been long since assured as a matter of social fact. Their original influence is not quite gone, for though our knights have now passed through the country gentle-man stage to enter the Civil Service, the professions and the lists of sport, to this day cavalry regiments retain their social *cachet*, and head the Army List.

It was inevitable that the new class of knights coming to the fore from the eighth to the tenth centuries should become a landed class, since, as we have seen, land was then both wealth and status. Therefore we meet at once the knight's benefice and fief, though in practice we shall do better to approach it by another route, via vassalage and commendation, for in reality, as matters developed at the time, these, like the knight himself, precede the fief. In the beginning the feudal bond is a purely personal one between lord and man, and the fief historically comes later as a means of giving effect to their relationship. Of all the fundamental elements which make feudalism none has a longer pedigree than vassalage, to be traced back in all probability to the *comitatus,* the war-band, of German tribes, described by Tacitus as early as the first century A.D. This, the group of chosen armed retainers (*comites*) about a war-leader, was a prominent feature of Germanic and therefore early Frankish society, and was unlikely to decline in importance in the endemic civil wars of Merovingian Gaul. The Carolingians, we know, made much use of 'vassals' both to acquire and keep their power and govern their over-mighty state, and encouraged their nobles and officials to have vassals in their turn, thus to bind society and their dominions the more closely to them. It is in this period, indeed, that the words *vassus* and *vassalus* come into general use to describe the sworn military retainer, whose status rises also as he becomes a mounted warrior, a knight—as he, above all, is required to do, and as he almost alone is able to do as a full-time retainer backed by the necessary resources. Personal relationships of vassalage were the means whereby the Carolingians, Charlemagne not least, eked out their inadequate administration, and when that administration broke down in the course of the ninth and tenth centuries they almost alone were left. Bishops and counts and others, no longer in any real sense the officials of a central authority, emerge as local potentates, and society coalesces about such local lordship. Everywhere men turned for protection to those greater than themselves; great men need vassals, mounted retainers, knights, even more than they did before; and new men arise to greatness, through opportunity and strong-arm methods. 'The king has now nothing save his title and crown ... he is not capable of defending either his bishops or the rest of his subjects against the dangers that threaten them. Therefore we see them all betaking themselves with joined hands[1] to serve the great. In this way they secure peace'—the words are those of a German prelate describing affairs in Burgundy about the year 1016.[2] It is now, in the ninth, tenth and early eleventh centuries, that as a matter of historical fact the new knightly ruling class establishes itself, that the new princely families, comital families and baronial families who are to make the future history of Latin Christendom emerge, and all are vassals one to the other to the top. Further, as the status of the vassal who is a knight thus steadily increases, and as he becomes ever more sharply distinguished from the peasant, whose military worth becomes less and he himself declines towards servitude, another and parallel development takes place in the all-important creation of the bonds holding men and society together. From Merovingian times there had been an act of

[1] *NB* and see below.
[2] Quoted by Bloch, *op. cit.*, p. 160.

commendation whereby one man placed himself under the protection of another. Now as the gulf between knights and peasants, upper and lower classes, widens, a special and elevated type of commendation is evolved out of the undifferentiated original, restricted to the high level of lords and vassals whose relationship it creates, and increasingly distinct from lower forms of commendation now also evolving and whereby the peasant and his progeny are bound to the soil and the lord of the manor. The former is that vassalic commendation which, if we seek to analyse, is one of the fundamental elements of feudalism, without which feudal society cannot be said to exist. It consisted in full of three parts. First came the crucial act of homage, a visual and symbolic ceremony wherein by the *immixtio manuum*, the placing of the joined hands between the hands of the lord-to-be, the supplicant became his man (French *homme*), his vassal. This act might be accompanied by a kiss to confirm it, emphasizing the element of a free compact between free men and to that extent social equals (one did not kiss one's serf). Second came the oath of fealty whereby the basic act of homage is hallowed by religious sanctions. Thirdly and finally, where appropriate— not of necessity since the feudal relationship now created can stand without it—came investiture, whereby the new vassal is symbolically invested by the lord with the fief to be held of him.

The relationship created by vassalic commendation is bilateral, a voluntary association between two free men, once created irrevocable save for a serious breach of obligation on either side, otherwise ending only with the death of either party. The principal obligation of the vassal is service, especially military service, which from an early date is knight-service. The principal obligation of the lord is the maintenance of his vassal. This can be done, and often was done, directly in the lord's household and at his table. The household vassal and the landless knight are more lasting features of feudal society than is commonly allowed, as one generation succeeds another, as there are more sons than lands available, and as young men of good birth but no patrimony must make a start. Nevertheless by the ninth century the most normal method of maintaining vassals—and the most important for historians since thereby feudalism becomes (like the Church) rooted in the soil, territorialized and thus with a new degree of permanence—was by a grant of land. Here then is that which is first called the 'benefice' (*beneficium*) and later the fee or fief (*feudum, feodum*), in post-Conquest England the knight's fee, in contemporary Normandy the *fief de haubert*,[1] and everywhere literally the foundation of feudal society. By it the lord provides the maintenance that he owes and from it the vassal obtains the means to provide his service. But it is not an outright grant: the vassal becomes the tenant of the lord. Vassalage itself is a personal relationship necessarily ending with the death of either party, therefore the fief reverts to the lord on the death of the vassal (and, similarly, on the death of the lord its continuing tenure will require confirmation by his heir). In the beginning the fief was not hereditary, nor can it ever become the outright property of the holder who is a tenant, while since also it is regarded as held conditionally in return for fealty and service, failure in either can lead to its confiscation. In all this we have much of the substance of medieval politics and nine parts of medieval law—and the latter at least will last, of course, far beyond the Middle Ages.

There is one other fundamental characteristic of feudal society, namely the castle, which among English-speaking historians requires more emphasis and attention than it commonly receives. The more one thinks about the castle, the more feudal it becomes. Properly defined as the private (as opposed to public) and residential fortress of a lord, it then appears an intensely feudal type of fortification, to be contrasted with those communal types of fortification which precede it—Iron Age fortresses, for example, or Roman camps, Viking camps, Anglo-Saxon boroughs, and walled towns and cities (the last existing also concurrently with it)—and with those purely military and national fortresses which succeed it—beginning in terms of English history with Tudor coastal forts. As a matter of historical fact

[1] Cf. p. 117 above.

also, the castle's existence as a viable military institution coincides exactly with the span of the feudal period. Its origins are to be found in northern France in the ninth and tenth centuries with the establishment of feudal society (in 864 Charles the Bald prohibited the construction of castles, *castella*, without permission); the local lordship of the feudal epoch came to be based on castles no less than upon knights; and the castle declines in importance with the decline of feudalism itself (a fact which may make the Indian Summer of English castles in the seventeenth-century civil war a significant pointer rather than an exception). It is true that the idea of the public nature of fortification for the public weal was never entirely lost in the Middle Ages, just as the concepts of public authority, sovereignty and kingship were never lost either, and in consequence the right of castellation was controlled; yet the castle is more or less unique in history in its combination of the dual role of residence and fortress, and it seems appropriate that feudal lords should live in castles. Certainly in the minds of contemporaries the castle was associated with that lordship which we call feudal, of which it was both the symbol and much of the substance. 'You shall have the lordship, in castle and in tower'—thus in 1173 in England the envoys of the Young King, seeking to win over the King of Scots by offering him the northern counties. The very word *donjon* (now debased to 'dungeon' in English, but not in French) applied by contemporaries to the principal tower which was the principal strength of many castles, and also contained the residential apartments of the lord, was derived from the Latin *dominium* meaning lordship. To this day in France, where with significance the word *château* is retained for the large country house of a gentleman, there, if you want to find the real thing as opposed to some later mansion, you must ask not just for *le château* but *le vieux château féodal*.

The most important comment to be made about that feudalism whose fundamental elements we have now described must be that as a social system it is positive not negative, cohesive not anarchical. Maitland as long ago as 1897 observed that 'There are indeed historians who have not yet abandoned the habit of speaking of feudalism as though it were a disease of the body politic', and himself went on to say, in a striking phrase that might well be framed above all our beds, 'feudalism means civilization'.[1] Matters have improved but little since, and it appears that no heresy is more long-lasting and pernicious than that which sees feudalism as a bad thing and, more especially, incompatible with monarchy and the state (though why the state should be a sovereign good is in any case another question). The mad concept of an inevitably revolting baronage, and of king versus baronage, and baronage versus king, as the themes of medieval politics, lingers on even in the highest places and not only in the classrooms of English schools where, it would seem, they cannot wait to get to 1485 to see a New Monarchy at last suppress the Overmighty Subject. The truth is otherwise, and feudal society is no more a manifestation of anarchy than it is of unrestrained and irresponsible exploitation. Dimly one may see the false train of thought: sovereignty (that sovereign good) fragmented, delegated and usurped in local lordship, personal relations taking the place of central authority as the principal bond of society, and, through the hierarchy of vassals, layer after layer interposed between the king or prince and the vast majority of his erstwhile subjects now the men of others. But, in so far as these things were ever true, they were not necessarily bad *sub specie aeternitatis*, and—more to our present point—they were the result, and not the cause, of the distintegration of the Carolingian state. To trace out and observe the origins of feudalism is to emphasize its positive and cohesive force. It was by means of vassalage, by making use, as it were, of nascent feudalism, that the Carolingians rose to power in the chaos of late Merovingian Gaul, and made of it something better, the Carolingian state and monarchy and empire, which historians generally revere. And when that state in western Frankia collapsed, society coalesced about local and feudal lordship, at the least as *faute de mieux*. Further, the developing bonds of vassalage were

[1] *Domesday Book and Beyond* (1960 paperback edition), pp. 267–8.

made as strong and sanctified as men knew how. God in this age
was not only on the side of waning Christian Kingship. 'By the
Lord [God] before whom this relic is holy, I will be to N. faithful
and true, and love all that he loves, and shun all that he shuns,
according to God's law, and according to secular custom . . . ' so
runs one early form of an oath of fealty, taken upon a sacred
relic. 'May the madness of infidelity be ever far from you; may
evil never find such a place in your heart as to render you unfaith-
ful to your lord in any matter whatsoever', thus a great lady to
her son, become the vassal of Charles the Bald, in 843. 'He who
swears fealty to his lord ought always to have these six things in
mind: what is harmless, safe, honourable, useful, easy, practicable
. . . The lord also ought to act towards his faithful vassal reci-
procally in all these things. And if he does not do this, he will be
justly considered guilty of bad faith, just as the former, if he
should be detected in avoiding or consenting to the avoidances of
his duties, would be perfidious and perjured', so wrote the
churchman and the scholar, Fulbert of Chartres, who died in
1029. To violate the mutual obligations of vassalage was to
commit a mortal sin: the concept of felony for the gravest
crimes was brought into English law after 1066 from feudal
custom wherein it denoted the most grievous offence of a breach
of fealty. One could go on, though there ought to be no need to.
To cite, as so many historians love to do, the inevitable instances
of broken faith and abnegated homage, no more detracts from the
normal force of feudalism to bind society together than to cite
the many instances of treason and disloyalty disproves the power
of nineteenth- and twentieth-century nationalism. It almost
seems that English historians suffer especially from anti-feudal
tendencies, as though perhaps, consciously or unconsciously
swayed by anachronistic nationalism and a misconception of
the Norman Conquest, they regard it as somehow 'foreign',
and alien to clean-limbed Englishmen. Perhaps for the same
reason they also try, as we shall see, to get rid of it much too
soon.

Certainly one cannot impute anti-feudal tendencies to kings

and princes, as is still commonly done in textbooks and even in other works. There is no dichotomy between kingship and feudalism, and to speak of feudal kings as being anti-feudal is a manifest contradiction in terms. Which brings us to the next point, namely that in the eleventh, twelfth and thirteenth centuries, feudalism was amongst the most potent forces working to bring about the foundation and development of states. By means of vassalage, as we have seen, the early Carolingians and Charlemagne acquired, maintained, and augmented their power, and so did their latter-day successors. It was by feudal power (for such it was) that, for example, the feudal states (for such they were) of Normandy and Anjou each rose to greatness within France, and broke out of it each to bestride its world like a colossus.[1] The Angevin Empire, after all, is not much less impressive than the Carolingian, and a good deal more sophisticated. The point is always missed by those books, and they are many, which treat of French history only in terms, anachronistic, of the larger unit of the French kingdom, and see all this achievement as a woeful, negative tale of weak kingship and over-mighty vassals.[2] The real point is that feudalism adds mightily to the powers of kings and princes. Nowhere in fact did kingship, which is older than feudalism, vanish in the holocaust of the ninth and tenth centuries, and even in France the monarchy was kept alive in the brave new world that follows as much as anything by feudal concepts, and by those concepts triumphed in the thirteenth century. The king was now not only God's anointed, he was also lord of lords, the feudal suzerain, and no one could or would deny it. Lords need vassals, but so also do vassals, even the greatest, need a lord, and the feudal pyramid must have an apex. In England an ancient monarchy not only survived the Vikings but greatly grew in strength, yet there too the monarch's powers were multiplied by Norman feudalism after 1066, for here too he became not king only but also feudal suzerain and universal landlord. It would be easy enough to stand textbook history

[1] See below pp. 178–84, 197–217.
[2] See Chapter X.

on its head and argue that the over-mighty power of kings in post-Conquest England is the result of feudalism. Even the Tudors and the early Stuarts centuries later (as every schoolboy really does know) derived a valuable prerogative from the feudal dues and from a reorganized Court of Wards. In the eleventh and twelfth centuries when it emerges, feudal monarchy is the 'New Leviathan'.[1]

If finally we seek, however briefly, to summarize at least something of the importance of feudalism to the history of the West, we must begin with the assertion that it is a prime factor in the revival of society after the ninth century, and also (one might almost say in consequence) a prime factor in the growth of states. These are large claims but they are not all. The feudal bond with its attendant obligations was reciprocal between lord and man, and if the rights of feudal lordship add greatly to the power of kings, who are the greatest feudal lords of all, so also the rights of vassals do much to protect their subjects. The working out and definition of the relationship between lord and vassal is not only very often the key to medieval political history but also a major theme of constitutional history, and many of our Western democratic liberties, where they survive, are the bequest of feudal barons quite properly standing up for their rights. It is curious that newspapers and liberals should dislike these men so much, and symptomatic of an ignorance of medieval history now becoming almost universal. The late American Professor Sidney Painter wrote a book entitled *Feudalism and Liberty*,[2] and in terms of English history Magna Carta is very much a case in point. It is indeed what it is sometimes called with derogatory intent, a 'feudal document', and in it one may find, as well as many other things, the principle of no taxation without consent.[3] Everywhere, too, the feudal doctrine that a vassal owes counsel to his lord shades off into a right to be consulted, and Magna

[1] R. H. C. Davis, *History of Medieval Europe*, p. 295.
[2] Baltimore, U.S.A., 1961. Strictly, this book is a collection of Sidney Painter's articles and addresses put together after his death as a memorial to him by his friend and pupil Fred A. Cazel, Jr.
[3] c. 12.

Carta[1] also needs to be included in any history of Parliament, and the origins of Parliament itself, in the beginning not confined to England, are very feudal. Because of these things, because, rather, feudal concepts were bred into the upper classes of European society and, therefore, into all other classes also, feudalism is neither lightly nor quickly to be dismissed. In spite of what seems the death-wish of English historians especially, it is a very long time dying and may, as one may hope, be not dead yet. Certainly it does not end with the appearance of national monarchies in the thirteenth century. Edward I was scarcely less a feudal king than William the Conqueror. If it is true that feudalism as a military system declines first (but is it? So-called 'bastard feudalism' in later medieval England looks remarkably like the real thing), it survives much longer as a social system, and longer yet in tenure and in law. Feudal tenure lasts in England until 1660 and in some respects beyond: feudal law, perhaps, until the nineteenth century: both, of course, in France until the Revolution. The concept of gentility, the ethical and social code of the gentleman, if gone now then only just, is or was the direct descendant of the code of chivalry. Chivalry now means chiefly an attitude to women, and much of both modern marriage and romantic love come out of the feudal past. So does a woman's right to dower. So does the age of 21 as marking the legal age of majority (for tenants by knight-service). So do the military traditions of European aristocracy, a territorial aristocracy and a landed gentry. These last sentences with which this chapter ends are merely random shots to show that feudalism is a basic and fundamental element in Western society, and not omitted even from the United States since they (in spite of Viking efforts) were founded in the seventeenth century and before it was too late. How many know, as one last parting shot, that when or if we pray with hands joined together we thus render our homage to God?

[1] c. 14.

CHAPTER VII

Reform in the Church

The principal result of the holocaust of the ninth and early tenth centuries was, as we have seen, a revival of society and of every aspect of it, and with revival came development, and with development change. It seems both characteristic and appropriate that this revival was first apparent in the Church, and, more specifically, in the monasteries. Nor is it surprising, for no institution had, or perhaps could have, suffered more than the Church and the churches in the war and depredation and social disintegration of the period. They, and the monasteries especially, suffered, as it were, doubly and trebly, for not only were they the obvious and invariable targets for looting and destroying raiders —so that in England, for example, as in Normandy, monasticism was virtually wiped out—but also they could not avoid the general demoralization of society and so became both invaded and exploited by the world. This last point needs immediate emphasis, for it explains what will be the principal demand of the new age for the freedom of the Church—freedom, that is, from secular exploitation and interference. That demand was nothing short of revolutionary both in practice and in theory, and in its implications was to prove political dynamite. In the old world the theocratic element in Christian Kingship, whether Carolingian or English, meant not only that the monarch was both priest and king, and the visible, consecrated ruler of the Church in his dominions, but also that Church and State, ecclesiastical and secular, were intermingled at every level of society for the good of each, to the point where they were one and indistinguishable. It is one of the results and tragedies of the reform movement which we now approach that Church and State, *regnum* and *sacerdotium*, will become, not separate powers but, rather, rivals for supremacy within and over what remains the entity of Christian society and Latin Christendom. The way is straight to wars between the Empire and the Papacy, which will happen, and to the murder of Becket as an English and Angevin postscript. Yet the historian (for whom especially to know all is often to forgive all) can see well enough how it happened, and can certainly understand the initial demand for the Church's freedom which leads to such tragic results. The paternalistic control, sometimes, as with the early Carolingians, even exploitation, of the Church within his realm by the Lord's Anointed for the public good, with his authority available for protection, reform and salvation, was one thing and respectable; but when, in West Frankia and the future France especially, that authority collapsed, to be devolved upon or usurped by local potentates in a disintegrating society fighting for its survival, the result could be, and often was, something very different and anything but respectable. In a localized world which could contain the exploitation or sheer robbery of ecclesiastical property, the system of lay 'advocates' of churches working as a mere protection racket, the gross scandal of lay abbots, the abuse of the right of appointments by unscrupulous lay patrons, a corrupt and worldly clergy, and a married clergy leading to hereditary church offices—in such a world pious and thinking men of vision might well regard the freedom of the Church from lay control, its separation from secular society which had engulfed it, as the essential pre-condition of a better life. Nor is it at all to be wondered at that such reform and such revival came first to the monasteries. The prestige of and belief in monasticism remained as it had been before, so that if you wanted to improve society you reformed or founded monasteries, rather as we, with less faith and logic, reform and found universities, and in any case monasticism in the West had once risen as the way of salvation by withdrawal from an evil world and now will so rise again.

The revival of society, then, began in the tenth century in the

Church, and within that it began in the monasteries as a movement of monastic reform. Though it was to spread over almost all
Latin Christendom, it began where it was needed most, in West
Frankia and Lorraine, in France and the Low Countries. Further
(and to counter any erroneous over-simplifications that may seem
to follow from what has been said above) it is important to stress
that it was, and necessarily, inspired and carried through as much
by laymen as by clerks. Thus in England, as an example, the
so-called Tenth-Century Reformation owed as much to King
Edgar 'the Peaceable' as to St. Dunstan or St. Ethelwold or St.
Oswald. In the beginning the tenth-century monastic reform
movement, which, of course, included the foundation and re-
foundation of houses as well as the reform of those then in existence, spread outwards, like ripples but gathering momentum,
from three main centres. These were Brogne, near Namur,
founded *c*.920, Gorze, near Metz, refounded *c*.933 and Cluny in
Burgundy, earliest and incomparably the most important of the
trio, founded in 910.[1] The influence of Gorze spread throughout
the area between Metz, Cologne, Verdun and Toul; that of
Brogne to Flanders and thence via Ghent and St. Omer to England: the influence, and more, of Cluny was to spread over
almost the entire West. Though men thus soon came to speak of
'Cluniac' monks, Cluniac monasticism, like that of Brogne and
Gorze, was, of course, Benedictine monasticism, based upon
St. Benedict's Rule, to which it sought to give perfect expression.
In fact, however, the Rule reached the reformers of the tenth
century through the modifying medium of St. Benedict of
Aniane and King Louis the Pious a century before, and the
monastic life which now spread over Europe with a new degree
of uniformity differed unconsciously from the original in the
increased time and effort expended upon the divine office and
liturgical exercises at the expense of both manual and intellectual
labour.[2] This contemporary trend, moreover, received further

[1] See Dom David Knowles, *Monastic Order in England*, pp. 27–30, and
the authorities there cited.
[2] Cf. above, p. 79.

and increasing emphasis at Cluny where—and thence in her satellites to only a lesser degree—elaborate ceremonial, with sumptuous accoutrements, set in magnificent buildings, became the outward and visible sign of Cluniac monasticism. The three-fold balance of St. Benedict's monastic day was lost thereby, for now there was little time for anything beyond the performance of an *Opus Dei* which could not be too dignified or splendid, but also there was scarcely any break in the steady stream of prayer to which the age attached so great a value. 'Worship the Lord in the beauty of holiness', and the genius of Cluny came to provide perhaps the richest expression of the concept of the Beauty of Holiness that the West has ever seen, stemming from the confident belief that all expense is justified in the service and worship of God to His greater glory. It was said that when in the thirteenth century St. Louis, King of France, visited Cluny, he and his whole court were suitably accommodated in the monastery without a single monk being turned out of his cell, and when, unforgivably at the Revolution, the great church of the monastery was demolished it took the contractors almost as long to pull it down as it had the monks' masons to build it. This, the third and final abbey church, was begun in 1089 and consecrated in 1132. It was then the largest in the West, with double aisles and double transepts, an ambulatory with radiating chapels, and a nave of sixteen bays. When later the great twin-towered narthex was added at the west end the whole church was nearly two hundred yards long. 'Let Christ be my witness that I have not exhibited these things in order that I may win praise, but in order that the spirit may be remembered': the inscription upon a particularly splendid but much later Suffolk parish church not far from where I write may remind us that the attitude of Cluny is not confined to any given period. Nor is its opposite, nor opposition to it. *Sancta simplicitas*, and Puritanism did not have to wait for the sixteenth-century Reformation to gain expression. The Cistercian monastic movement in the twelfth century began as, amongst other things, a conscious and articulate reaction against the opulent magnificence of Cluniac customs which, in the words of St. Bernard, 'while they attract the eyes of the worshipper, hinder the soul's devotion'.

This, however, was in the future. Meanwhile, in the tenth and eleventh centuries, Cluny carried almost all before her, and as a force almost wholly for good. The abbey was founded in the year 910 by William, Duke of Aquitaine, and placed under its first abbot, St. Berno. In the duke's foundation charter it was laid down that 'With a full heart and mind the monks shall build an exceeding pleasant place, so far as they can and know how.' The simple object was that here should be lived the perfect religious life, under the Rule of St. Benedict, and to this end, from the beginning, the monastery was to be free from all secular control and interference. To achieve this aim the duke called in aid the highest authority there was, and to keep out intruders placed his new foundation under the direct protection of the Papacy. From these beginnings the fame and reputation of the excellence of Cluny, lying at the crossing of important routes, and governed by an extraordinarily distinguished line of abbots who included four saints among the first five, spread in all directions—unintentionally, slow at first, then gathering momentum. Neighbouring rulers and princes called upon Cluny to reform other houses, and they in turn reformed others increasingly far flung, and all such became her dependants. St. Odo, the second abbot (926–42), in particular, became the itinerant apostle of reformed and Cluniac monasticism, travelling the length and breadth of France and Italy on his mission, part self-imposed and part imposed upon him. Other travellers came and saw the light themselves, then sought to kindle it at home. The story of the visit to Cluny in 1075, and its outcome, by the Norman magnate William of Warenne and Gundreda his wife, which he himself related in his foundation charter for St. Pancras at Lewes in Sussex, has often been told yet requires repetition as typical: 'We went to many monasteries in France and Burgundy to offer our prayers, and when we had come to Burgundy . . . we turned aside to the monastery of Cluny, a great and holy abbey in honour of St. Peter, and there we adored and besought

St. Peter. And because we found holiness and religion and so great charity, and we were so honourably received by the good prior, and by all the holy convent, who took us into their society and fraternity, we began to have love and devotion for that order and that house above all other houses which we had seen. But the lord Hugh, the holy abbot, was not at home. And because my wife and I had long before, and then the more greatly, desired, with the advice of the lord Lanfranc, the archbishop,[1] to found a house of religion for our sins and for the safety of our souls, it seemed to us that for no order would we so willingly do this as for that of Cluny. . . .' In this way, in due course (abbot Hugh was at first reluctant to send any of his monks to England 'on account of the long distance of that strange land and especially on account of the sea'), St. Pancras at Lewes was founded and colonized from Cluny, to be the first Cluniac house in England.

It has been calculated that in the end some 1,450 religious houses formed the 'congregation' of Cluny, all following with absolute uniformity the 'customs of Cluny', *i.e.* the Cluniac usage of St. Benedict's Rule, all directly subject to the abbot of Cluny who, as the only Cluniac abbot, professed the monks and appointed the priors of all the other houses, and all exempt and free from any other authority than his and that of the See of Rome. In this way, the Cluniacs became the first of the monastic 'orders' with centralized control, as opposed to the individual autonomy of original Benedictine houses, yet impressive and important though this is, the influence of Cluny went far beyond the huge congregation of priories directly dependent upon her. Indirectly also, her influence seemed to know no bounds. The English monastic reformation of the tenth century, as an instance, was in one sense independent and spontaneous, yet in the event was influenced by Continental models, from Brogne via Ghent and St. Omer, as we have seen, but also and not least from Cluny especially via the Cluniac house of Fleury-sur-Loire. In the new duchy of Normandy also, monastic reform, which there as in England was in fact the revival of what was

[1] *i.e.* of Canterbury.

defunct, came in the tenth century and early eleventh first from Ghent and then and more substantially from Cluny. 'The decisive moment in the history of Norman monasticism'[1] (and Norman monasticism will not for long be confined to Normandy) came in 1001 with the invitation and appointment by Duke Richard II, 'the Good', of William of Volpiano to reform the ducal foundation of Fécamp. William was a Cluniac monk and abbot of St. Bénigne at Dijon, and though at first he hesitated, observing that the Normans had hitherto been more apt to destroy than build the temples of the Lord, come he did, and from Fécamp his influence and that of Cluny spread over all the duchy. Much of Germany, too, through the agency of the re-formed house of Hirsau is another case in point. By the second quarter of the twelfth century abbot Hermann of St. Martin at Tournai (1127–1132) could write that it was scarcely possible to find a monastery in France or Flanders where the Customs of Cluny were not observed.

Cluny thus becomes one of the great religious forces in the history of the West and, more particularly, a striking manifesta-tion of the revival of Latin Christendom in the tenth and eleventh centuries. Nowhere, in fact, could the influence of monasticism be confined within the cloister, and more and more monasteries were directly or indirectly Cluniac. Princes and lords were the founders and the patrons, monastic bishops were a feature of the age, and thus not only shepherds of many souls but also coun-sellors of the great. The abbots of Cluny walked with emperors and kings, and Cluny became the spiritual and moral centre of the West, the Papacy notwithstanding. Nor can the role of Cluny be seriously denied as at least the harbinger and herald of the general reform movement within the whole Latin Church to which we must now turn. It is true that by the eleventh century Cluny, by sheer success, was so much a part of the 'Establish-ment' as to deny her any leadership then in a movement primarily dedicated to the freedom of the Church from secular encroach-ment; yet Cluny, too, was free, and allied also to the Papacy.

[1] Knowles, *Monastic Order in England,* p. 84.

Also she had prepared the minds and hearts of men for something more. Not even in the eleventh century could monasticism
by itself provide all that the Church should offer or society need.

Any account of the so-called Gregorian or Hildebrandine
reform movement of the Western Church in the eleventh and
twelfth centuries must necessarily contain the dramatic events
of the Investiture Contest to which it led, of the head-on collision
of Church and State, and more particularly of Papacy and
Empire. Yet also in a book like this, chiefly concerned with the
evolution of Europe and the medieval foundations of the modern
West, causes and results are more important than any narrative
of what happened. It may serve best, therefore, first to mention
briefly outstanding events and dates, and then turn to a more
detailed consideration of how these things could ever have come
to pass, and with what consequences for the history of Latin
Christendom. Thus, in 1073 Gregory VII, the former Hildebrand, from whom, though it does not begin with him, the
movement takes its name, was elected to St. Peter's chair. In
1075 Pope Gregory issued his decree against investiture: it was
not the first such decree, but it came as a particular challenge at
that moment. The Investiture Contests which then follow were
not, of course, confined to Germany but were common to all
Latin Christendom, yet, for particular reasons, it was in and
with Germany that the issue was most bitterly, and literally,
fought. Henry IV of Germany (1056 to 1105) in response summoned an ecclesiastical council which renounced obedience to
Gregory as Pope. Gregory's answer was the excommunication
and deposition of Henry, and the result was civil war in Germany
as every discordant element took up arms against the king for
reasons of their own. There followed the dramatic and famous
submission of King Henry, barefoot in the snow, to Gregory at
Canossa, on 25 January 1077. This, however, was by no means
the end. In 1080 Gregory excommunicated and deposed Henry a
second time, and Henry in his turn deposed the Pope, having
another, *i.e.* an anti-Pope, elected in his place. In the next year,

1081, the king invaded Italy, and in 1084 captured Rome. Gregory from the castle of St. Angelo summoned his Norman allies from the south of Italy, Rome was sacked, and Gregory withdrew with them to the new Norman kingdom. He died at Salerno in 1085, an exile from his city and his see. The struggle, however, continued after the death of Gregory, and also after the death of Henry IV in 1105. Not in fact until 1122, in the Concordat of Worms, was a settlement reached (along the lines of an earlier settlement at Bec with Henry I of England in 1102), and even then the civil wars in Germany continued for another thirty years until 1152.

And how on earth (for, surely, not in heaven), we may ask, did all this come about thus to tear the very fabric of the old world asunder, with deposed kings and emperors in arms against the Pope, and Rome sacked as hitherto only by barbarians and heathen? Part of the answer we have seen already in the close intermingling of things secular and ecclesiastical in the old world of Carolingian and Christian kingship, in the results of the breakdown of Carolingian society, and in the consequent and justified demand for the freedom of the Church. Reform and revival along these lines came first to the monasteries, but with it as yet no friction between secular and ecclesiastical, no dispute between God and Caesar, no confrontation of the German Empire and the Papacy. Clearly to reach that point we must go further and examine in more detail the growing reform movement within the Church outside the monasteries. That Church, of course, had been invaded and distorted by the world only less than the monasteries, and by the tenth and eleventh centuries stood in great need of reform. Yet also we must notice that here too, as with the monasteries, reform in the beginning came as much from laymen as from clergy, and very little from the un-reformed Papacy itself—which, in turn, is part of the tragic paradox of the whole affair.

If we go back to the beginning of the general reform movement, we find that there were two evils in particular which early critics assailed, more than investiture which comes only later into the centre of the storm. These were clerical marriage and simony, and both, if followed through, will lead us to the heart of the controversy. Let us take first clerical marriage and the opposite principle of celibacy, which have now once again in our own day become a live issue in the Roman Church. Why then was the principle of clerical celibacy held to be so important in the eleventh century? For one thing, it of course reflects the ascetic ideals of the age. Monasticism was universally regarded as the ideal state, and monks, who, amongst other things, abjured the Flesh, as the spiritual élite. Ought not, then, the ordinary, secular clergy, in sore need of moral regeneration, to mould themselves more closely upon their perfection in this particular respect? It was, moreover, a particularly important respect—and here we approach the heart of the matter—for the clergy, it was held, are not, or should not be, as other men, but as a race apart. The priest, and he alone, administers the Sacraments through which salvation lies. He stands as mediator between God and man. He is both different and superior. And here we meet, as in other places, that concept of hierarchy fundamental to medieval (and later) society. Hugh of Flavigny composed a proper order of precedence to be followed on the Day of Judgement, which ran as follows: first, St. Peter, Prince of the Apostles, second, St. Paul followed by the rest of the Apostles, next holy hermits, next perfect monks, then good bishops, then good priests, penultimately good laymen, and, last of all, women. The order is in many ways illuminating for the student of the times, and *mulier est hominis confusio* even to Chaucer's Chanticleer, but what matters to us here is that in it all priests precede all laymen. The idea of the superiority of the clergy, combined with prevailing asceticism, is bound up in the principle of celibacy, and the former leads to the very centre of the Investiture Controversy. There were other considerations also. The priest should surely be free from earthly entanglements so far as in him lies in order to concentrate wholly upon his superior functions and the cure of souls—and any man who has sought to work against a background of domestic noises may the more easily grasp the point at issue here. One cannot serve two masters. One cannot serve both God and Man. By how much the less, then, can one hope to serve both God and Woman? There was one other matter also, less timeless but very pertinent to the conditions then prevailing. Married clergy could and did lead to the scandal by any standards of hereditary spiritual office, and with that there is all too unlikely to be much sense of vocation or inspiration by the Holy Spirit, or much discipline, or much hope of reform.

The issue of celibacy, therefore, contained the concept of the superiority of the spiritual power over the temporal, and also touches upon the vital issue of appointments to spiritual office. And in this latter we meet simony. Simony is the sin of Simon Magus, who, the Bible tells us, offered money to St. Peter for the gift of the Holy Spirit. It is, then, the sin of the purchase of spiritual office: there is no doubt of its prevalence in the tenth and eleventh centuries; and it is almost impossible to do justice to the vehemence with which the reformers of the day denounced it. It leads, of course, even more directly than celibacy, straight to the centre of the coming controversy and the demand for the Church's freedom from secular control, more especially when, as time went on, simony came to be more broadly interpreted to cover almost any intervention by the laity in clerical appointments notwithstanding all the time-honoured precedent and practice of the past. Such is the position, for example, in the influential mid-eleventh-century work, *Contra Simoniacos*, of Cardinal Humbert, a member of the reforming party who saw secular domination of the Church as the prime cause of corruption. Bishops, he wrote (and bishops especially, together with abbots, inevitably become the key figures, the control of whose appointment was essential to both sides), bishops ought to be first of all elected by the clergy, then acclaimed by the people, and finally consecrated by the metropolitan. But now the right order is reversed: the king, a layman, elects, the metropolitan consecrates, and, last of all, the clergy and people must give their assent whether they like it or not. Further still, Humbert inveighed against the significance of the investiture of the bishop by the king. The king bestows the staff and ring, the symbols of spiritual authority, upon the bishop, and thus, a mere layman, presumes to celebrate a sacrament by conferring the grace of the episcopal office.

And so with Cardinal Humbert we reach investiture, the lay investiture of clergy, part of the larger whole of secular domination against which the reformers set their faces, their voices and their pens, but a crucial part and so, by the general usage of historians, giving its name to the impending 'Investiture Controversy'. Inevitably, we may feel, in a feudal world the Church, which is ever of this world if not of the next, was heavily feudalized, and in no way were its higher echelons at least more enmeshed in secular society. Bishops and abbots, as the lords of great estates, magnates and counsellors, endowed also with great liberties which involved the responsibilities of local government, were required like other lords to be the vassals of the prince or king, and therefore to do homage like the rest. Against this also the reformers will inveigh, and not unreasonably (though largely in vain) since prelates have at the least, so to speak, another dimension and are different from secular vassals who are above all warriors and armed retainers. So too, and in particular, the investiture of prelates by lay lords was different, and in the prevailing climate of opinion could now be seen to have intolerable implications. Investiture was that part of the ceremony of commendation wherein the new vassal symbolically received the fief from the lord, thereafter to be held of him who conferred it.[1] Prelates at this time were commonly invested with the ring and pastoral staff as the symbols of their office, accompanied by the words 'Receive this church'. In a society much dependent on symbols and visual ceremonies the implication seemed inescapable not only that the prelate held his church and office from the ruler who thus bestowed them, but also that he derived his very spiritual authority from a mere temporal lord. In spite of all the teaching, the preaching and the precedent of anointed Christian

[1] Above p. 121.

kingship in the past, this now seemed intolerable to some, and in any case, in the new world of eleventh-century feudal Europe, by no means all rulers were anointed kings. It was perhaps less certain how far divinity sat with counts and dukes.

The wind of change now blowing within Christendom was revolutionary, for in so many ways the 'right order' of the world which the reformers sought was the reverse not only of current practice but also of all past precedent and custom. For this reason amongst others one should not suppose that in the eleventh century every cleric sought reform. On the contrary, for long the *avant garde* of the reformers remained a minority in the Church, while the entrenched old order continued in its ways, not all of which in fact were reprehensible by every standard. As late as the later eleventh century and the pontificate of Gregory VII himself, one may call to mind so splendid an example of a bishop of the old school as Odo of Bayeux, half brother to the duke and king, his companion on the battlefield at Hastings, afterwards earl of Kent and amongst the very greatest temporal lords in England. Men said (and cf. Wolsey) that he had his eye on Rome itself. Or again as a lower and an earlier instance there is Ordericus Vitalis' anecdote about the Norman secular clergy who lived like laymen with arms and concubines, and when reform came proved more willing to give up the former than the latter. What was wanted if reform was to become universally effective was not only an intellectual base, which the reformers, on their way to acquiring a near monopoly of intellectual opinion, had no difficulty in providing, but also a central code backed by a central authority. We must turn, therefore, to canon law and to the Papacy.

It is no accident that the eleventh century saw a great increase and development in the study of canon law. Most reformers, ecclesiastical reformers not least (as in the sixteenth century), have their hearts and minds fixed upon the past, and advance backwards in search of its authority and simplicity. The eleventh-century reformers sought precedents and justification for their convictions in the ancient law of the Church, *i.e.* in canon law.

But canon law itself in this age was an heterogeneous accumulation of ill-organized materials—excerpts from the Bible, from Roman Law, from the Fathers, with papal letters and decretals, and the canons and decisions of past councils of the Church. The need was for organization and this was an organizing age: it was also an intellectual age, with a revived interest in law and jurisprudence to provide the order and the justice which men wanted.[1] Thus the characteristic products of the growing body of contemporary ecclesiastical lawyers were handbooks and digests of canon law, collections and *summae* of laws and decretals, systematized and arranged conveniently under subjects and headings and sub-headings for easy reference and use. Hence, for example, the *Decretum* of Burchard compiled in Germany about 1000, and others similar later in the century compiled increasingly, and significantly, at Rome. Compiled at Rome significantly for two reasons: first, because each of these digests and collections of canon law tended to reveal and emphasize the ancient authority and power of Rome; and, secondly, because as the century advanced Rome came increasingly to take over the direction of the reform movement, which itself became increasingly associated with the concept of Papal Supremacy—a concept, of course, very ancient but now expressed at least in practice in a revolutionary way. We may see the connection between reform, the Papacy and canon law the more clearly in an anecdote told by Peter Damiani, Cardinal Bishop of Ostia and a leading member of the reforming party. According to him, Hildebrand, *i.e.* the future Pope Gregory VII, had often asked him to make a note in the course of his studies of anything he discovered touching the rights and powers of the Apostolic See, so that he, Hildebrand, might compile a collection of such authorities for future reference. Later, we know that Gregory as Pope kept on his desk a file of such authorities, and it was doubtless from this source that he was to copy into his register, about 1075, his famous *Dictatus Papae*, whose principal headings relating to papal power form an index of papal authority. Twenty-seven in number, they

[1] Cf. below p. 223.

are all of them potent maxims—that the Roman Church was founded by God alone; that he [the Pope] can be judged by no one; that the Roman Church has never erred and, by the testimony of the Scriptures, it never will—and some are statements about which the Investiture Contest will be fought: that the Pope may depose emperors; and that he can absolve subjects from their fealty to unjust rulers.

This, however, is to anticipate. It was the reformed Papacy that was to lead and direct the reform movement in the later eleventh century, but in the beginning of that century the Papacy itself was in need of reform. That the Papacy came late into the reform movement of the Church explains such facts as that William the Conqueror and Lanfranc, though both convinced reformers in their day, could yet have little sympathy with what appeared to them as new-fangled notions of the practice of Papal Supremacy. The pace of change at this time was such that within one generation those formerly in the van could find themselves at the end fighting a rearguard action. By the early eleventh century the Papacy itself, the bishops of Rome, like other bishops elsewhere had fallen under the domination of secular lords; and not under that of respectable princes like the King of the Germans or the English or the Duke of the Normans, but under the control of the local nobility about Rome who set up Popes in their own image and in accordance with their own factions. Matters were at their worst in the year 1046 when there were no less than three Popes or rival claimants to St. Peter's chair. To end the scandal, the Emperor himself, Henry III of Germany, a pious prince and convinced exponent of ecclesiastical reform, intervened, summoned the Council of Sutri, and through it deposed all three competing Popes, appointing another in their place, the worthy and reformist Clement II. Here surely we must pause a moment to observe an Emperor thus summoning ecclesiastical councils to depose and elect Popes, and since these things were done in the interest of reform we also find again the tragic paradox of things. The reformed Papacy will attack temporal control of the Church and in so doing break the power of German kings and emperors, yet a series of reforming Popes from Clement II to Leo IX and Victor II were elected under imperial influence before the death of Henry III in 1056.

The Papacy therefore, between 1046 and the election of Hildebrand as Gregory VII in 1073, went from strength to strength, at one and the same time taking over the leadership of the reform movement and giving practical expression to its ancient claims to supremacy within the Church, imposing reform and its own authority alike by the dual means of councils and papal legates, and developing in Rome the papal *curia* of central government, which now included the most eminent spirits of reform—Cardinal Humbert, Peter Damiani, and Hildebrand himself. Reform, and papal authority as the means to the end of reform, became the order of the day. But also as the reform movement becomes increasingly associated with the active assertion of papal supremacy, one can see a shift of emphasis, from the imposition of discipline within the Church to an attack upon the temporal power which presumes to interfere—upon those who, in vivid reformist terminology, 'dare to defile the bride of Christ'. The shift is shown in increasingly severe decrees against simony and in Humbert's *Contra Simoniacos* already referred to, but also and especially in the efforts now made to ensure that elections to the Papacy itself must, above all, be free— free of secular interference including that of the supreme temporal power of the emperor, notwithstanding its beneficial effects in the past. Hence the Election Decree of 1059 which gave all real power to the developing college of cardinals and largely ignored imperial rights dating back to Otto the Great. In this great matter also the Roman reformers were much helped in practice, and enabled to establish valuable precedents, by a minority in the German monarchy, and therefore the absence of an emperor, which followed the death of Henry III in 1056. In the event both Alexander II (1061–1073) and Gregory VII, the former Hildebrand, were elected Pope without reference to imperial authority.

We come therefore to Gregory VII and he who was or was

made his principal opponent, the new king, Henry IV of Germany, in whose confrontation the Investiture Contests reach their ultimate height with the attempted deposition of each by the other and open war between them. Obviously there is still a great gap between these things and all that has gone before, and we have not therefore finished either an explanation of how they came to pass or of the extent to which Gregory's policy was revolutionary both in practice and in theory. To some extent, of course, the gap is filled by personality, which can never be left out of history (we may say, indeed, that the principal weakness of medieval history is that we know so little of personalities in a period when they matter most, with such vast power concentrated in the hands of so few). While Henry IV was a not unworthy opponent to stand fast upon the ancient ways against the advance of new-fangled papal notions, Gregory was a man with the utter conviction required to put theories into practice, and the courage to attack opposition. 'Cry aloud: spare not, lift up thy voice like a trumpet and declare unto my people their transgressions!' And also, 'Cursed be he that keepeth back his sword from blood!' Again it must be repeated that the Investiture Contests were by no means confined to Germany, but were most crucial and most bitterly fought there for two reasons: first, because of the particular degree to which the German monarchy was dependent upon the German Church for its government and therefore the importance to it of the control of the election of prelates; and second, because of the uniquely intimate relations between the German kings as emperors with the Papacy.[1] The Pope crowned the Emperor and the Emperor was the protector of the Pope with rights in his election, in witness whereof, though Gregory might cite doubtful precedents for the papal deposition of kings, only some thirty years earlier the Emperor Henry III had deposed and appointed Popes at the Council of Sutri.

The open breach between Gregory and Henry began, significantly enough, with a dispute over the election of the archbishop of Milan, for Henry was King of Lombardy like his

[1] See further, Chapter VIII.

predecessors. In this matter of ecclesiastical elections and appointments, which we have already discussed, it is easy enough to see and understand the position of both sides: the importance of freedom to a reforming Church convinced, not without reason, that secular interference was the root cause of corruption; and the importance of control for the established monarchies and principalities, Germany especially, dependent upon the governmental and administrative services of literate churchmen, to say nothing of the military and other services (including counsel) owed by those who were by merely temporal standards amongst the greatest magnates in the land. The Church simply was too integral a part of contemporary society to be wrenched apart. Further, all precedent and practice for centuries past was on the side of kings and secular princes in these things; but for Gregory and his supporters what mattered was not antiquity but right—'The Lord hath not said "I am tradition" but "I am the truth".'

Again there is, of course, nothing new in the concept of Papal Supremacy within the Church, though there was something new in practice, more especially in the context of the immediate past, in the degree now of its active assertion, by what is becoming the centralized government of a Universal Church at Rome, in the local affairs of local churches hitherto presided over by anointed rulers part priests as well as kings. Here we reach the heart of the Investiture Contests, in the conflict of what have become two rival powers, spiritual and temporal, in practice centred upon appointments to ecclesiastical office and the issue of the freedom of the Church from secular interference, but in the realm of intellectual theory amounting to a contest for the supremacy of the one over the other, and thus for the dominion of the world. In this the Papacy under Gregory took the initiative and the offensive, and in this was revolutionary both in theory and in practice. For hitherto the prevailing doctrine had been that which was derived from Pope Gelasius I (492–6), the doctrine of 'the two swords', that the two powers spiritual and temporal were each ordained by God and held their distinct authorities direct from Him. The mosaic of Pope Leo III (795–816, and he who crowned Charlemagne) in the Lateran Palace thus shows St. Peter investing the Pope with the *pallium* as the symbol of spiritual authority, and Charlemagne with a banner as the symbol of temporal. 'Render unto Caesar the things that are Caesar's, and unto God the things that are God's', and Caesar also is divine through the sacrament of his coronation. Thus Ethelred's laws declare in early eleventh-century England that 'a Christian king is Christ's deputy among the Christian people.'[1] Thus, too, Henry IV's proud and dignified rejoinder on the occasion of Gregory's excommunication and deposition of him in 1076: 'You have dared to touch me, who, although unworthy, have been singled out by unction to rule, and whom, according to the traditions of the Holy Fathers, God alone can judge.' The latent problem, now made manifest, was that under the Gelasian dispensation the two powers spiritual and temporal must agree. So Peter Damiani wrote: 'The heads of the world [*i.e.* the Emperor and the Pope] shall live in the union of perfect charity ... the two persons ... shall be so closely united by the grace of mutual charity that it will be possible to find the king in the Roman pontiff, and the Roman pontiff in the king.' But if they should disagree, what then? For Gregory in such a case there was no question but that the spiritual should prevail because of its innate superiority. Gelasius himself had written that of the two powers spiritual and temporal, 'the burden of the priesthood [*sacerdotes*] is the heavier, for they must render account for kings as for themselves in the day of judgement'. All the world acknowledged the supreme authority of the Roman pontiff in matters of faith and morals, which must therefore give him authority even over kings and emperors. 'If I therefore have to represent you', Gregory once wrote, echoing Gelasius, to William the Conqueror, Duke of Normandy and also King of England, 'If I therefore have to represent you at the dread tribunal before the Just Judge who is not deceived, the Creator of every

[1] VIII Ethelred II, 2:1. A. J. Robertson, *Laws of the Kings of England from Edmund to Henry I* (Cambridge, 1925), p. 119.

living being, pray heed and consider whether it is right or possible for me not to be greatly concerned for your salvation, and whether it is right or possible for you not to obey me promptly in order that you may secure your own salvation.' Papal Supremacy in this sense, moreover, was derived direct from the basic authority of the Petrine texts, where in St. Matthew's Gospel the words of Our Lord to St. Peter were not only 'That thou art Peter, and upon this rock I will build my church; and the gates of hell shall not prevail against it,' but also 'And I will give unto thee the keys of the kingdom of heaven: and whatsoever thou shalt bind on earth shall be bound in heaven: and whatsoever thou shalt loose on earth shall be loosed in heaven'. The Pope as the successor of St. Peter thus had beyond question the power of 'binding and loosing' on earth and in heaven, of absolving sin and also of condemning by excommunication, which cut off the sinner from the body of the Church, from sacraments and salvation— and how should anyone in the latter case have rule over a Christian people? Thus not only the excommunication but also the deposition of Henry IV of Germany lay within the competence of the Apostolic See—and thus Gregory VII in the tremendous proclamation of his sentence: 'Blessed Peter, prince of the apostles, mercifully incline thine ear, we pray, and hear me, thy servant . . . by thy favour, not by any works of mine, I believe that it is and has been thy will that the Christian people especially committed to thee should render obedience to me, thy especially constituted representative. To me is given by thy grace the power of binding and loosing in Heaven and upon earth. Wherefore, relying on this commission, and for the honour and defence of thy Church, in the name of Almighty God; Father, Son and Holy Spirit, through thy power and authority, I deprive King Henry, son of the Emperor Henry, who has rebelled against thy Church with unheard-of audacity, of the government of the whole kingdom of Germany and Italy, and I release all Christian men from the allegiance which they have sworn or may swear to him, and I forbid anyone to serve him as king . . . And since he has refused to obey as a Christian should, or to return to God

whom he has abandoned . . . I bind him in the bonds of anathema
in thy stead. I bind him thus as commissioned by thee, that the
nations may know and be convinced that thou art Peter and upon
this rock the Son of the Living God has built his Church, and the
gates of hell shall not prevail against it.'

To deny the Pope is to deny Peter and to deny Peter is to deny
Christ, whether in things spiritual or temporal. The logic is
impeccable given certain premises none of which are new and all
of which are ancient, yet the result of its application is revolutionary. For where is Christian Kingship now and the monarch
as the Lord's anointed? There was, of course, opposition even at
this high intellectual level of political theory and theology, the
so-called Anonymous of York pitching the claims of sacerdotal
kingship higher than ever a Tudor or a Stuart or a Bourbon
would dare to do, and denying (not in the sixteenth century but
in *c*.1100) any supremacy or primacy of Rome even within the
Church, where all bishops are equal. Yet in the main the papal
thesis and the reformist cause carried the intellectual opinion of
the day, and though in the event 'that divinity that doth hedge a
king' did not vanish in the eleventh century, nor was the balm
washed from the anointed head, Gregory and his supporters
were at pains henceforth to deny that sacerdotal element in
kingship which the Church itself had first pronounced and
preached. They were not afraid to pass logically from the assertion of the inherent superiority of the spiritual power to the
assertion of the inherent inferiority of the temporal, based, unless
blessed by the Church, not upon divine authority but upon force
or worse.

The revival of the Church in the eleventh and twelfth centuries, the Hildebrandine, Gregorian reform movement and
the Investiture Controversy, are of importance not only for the
student of the times, nor only for the timeless question of the
proper relationship of God and Caesar, things spiritual and
material, but also in their results as factors in the development
of Europe and the West. To some questions, including the most

important, the immediate answers both at Bec and Worms were compromises, and indeed they had to be. The question of the right relationship of Church and State, *regnum* and *sacerdotium*, at the highest level of emperors, kings and princes with the Papacy, was shelved, or rather, 'left to fester',[1] since, of course, it will be raised again. At a lower level, the crucially important practical question of the investiture and appointment of prelates also ended in compromise, nor could it have been otherwise since bishops especially were vital to both sides. Lay investiture with ring and staff, the symbols of spiritual authority, was given up, and one should pause to emphasize the importance of this in principle before going on to say that in practice the secular power was usually able to control the choice of personnel. The problem of the dual allegiance of prelates in particular and churchmen in general was recognized rather than solved by the increasing distinction made between 'temporalities' and 'spiritualities', so that prelates were still vassals for their lands held in lay fee, and for their temporal possessions clerks must render whatever services and obligations other men would do. The blatant scandal of simony was suppressed in the narrow sense of the payment for spiritual office, though not in the broad sense of any secular interference in ecclesiastical appointments, and, more covertly and discreetly than before, money could still move mountains in the papal *curia* as in other courts. The problem of clerical marriage proved harder because more diffused, but in the end celibacy triumphed, though more easily obeyed in the letter by renouncing marriage than in the spirit by renouncing concubines. And as it proved difficult to withdraw the clergy from the lot of common humanity, so it proved impossible to withdraw the Church from secular society, to separate Church and State. The issue of clerical immunity from secular jurisdiction remained to be bitterly fought, not least in England; prelates must still do homage; clergy will continue to serve the State and princes to reward their clerical administrators with ecclesiastical prefer-ment, so that a fourteenth-century Wyclif will inveigh against

[1] C. W. Previté-Orton, *Shorter Cambridge Medieval History* (1953), i, 500.

'Caesarian' bishops as vehemently as ever the Gregorian reformers had done.

There are still other matters. Papal Supremacy within the Latin Church became increasingly a reality, and with a new dimension, as Rome takes on the task of active government of a Universal Church. With this there went also an even larger yet less easily defined role for the Papacy as the leader of Latin Christendom—as when, for example, Pope Urban II launched the First Crusade in 1095. Further, such papal leadership of the West reflects a profound change in the attitude of the official Church, which thus turns its back upon the ancient monastic concept of withdrawal from the world as the spiritual ideal. Yet if one seeks to render any kind of profit and loss account, all was not gain for the Church and the Papacy as the result of the Investiture Contests. The new spirit of clerical separatism, while in practice by no means entirely successful, could and did lead to a new spirit of anti-clericalism, while the Papacy also lost much of its hold on the affections, as Rome, where men had formerly sought St. Peter in devotion, became increasingly the business centre of a bureaucratic ecclesiastical government. One cannot easily love bureaucracy. The change is nowhere better discussed and put than by Southern in his *Making of the Middle Ages.*[1] 'Almost without exception the Popes between Gregory VII and Innocent III [1198–1216] were practical men, and most of them had already had long experience in papal business as legates or chancery officials before their election ... There is no saint among the twelfth-century Popes ... The men who lived in Rome in the twelfth century, from the Pope downwards, did not get much mercy from their contemporaries. They were the objects of attacks which we should regard as both scurrilous and indecent. The picture in the *Gospel according to the Mark of silver,*[2] of the Pope gathering his cardinals together and stimulating them in Biblical phrases to fleece the suitors at the Papal court— "For I have given you an example, that ye also should take gifts

[1] *E.g.* pp. 152–3.
[2] A well-known satire of the time.

as I have taken them", and again, "Blessed are the rich, for they shall be filled; blessed are they that have, for they shall not go away empty; blessed are the wealthy, for theirs is the Court of Rome"—would seem today a crude piece of anti-religious propaganda; but it was a piece of twelfth-century writing of perfect respectability and orthodoxy.'

Finally, there remains one other result of the Investiture Controversy, outside the realm of ecclesiastical institutions and in the sphere of straight political history, which as a factor in the development of Europe may seem of the greatest importance. In Germany, to which we must next turn, the direct result of the conflict was nothing less than the collapse of a political society and the permanent weakening of the German monarchy and Empire. The political fragmentation of Germany so familiar to all school students, the failure not so much to coalesce as to retain early medieval cohesion, is attributable to the Investiture Controversy, and it is this rather than the Thirty Years War which explains the later German problem. It does not seem any exaggeration to maintain that to modern German history—and therefore, for this reason alone, to much of modern European history—Gregory VII and Henry IV are as relevant as Frederick the Great of Prussia or Bismarck or the Kaiser.

CHAPTER VIII

Germany and the German Empire

In the post-Viking age of revival, development and expansion in every sphere, and in the 'central' or 'high' Middle Ages from the tenth to the thirteenth centuries, a principal theme is the formation and development of states, the expansion of secular government. Out of this process will emerge the political pattern so familiar to the student of the 'modern' period of European history—England and France going from strength to strength, Germany and Italy both divided, Poland, Hungary, Bohemia in the east towards Russia and Byzantium, Christian Spain recovering the Iberian Peninsula from the Moslems and the Moors. But because the outcome is so familiar it is important not to be hypnotized by it nor to write or view the history of the times blinded by hindsight and conditioned by modern, and therefore anachronistic, standards. In particular, there is surely nothing either sacred or inevitable about the nation state. The 'nation' is and always was a vague conception, and one of the main lessons of history is that what happens is by no means necessarily foreseen or planned. That France will have evolved as a principal and united national monarchy by the end of the thirteenth century,[1] for example, is of course an immensely important fact in the history of Europe and the West, and we are justified in studying how this came about; but it does not follow that the end was foreseen, nor that from the beginning her kings consciously strove to achieve it, as so many history books seem to imply either that they did or should have done. Similarly, the fact that the German kingdom during this same period, in spite of

[1] See Chapter IX below.

much initial promise, in the end fragmented, is again a controlling factor of immense importance in all subsequent European history, but to write of this in elegiac terms of timeless tragedy is another matter, bending the past in the interest of our own assumptions. One may not unfairly quote in this connection a sentence from the Introduction of J. W. Thompson's influential and distinguished *Feudal Germany*:[1] 'The tragic result was the conversion of the once strong and magnificent German kingdom into a rope of sand, a confused and jarring chaos of small and warring states ruled by petty dynasts neither materially able to accomplish great things nor morally capable of understanding that high things are to know, that deep things are to feel.' We need not stoop to putting the question of whether those 'great things' which a united Germany, or any other nation state, has been materially able to accomplish have really been so unquestionably beneficial to mankind; but since the attitude underlying J. W. Thompson's approach is very prevalent amongst historians, whether rejoicing at the achievement of French political unity or bewailing the eventual 'failure' of the German kingdom, we may ask by what divine decree it is that the modern nation state is right and anything different, especially if it is smaller, self-evidently wrong. It does not seem so obviously apparent why life in Baden-Baden should be held inferior to life in Bismarck's Germany, or life in the county of Anjou to life in the kingdom of France under Louis XIV or Philip the Fair. Certainly in this period we have other units than the big and 'national' units to observe. The process of political development and the evolution of states is for long more apparent in the smaller units of Normandy, Anjou and the other French feudal principalities than it is in the larger unit of France, or in Flanders than in Germany. Again, one of the principal manifestations of the growth of governmental techniques and machinery in this period is found outside the context of secular states altogether, in the growth of papal government, of papal monarchy. We shall miss much of this, and thus get our history wrong, if we think only in terms

[1] New York (first published 1928, republished 1962), p. xvi.

of the large 'national' units which are eventually (in some cases long centuries later) going to emerge triumphant, as we shall also very likely and very often misinterpret the motives and policies of rulers who, if they knew where they were going, were looking in directions different from ours and with other eyes.

In this chapter, then, we shall deal with the history of Germany down to the thirteenth century. The German kingdom was in fact the first and most powerful monarchy to emerge on the mainland of Europe from the chaos of the ninth and tenth centuries, so that much of the future of Latin Christendom might have seemed to lie with it. 'If there was one thing about which a critical and well-informed observer ... [in the later tenth century] ... might have felt confident in making a prediction, it was that the future of Latin Christendom lay in the hands of the rulers and people of the German-speaking lands.'[1] In the event it was not to be, but the 'misfiring of German leadership in Europe' and the political fragmentation of Germany which is established by the end of our period is scarcely of less importance for the future as it turned out than any German leadership might have been. Further, the fact that the kings of Germany from the time of Otto I and the year 962 were Emperors also, and the successors of Charlemagne, gives another dimension to their history, so that their eventual political failure and their defeat at the hands of the Papacy mean not only the decline of the German kingdom but also the decline of the medieval Empire in fact if not in theory. Yet the contribution of Germany to the political history of Europe and to the origins of the modern West is not simply as a negative factor causing subsequent reactions not least in the nineteenth and twentieth centuries, for also in this period the remarkable and very positive achievement of the eastward expansion of the German peoples took place, beyond the Elbe, to the confines of Russia and beyond. This represents not only the expansion of Germany but also the expansion of Latin Christendom, and altered the map of Europe, religiously, politically and even ethnically for all time, with

[1] R. W. Southern, *Making of the Middle Ages*, p. 19.

results running deep to the present day. The rise and decline and expansion of Germany, therefore, between the tenth and thirteenth centuries is worth some moments of our time as students of the present, let alone as students of the past.

The history of what will be Germany (Map 6) begins officially, so to speak, in 911 with the election as king of Conrad, Duke of Franconia, on the death of the last Carolingian King of the East Franks, Louis the Child. To see the significance of this it is necessary to go back to the Treaty of Verdun in 843,[1] whereat the inheritance of Charlemagne had been divided into three, the kingdom of the West Franks (later France), the Middle Kingdom of Lorraine, Burgundy and north Italy, and the kingdom of the East Franks beyond the Rhine. It was to this last area that Conrad succeeded, and the act of the German tribes there in electing him as their king instead of giving their allegiance to the surviving Carolingian Charles the Simple, King of the West Franks, thus marks, for the historian, a decisive step away from the past towards the future. The East Frankish kingdom will be Germany (and from now on we shall call it so for brevity's sake), though at this time there was no such name for it, and not until the eleventh century will the usage of the word *Teutonici*, Germans, be established to describe its diverse peoples. These peoples were not one but four 'nations', Franks, Saxons, Swabians and Bavarians, settled (though these things are never neat and tidy) in the four semi-tribal or 'stem' duchies, of Franconia, Saxony, Swabia and Bavaria respectively, into which this original Germany was divided. That particularism which marks German history thus has early beginnings, though doubtless we should not emphasize them too much since everywhere in medieval history division necessarily precedes unity. It is what happens subsequently which determines coalition and cohesion, though with this qualification we may accept J. W. Thompson's dictum as a text for the history of Germany: 'The particularism which has characterized German history finds its root in the important fact that no ruling house ... has ever

[1] Above p. 106. See also Map 5.

Germany and the Empire, c 1190

Lübeck
Pomerania
Saxony Brandenburg
Rhine
Gau
Cologne
Elbe
Kingdom
of Poland
Lorraine Nassau
Mainz Main
Worms Franconia Bamberg Bohemia
Alsace Waiblingen Moravia
Toul Danube
Freiburg Augsburg Austria Slovakia
Besançon Swabia Bavaria
Cluny Trans Jurane Constance
Burgundy
Rhone
Kingdom of Hungary
Kingdom of Milan Cortenuova
Burgundy Brescia
Roncaglia Legnano
Alessandria Danube
Lombardy Venice
Provence Romagna
Pisa Zara
Tuscany Papal States
March of Ancona
Sutri Spoleto
Rome Anagni
San Germano
Benevento
Melfi

Kingdom of Sicily

Palermo

MAP 6

succeeded in overcoming the original and primordial heterogeneity of the German race.'[1]

Nevertheless, for the first century and a half and more of German history after 911, most notably in the reigns of Henry the Fowler of Saxony (918–936) and his son Otto I, the Great (936–973), we have nothing but a success story in our present context of the growth of medieval states, achieved by the political agency of monarchy and the traditions of Germanic and Carolingian kingship. The parallel is with England, for in Germany as in England the monarchy did not wane but waxed during the early tenth century, and emerged from these testing times strengthened and triumphant above all through successful warfare. Further, in both cases, to press the parallel a little further, what the historian may see as the units of potential particularism—the stem duchies in Germany and in England the former kingdoms of the Heptarchy wiped out by the Danes— were something other than the dynamic feudal principalities of France, in whose favour all contemporary forces seemed to work, and belonged, it might seem, to the past rather than to the future. Certainly the duchies could be and were contained and bound closer to a common monarchy by personal policies characteristic of the age, the exaction of obligations and services due to the king, the maintenance and acquisition of royal lands and the appointment of dependent counts and bishops within them, marriage alliances and the appropriation of the dukedoms themselves where possible for members of the royal family. So too in Germany, as again in England but not France, it is evident that the territorial extent of the kingdom, in the beginning from the Rhine to the Elbe, was not beyond the capacity of contemporary kingship to control, and that fact in turn is very relevant to the crucial element of military prestige, itself contributing vastly to the growing power of German kings. Kings at this date might be anointed and consecrated by the Church but they were also primarily war-leaders, which indeed, in the beginning, made them qualified as the Church's protectors. In Germany the

[1] *Op. cit.*, p. xiii.

particular threat and the terror of the times was not so much the Vikings as the Magyars.[1] Henry the Fowler's victories over both, and especially over the latter at the Unstrut in 933, led his followers, we are told, to hail him as emperor, while Otto's great and decisive victory over the Magyars at the Lechfeld in 955 leads straight to his imperial coronation at Rome, in 962. As the saviour of Christendom Otto, henceforth 'the Great', was worthy to be given the mantle of Charlemagne.

In getting so far we are also going too fast. By the later tenth century and the later years of Otto's reign there had also been a great extension, both of the German kingdom and of the territory ruled by her kings, to the west, the south and the east. To the west, Henry the Fowler annexed Lotharingia from the Middle Kingdom, to which the imperial title had come to be attached (and in the shadowy Middle Kingdom, as in these events, we can begin to see something of the origins of the later problem of French landward frontiers). In this direction, Henry's son and successor, Otto I, was able to extend his control over Burgundy, and then, in 951, annexed the last province of the former Middle Kingdom by invading Lombardy and becoming King of the Lombards as Charlemagne had been before him. Very reminiscent of Charlemagne also, in his conquest and militant conversion of the Saxons, was Otto's expansion eastwards beyond the Elbe to conquer and convert, planting churches as he went, the heathen Slavs or Wends. Otto the Great thus began the eastern expansion of the German people and also in so doing, like Charles the Great, expanded the bounds of Christendom. Furthermore if, after Lechfeld, the Magyars settled in Hungary managed to remain autonomous, to accept Latin Christianity under Stephen I (997–1038) and to become an independent kingdom in 1100, they were nevertheless under sustained German influence, while the future Bohemia and the future Poland both accepted not only the Roman faith but also Otto I's overlordship, the one in 950 and the other in 967.

The government of this pre-Gregorian and predominantly

[1] Above p. 94.

pre-feudal Germany was the exemplification of Christian King-ship. Though the Salian dynasty, who in the person of Conrad II succeeded the Saxon house in 1024, made use of a class of out-right royal officials, the so-called *ministeriales*, of semi-servile origins, such royal administration as there was throughout this period down to the Investiture Contests was heavily dependent upon the Church. This is the 'Ottonian system' of the text-books. The monarch who was both priest and king had his Church at his disposal to aid him in his government of the Christian people, and nowhere was this now ancient alliance of Church and State to the point of total integration made more man-ifest than in Germany. Pope John X himself had declared that the appointment of bishops pertained to the king alone, and the abbots of the great royal abbeys, whom the king as founder and patron also appointed as of right, were no less important. In an otherwise illiterate age, clerics stood at the king's right hand for the purposes of counsel and administration as well as of salvation, and throughout his realms the great churches, monastic and cathedral, richly endowed not only with lands but also with liberties and immunities, governed their franchises to the honour of God and on the king's behalf, responsible for justice, taxation and military service.

The Ottonian system, personal and theocratic, finds its most perfect expression in the case of Bruno, brother to the king, also archbishop of Cologne, Duke of Lotharingia, chancellor of the kingdom and, withal, a cultivated man of letters. He may serve also to introduce the Ottonian Renaissance of which in his own person he stands as a distinguished example. In the kingdom now stabilized and extended, and, above all, freed from the menace and devastations of the Magyars, governed in practice largely by literate and educated clerics, its king the greatest prince in Latin Christendom, and king also of Lombardy in Italy from whence came classical learning and tradition, there was, and not surprisingly, a notable revival of art and letters. It was, like the Carolingian Renaissance which preceded it,[1]

---

[1] Above p. 47.

eminently practical in motivation, not primarily for the love of learning for its own sake but for the better service of the Christian faith and Christian people, as with archbishop Bruno's school for the training of future bishops of the Empire. And all these echoes of Charlemagne so clear to the historian sounded also in the ears of the contemporaries of Otto the Great, the saviour of Christendom, who in the beginning had been crowned and anointed in the chapel of the great emperor's former imperial palace at Aachen. The memory and the concept of a Latin Christian Empire had never died in the dark days following the deaths of Charles the Great and Louis the Pious, and the Roman Church especially, never in greater need of a protector, continued to search for him whom it found in Otto. Thus it came about, in a way again reminiscent of Charlemagne, that after Otto had invaded Italy in 961 at the Pope's invitation to defeat his enemies, he was crowned Emperor by John XII in St. Peter's at Rome in February 962. The Donations of Pepin and Charlemagne were confirmed by the new Emperor, who was officially designated amongst other things the protector of the Papal State in Italy.

Renovatio imperii Romani, and the 'Roman' Empire now established as a conscious revival of Charlemagne's was to last until 1806. Yet from the beginning it was different, and different especially in the much wider gap (which we might almost call, in modern jargon, credibility gap) which existed between the theory and the practice. No longer the Empire of the Franks whose dominion very nearly coincided with the boundaries of Latin Christendom, it was in reality a German Empire, the actual power-base of Otto and his successors as Kings of Germany and Kings of Lombardy according ill with theories of universal monarchy or at least of secular primacy in the West. 'You are our Caesar, emperor of the Romans and Augustus', wrote Pope Silvester II, the former and learned Gerbert of Aurillac, to his former pupil, Otto III, who appointed him; and the splendid titles of Caesar and Augustus and Emperor of the Romans will be endlessly reiterated, not least by a Frederick I in the twelfth century and a Frederick II in the thirteenth, though then, sadly enough, chiefly as defensive counter-propaganda against the claims of a hostile Papacy. Yet the reality was otherwise, and the future was against it, even without the lethal enmity of the universal Apostolic See, as the national monarchies of France and England grew in stature and in power. Richard I of England and Normandy, Anjou and Aquitaine, might become the vassal of the Emperor in a hard-pressed moment, but when earlier in the twelfth century Rainald Dassel, chancellor of the Emperor Frederick I, referred disdainfully to other kings as 'kinglets' (*reguli*) there was a storm of diplomatic protest. 'And who then', demanded John of Salisbury from England, 'appointed the Germans to be judges over nations?' By the end of the thirteenth century, and the end of our period, the lawyers of Philip the Fair in France will state with deliberate precision that 'the King of France is Emperor in his kingdom'.

Already, indeed, we cannot avoid the question dear to examiners: whether the Italian and/or the Imperial connection brought harm to the German kingdom? Both are interconnected, and there can be little doubt that they did. Apart from other and lesser considerations, notably the diversion of German interest and resources from proper German affairs, both brought the Kings of Germany into uniquely close relations with the Papacy, and it was the Papacy which was to weaken to the point of destruction the German kingdom and the German Empire between the late eleventh and the thirteenth century. With the bitter and revolutionary struggle between Church and State, *regnum* and *sacerdotium*, which reaches its first culmination in the Investiture Contest of the late eleventh century we have dealt before, and noted that the storm broke particularly over Germany.[1] Nowhere by the time of Gregory VII did the old world survive so vigorously and unchanged as in Germany, nowhere was the relationship of Church and State closer, or, in the new climate of opinion at Rome, the subservience of the former to the latter more complete. Further, and as we have seen, as the Papacy increasingly

[1] Above, Chapter VII.

assumed the leadership of the reform movement in the Church, it appeared to the reformers of paramount importance that appointments to the Holy See should, above all, be free of secular interference, yet alone among secular rulers the German kings as Emperors had established rights in Papal elections since the time of Otto I. Otto himself, and Henry III after him at the Council of Sutri in 1046,[1] had deposed Popes as well as appointing others. Further still, if the Papacy, as it were in self-defence, was to claim in the last resort supreme temporal as well as ecclesiastical authority, this was because no other temporal ruler could make a similar claim as Emperor of the Romans, Caesar and Augustus. We have seen, too, the strong element of tragic paradox in the situation, since reform had been brought to the Papacy in the first place by the Emperor Henry III. Nevertheless the challenge when launched by Gregory VII in 1075 proved fatal to Germany, for the monarchy as then constituted could not exist without the Church, and in any case the papal excommunication and deposition of Henry IV was an invitation to every particularist and opposition element in Germany and Italy to throw off their allegiance to the king. The result was civil war in Germany, with rival factions (most notably Guelf and Ghibelline) and even rival kings contending, for three-quarters of a century until the accession of Frederick of Hohenstaufen (like some German Henry Tudor) in 1152. By then 'the power of the monarchy had been shaken to its foundations . . . the old order had passed beyond recall. In a welter of war and rapine and confusion, Germany had passed over into a new age; it had undergone a revolution, which left its marks for all time on German history.'[2]

In fact, German particularism as an increasingly established political condition began in these years, and the Germany of the princes has its origins in the Investiture Contest and the struggle between Gregory VII and Henry IV. In spite of the efforts of

[1] Above, p. 143.
[2] G. Barraclough, *The Origins of Modern Germany* (Blackwell, Oxford, 1946, 1952), p. 134.

Frederick I ('Barbarossa', 1152–90), Henry VI (1190–97) and Frederick II (the Great, 1197–1250) to revive both, the rest of the history of the German monarchy is an anti-climax until the late nineteenth century, and the rest of the history of the medieval Empire no less an anti-climax until its eventual extinction in 1806, in spite of the dreams of many, including the poet Dante in the fourteenth century. The civil wars of the late eleventh and early twelfth century played the part in the history of Germany of the ninth and tenth centuries in the history of the kingdom of the West Franks, *i.e.* France: with the collapse of central authority and the disintegration of the old order, society regrouped itself on the basis of local, military and feudal lordship. Although the western provinces of Lotharingia and Burgundy had inherited a form of embryonic Carolingian feudalism from the Carolingian past, the rest of Germany had not, and the monarchy which had grown up and prospered was of the old, Germanic and pre-feudal type, a political nexus of the king and his free subjects, some of whom were magnates, cemented by the Church. Now all that was gone with the wind of change, and a new and fully feudal society emerges in Germany for the first time, based on the new realities of castles and knights and vassals, and led by new men—for it is now significantly that the princely families of the future Germany first come upon the stage of history: the Hohenstaufen who become the new ruling dynasty in 1152, the Zähringen, the Wittelsbachs and the Hapsburgs among others. Further, in the circumstances of the wars the new German feudalism augmented the powers of the princes but, in contrast, for example, to Norman England after 1066, stopped short of the king who was therefore to a degree cut off from his former subjects now the vassals or serfs of other lords than he. Nevertheless it is certainly worth emphasizing that these developments in Germany are not to be used to perpetuate the myth and heresy that feudalism and monarchy are antithetical forces, the former inevitably a negative factor leading to particularism and political anarchy. In the first place, German feudalism was the result and not the cause of the civil disorders and civil wars of the late eleventh and early twelfth centuries: in the second, the revival of the monarchy by Frederick Barbarossa, himself one of the new feudal princes, was attempted by what can only be called feudal means, the king seeking to establish himself as the feudal suzerain and lord of lords on the model of the 'New Leviathan' in France and England.[1] Moreover, the eventual failure of the twelfth-century revival of the German monarchy, and with it the German Empire, was due not to the feudal particularism of German princes, but once again to the fatal Imperial and Italian connections, bringing about a second round of hostilities with the Papacy which this time destroyed the Hohenstaufen even more effectively than it had formerly destroyed the Salian kings.

In Italy, in Lombardy, royal and imperial power had been weakened as much as in Germany by the mid-twelfth century as the result of the Investiture Contests, and here Frederick Barbarossa achieved no more than a modified failure. Here he received the one great military defeat of his reign at the Battle of Legnano in 1176, and his defeat was at the hands not of feudal princes but of the Lombard cities with the support of the Papacy and its Norman allies from Sicily and the south.[2] Frederick perforce made his peace with the combined cities, the Lombard League, at Constanze in 1183, recognizing many of their liberties and privileges in return for their allegiance. And here, while we note the immediate arousal in this post-Gregorian world of Papal opposition to any revival of German and imperial power in Italy and adjacent to the Papal States, we should also pause to wonder at the spectacle of imperial defeat, albeit with papal aid, by the city states, the communes of north Italy—Milan especially, with Pisa, Genoa, Pavia, Lucca and Arezzo—as symptomatic of the great revival of trade and commerce in twelfth-century Europe, and of the wealth and therefore power accruing from it. It is a manifestation also, one may surely feel, of that constant feature of almost every historical period, the rise of the middle classes. Meanwhile matters were made worse by the next and

[1] Cf. p. 127 above.
[2] For the Normans in southern Italy and Sicily, see p. 207 below.

most brilliant move of Barbarossa in his Italian policies. In 1186 he negotiated the marriage of his eldest son, Henry, to Constance, the heiress of the Norman Sicilian kingdom in the south. When William II of Sicily died in 1189, and when in the next year Frederick I died also (tragically by drowning on his march towards Jerusalem in the cause of the Third Crusade), Henry VI as the successor of both was the claimant to the rich Sicilian kingdom in right of his wife as well as King of Germany and Lombardy. The results, in spite of his brilliance, and exacerbated by his sudden death in 1197, were in the event disastrous. 'From 1190 for sixty momentous years the attempt to incorporate Sicily into the Empire absorbed imperial energies, directing attention increasingly from Germany, leading to ever new entanglements, until in the end it pulled down the structure Barbarossa had raised, destroyed the Hohenstaufen dynasty and enduringly crippled German government: from the strain of these years Germany never recovered.'[1]

The attempted union of Sicily to the Empire not only caused the Emperors increasingly to neglect Germany in favour of their new possession, but also, it is neither too much nor yet anachronistic to say, threatened the balance of power in Europe. The tragic death of Henry VI in 1197 at the age of thirty-three, leaving a three-year-old minor, the future Frederick II, to succeed him, caused a disputed succession and a civil war in Germany, and brought also the modernistic intervention of the rival great powers, the French kingdom and the Angevin Empire, in German affairs in support of rival candidates. Even more important, it brought about the intervention of the Papacy, long-since alarmed at the union of Sicily and the Empire which at one stroke cut off the ancient papal alliance with formerly Norman Sicily and threatened the independence of the Papal States and Rome by encirclement. In the event papal intervention proved decisive in preventing the union and, in the process, destroyed the ruling house of Hohenstaufen root and branch, and with it the German monarchy, this time finally. By 1250 Frederick II, the

[1] Barraclough, *Origins of Medieval Germany*, p. 197.

medieval Frederick the Great, whom men called *Stupor Mundi*, the Wonder of the World, was defeated and dead in far-off Sicily, and neither his Empire nor his kingdom in Germany ever recovered. The spectacle thus of the Vicar of Christ in the thirteenth century striking down and extirpating the theoretical temporal head of Latin Christendom, and his sons after him, is not edifying, and was done with a vituperation distasteful to this day ('There has arisen out of the sea a Beast full of words of blasphemy . . .' etc., thus Gregory IX, and one is reminded a little of fascist beasts and hyenas). Yet there are mitigating circumstances to be considered, and the historian, of all people, is under compulsion to see both sides of every question, and as many other sides as there may be. For one thing, personalities do affect policies, never more so than in the Middle Ages, and even in a timeless institution like the Papacy. It is therefore worth recording that, if Gregory IX rejected any and all co-operation with Frederick and the Empire, his predecessor, Honorius III, had embraced it. Moreover, Frederick's personality, with his blasphemous words, heretical views and ruthless scientific curiosity, seemed to give substance to Gregory's vision of the Anti-Christ. And further, there was of course a point of view and principle entirely sincere and logical as the motivation of Gregory's policy. The Pope was at least the supreme spiritual head of Latin Christendom, entrusted with the keys of the kingdom of heaven and the power of binding and loosing, ultimately responsible for the salvation of men. To exercise aright these sovereign powers it was essential that the Supreme Pontiff should be free of secular pressure and interference, including that of the Emperor who in any case and in reality was by now only one power among others. To achieve this essential independence the Pope must be physically free in his own city of Rome, and the freedom of Rome secured by the independence of the Papal States, though both were currently threatened with engulfment by a hostile Empire. Thus by a logical process of thought which will continue to the nineteenth century (and its underlying principles longer), 'the temporal security of the Papal States was but the necessary condition of the spiritual freedom of the Church.'[1]

Yet notwithstanding the negative fact of the political failure of the German kingdom and Empire, what has been called 'the greatest deed of the German people during the Middle Ages' still remains to be recorded, and, moreover, took place coincidentally with that failure itself. For although the eastward expansion of Germany beyond the Elbe (Map 7) has its beginnings under Henry the Fowler and Otto the Great ('Henry I committed Germany to the policy of a thousand years'[2]), their advance was wiped out by the great Slav risings of 983, 1018 and 1066, and the achievement in the end, like so many other medieval achievements, was that of the twelfth century especially, though continuing into the thirteenth and fourteenth. Further, that achievement was brought about, significantly enough, not by the kings but by the German people, knights and monks, merchants and peasants, under the leadership of the German princes, notably Henry the Lion of Saxony, Adolf of Holstein and Albrecht the Bear. In sum, the area of Germany was increased by two thirds, partly to the south-east but most notably in the north along the Baltic by the conquest and colonization of the lands of the heathen Slavs or Wends, who had moved in from behind during the great period of the migration of the German tribes themselves during the fifth and sixth centuries, and were now conquered, suppressed, and forcibly converted to Latin Christianity. During the twelfth century, especially in the middle years, the frontier of Germany in the north was rolled forward from the Elbe, where Charlemagne had left it, to the Vistula, and the provinces of Mecklenburg, Brandenburg and Pomerania were occupied. Thereafter in the thirteenth and fourteenth centuries, through the agency of the crusading Order of the Teutonic Knights, German power and militant Christianity occupied Prussia (which thus belatedly enters European history) and

[1] R. H. C. Davis, *History of Medieval Europe*, p. 377.
[2] Thompson, *Feudal Germany*, ii, 479–80.

German eastward expansion and colonisation

Denmark

Königsberg

Oldenburg
Neumünster
Holstein
Trave
Lübeck
Ratzeburg
Hamburg
Lauenburg
Lüneburg
Saxony
Elbe

Doberan
Stralsund
Rügen
Rostock
Wismar Eldena
Schwerin

Greifswald
Kolberg
Kammin
Pomerania

Oliva+
Danzig
Elbing
Marienburg
Prussia
Marienwerder

Havel
Uckermark
Stettin
Stargard
Kolbatz

Pomerelia

Kulm
Thorn

Vistula

Weser
Aller
Salzwedel
Stendal
Altmark
Brandenburg
Brunswick
Brandenburg
Magdeburg
Halberstadt
Flaming
Goslar
Zerbst
Köthen
Halle
Leipzig
Naumburg
Pleissnerland
(Vogtland)
Altenburg
Meissen
Plauen
Eger

Lebus
Neumark

Frankfurt
Guben
Jüterbog
Jonas
Lausitz
Elster
Görlitz
Meissen
Bautzen
Zittau

Posen
Warthe
Oder
Glogau
+Leubus
Liegnitz
Breslau
Brieg
Silesia

Poland

Gnesen

Thuringia

Saale

Franconia
Bamberg
Nürnberg

Eger
Eger

Prague
Bohemia

Elbe
Vistula

Moravia

Regensburg
Ingolstadt
Straubing
Landshut
Passau
Munich
Bavaria
Salzburg

Danube

Linz
Austria
Vienna
St.Pölten

Morava

Hungary

Danube

Styria

Carinthia

MAP 7

moved on through Courland, Estonia and Livonia to the Gulf of
Finland. In the end even the prowess of the Teutonic Knights
was defeated by the limitless snowy wastes of Russia, and the
student who wishes to gain something of the experience of this
part of the story would do well to see Eisenstein's great film
'Prince Alexander Nevski' (making proper allowance for the
element of hostile propaganda, which chiefly serves to underline
the relevance of medieval history to the present). But in the main
the eastward expansion of Germany in and after the twelfth
century was permanent, altered the map of Europe for the last
time, filled in, as it were, the gap in Latin Christendom of the
Slav lands, and finally established the modern political and
ethnic pattern of northern Europe. It was not just conquest but
crusade and holy war, and not just these things but also a great
colonizing movement whose closest historical parallel (including
the tragedy of the displacement, exploitation and suppression
of the native inhabitants) is perhaps the gaining of the American
West in the nineteenth century.[1] Its fundamental causes are thus
to be found in the general conditions of expansion obtaining in
Latin Christendom in the twelfth century,[2] including an expanding population, an expanding trade and commerce, land-hunger
marked by the taking in of former waste and then the overflow
to new lands, as in Germany beyond the Elbe and the Crusading
States in Outremer. It has been calculated that in Silesia some
1,200 villages were founded between 1200 and 1350 and some
1,400 in Prussia during the same period, while the total require-
ment for the settlement of these two provinces alone must have
been some 300,000 peasants. Such numbers, there and elsewhere,
came, seeking new land, new wealth, new opportunities, and new
status (for in the east men, both princes and peasants, were free
of the confinements of the feudal and manorial west). We hear of
contractors, 'locators', who undertook to plant villages and supply
the settlers for them, and we hear, echoing down the centuries,

---

[1] Comparisons are continuously illuminatingly made especially by the
American J. W. Thompson in his *Feudal Germany* (vol. ii).

[2] Cf. p. 219 below.

proclamations and appeals to attract immigrants, as this from
Saxony, probably in the year 1108: 'They [the Slavs] are an
abominable people, but their land is very rich in flesh, honey,
grain, birds and abounding in all products of the fertility of the
earth, when cultivated, so that none can be compared unto it.
So they say who know. Wherefore, O Saxons, Franks, Lotharing-
ians, men of Flanders most famous—here you can both save
your souls, and if it please you, acquire the best of land to live
in.'[1] Such advertisements, promising both salvation in the next
world and material well-being in this, appealed to all sorts and
conditions of men, and were meant to. In the words of an old
Flemish song, 'Let us ride to the eastern lands, conditions are
better there.' There were new commercial centres in the east
also, as well as peasant settlements and princely potentates, and
these were the contribution of the German merchants to the new
Germany, the great trading cities founded along the Baltic shore
from Lubeck via Wismar, Rostock and Stralsund to Kolberg.
The merchants indeed got further than the peasants, to the gulfs
of Riga and Finland, for this way lay a great trade route to the
East (followed by the Vikings long ago) through Kiev and
Novgorod. In the fullness of time the Hanseatic League will arise
out of these new German towns and ports and the descendants of
these men.

Much of the future history of Germany, without exaggeration,
lies in the new lands of the east, and we have seen, as instances
merely, the origins of Brandenburg and Prussia in the north,
just as Austria finds its origins in Charlemagne's East March
(Ostmark) and subsequent eastward expansion in the south.
Indeed in this chapter we have seen, both negatively and
positively, the pattern of the future formed no less certainly than
in those other chapters which precede and follow it. The condition of a Holy Roman Empire which survives until 1806 as
neither an empire nor Roman nor holy finds its explanation in
these years, and a divided Germany of the princes, whose
reunification and its consequences dominate the most recent

[1] Cited by Thompson, *op. cit.*, ii, 497.

period of European history, is the result neither of the Reformation nor the Thirty Years War but of the medieval contests between that Empire and the Papacy. One may wonder, too, at the present division between West and East Germany, set against the history of German expansion eastward, and that constant and triumphant striving, also, is directly relevant to the German invasion of Russia in the Second World War. It is possible, indeed, without being apocryphal, to suggest that an ignorance of the medieval history of Germany is even more lamentable than an ignorance of the medieval history of other lands, for certainly it illuminates both the present and the recent past, and if we are unknowing others are not. Prussian court painters of the late nineteenth century loved to depict the legend of the Emperor Frederick Barbarossa, who had never died but slept to be awakened by ravens when Germany should again be united. The German army in the last war gave the code-word 'Barbarossa' to their Russian campaign, and Adolf Hitler called his Nazi state the 'Third Reich' because the first was the German Empire of Otto the Great and his successors, and the second that of Bismarck and the Prussian Kaisers.

CHAPTER IX

France

From Germany we turn to France, in many ways the fount of medieval civilization, and whose outline political history in this same formative period, from the tenth to the thirteenth century inclusive, is the reverse of that of the former, beginning with disunity and particularism—the France, so to speak, of the princes—and ending with a powerful, unified national monarchy. Throughout, the monarchy may be taken as the unifying theme, and by its power the progress of French political unification may be measured. In the beginning, in the late tenth century, it is often said (though wrongly), the king of France was no more than *primus inter pares* in his kingdom. By the end, Philip IV (1285–1314) and his lawyers will declare that 'the king of France is Emperor in his kingdom', and will speak also of 'the plenitude of royal power'. The French monarchy of Louis XIV can already be glimpsed in that of Louis IX, St. Louis (1226–70), of whom it has been said that he set France firmly on the road to royal absolutism, and his monarchy in turn was made possible by the achievements of the more pedestrian Philip II, 'Augustus' (1180–1223). During this time also, yet not obviously connected with these political developments (and so warning us against too obvious inferences), France and northern France especially took the lead in the evolution of a medieval culture, in thought and learning in her schools and universities, in art and architecture, in feudalism and in chivalry (as in war and the Crusades). What can often seem French arrogance in Anglo-Saxon ears and eyes is based upon past achievement, medieval as well as 'modern'.

But what is France? For this emergent nation state and

national monarchy we must return not only to the Franks, whom Germany also can claim as founders, but also and more particularly to the later Carolingian period and to the Treaty of Verdun in 843.[1] From that division of the Carolingian inheritance the kingdom of the West Franks will be France as the kingdom of the East Franks will be Germany, with the Middle Kingdom lying in between them. No area of Latin Christendom suffered more in the ninth and tenth centuries than West Frankia from the incursions of the Vikings, together with those of the Magyars, and of the Moslems in the south. Largely for this reason, combined with the incapacity of kings to give protection over so large an area against so great a threat, political disintegration did not stop in the future France in 843 as in the future Germany. Nor were the divisions of the kingdom ancient like the German quasi-tribal duchies, but the more or less new creations of the urgent times. With the decline of central authority society regrouped itself on the basis of local, military and feudal lordship, and it is here and now, as we have seen, that the origins of feudal society in France (and thus in Europe) are to be found.[2] Nowhere else were the ninth and tenth centuries so great a watershed in history than in France, which may to some extent instinctively account for Pirenne's thesis, that here, and not in the original Germanic invasions of the fifth and sixth centuries, lies the real break between classical and medieval.[3] Everywhere in the provinces of a crumbling kingdom new men appeared to carve and hammer out new principalities, often based upon ancient administrative divisions, their own authority doubly derived, in part from royal powers once delegated to Carolingian counts and bishops and now usurped, and in part from the new facts of feudal lordship. 'War made them conspicuous, grants of land established their position, marriage consolidated it, and the acquisition of ancient titles of honour cloaked their usurpations'[4]—thus

[1] Above, p. 106. See also Map 5.
[2] Above, p. 108.
[3] Above, p. 105.
[4] R. W. Southern, *Making of the Middle Ages*, p. 82.

Southern on the new men of the age, the new comital families and feudal princes who now arise from the ashes of the Carolingian world. Their world was local: they answered local needs and exploited local situations, and beside them stood (sometimes, indeed, to be numbered among them) the local bishops and the local abbots of an equally localized Universal Church. In the brave new world of feudal France, castles and churches, often side by side, stood as the symbols and the substance of political and ecclesiastical authority, often indistinguishable. And the bonds of society were as intensely personal as the communities newly formed were local: one served one's lord, whether lay or clerical, and the local saint was no less potent in the affairs of men than the local lord. Personal ties, indeed, took precedence over territorial divisions, which in this reformation of society were blurred: you might be uncertain where you were, but you knew whose man you were, and whose lordship you were in. It was an age thus, in the beginning, of the open frontier, and an age also of the open society, where not only survival but also greatness, lordship, went to the fittest and the strongest, and where anything could happen and very often did. An age, too, which combined its localism with an extreme mobility as the upper classes and their innumerable retainers (in a society where the household rather than the family was the basic unit) were constantly on the move, to govern and administer, to pray on pilgrimages, and to fight. As Marc Bloch[1] pointed out to resolve this seeming paradox, 'When transport is difficult, man goes to something he wants more easily than he makes it come to him.' He also pointed out in illustration that the kings of this first feudal age 'positively killed themselves by travel,' and an English historian some years ago caught the note exactly by remarking that life at the ceaselessly itinerant royal court (or, one may add, in the peripatetic household of any other magnate, clerk or lay) must have been like a grand but perpetual picnic.[2]

[1] *Feudal Society*, p. 62.
[2] D. M. Stenton, *English Society in the Earlier Middle Ages* (London, 1952), p. 17.

Extreme formality with informality, trumpets and the reek of horses, splendid garments in the rain, like a huntsman in December, with such and other contradictions this age, like any other, is replete.

It seems symptomatic of a new age and a new world that in 987, after the death of Louis V from a fall at hunting, the now ancient Carolingian ruling house he represented was replaced by a new dynasty in the person of Hugh Capet, son of Hugh the Great, 'duke of the Franks' (and greater than the kings thereof), and ancestor thus of the Capetian kings who rule henceforth throughout our period and to 1328. But for long political reality in France is not the kingdom but the powerful and near-autonomous feudal principalities into which it was divided, and now, in the late tenth and eleventh centuries, in process of formation—Normandy, Anjou and Flanders, Champagne and Chartres, Brittany, Aquitaine, Toulouse and the rest (Map 8). The political dynamic of the age works at first in their favour rather than in that of the kingdom, for the small units rather than the whole; nor.is there anything inherently wrong in this to be regretted, and those books, and they are many, which write of early medieval French history only in terms of the kingdom, and thus see it all negatively, through a glass darkly, as the history of weak kings and over-mighty subjects, miss most of the truth and almost all the fun. The truth, of positive endeavour and achievement, is otherwise, and is clear enough if we will once cast off modern political assumptions of which contemporaries had not heard, and accept and understand those things, inconceivable at first sight to us, but which contemporaries took for granted. The Duchy of Normandy or Aquitaine, the County of Anjou, Flanders or Champagne, these emergent entities and facts were real, immediate, viable: the kingdom of the French, as something comprising these and other principalities, for long was not.

Reality is best approached and realized through the several histories of the several feudal principalities (in which, most happily, French historiography abounds), though in practice

France, c.1000

Flanders

Lower Lorraine

Maas

Rhine

Upper Lorraine

Amiens
Ile de France
Beauvais

Rouen

Laon
Rheims
Chalons

Normandy

Marne

Paris

Chartres

Seine

Brittany

Maine

Champagne

Orleans

Blois

Loire

Armancon

Seine

Dijon

Anjou

Touraine

Cher

Berry

Duchy of
Burgundy

Poitiers

Duchy of
Aquitaine

Limoges

Vienne

Loire

Saône

Kingdom of
Burgundy

Dordogne

Perigord

Auvergne

Rhone

Bordeaux

Lot

Garonne

County of
Toulouse

Tarn

Duchy of
Gascony

Toulouse

March of Gothia

Roussilon

Spanish March

MAP 8

within the scale of this present book one or two only must suffice. Since in fact it will be necessary to speak of the Duchy of Normandy in the next chapter, we may take here the County of Anjou as our first example, for 'perhaps more simply than anywhere else in Europe, the shaping of a new political order may be seen in the valley of the Loire', and the history of Anjou from the late tenth to the mid-twelfth century 'provides a rich portrait gallery of the makers of a medieval "state" '.[1] Anjou was the creation of its counts, and they were typical of the age and place in being new men emerging from obscurity in the darkness of the ninth century. The first member of the future comital family in history and thus its historical founder is one Ingelgarius, of whom little enough is known save that he gained the first footing for his house in the Loire valley and fought both the Bretons and the Danes. He was succeeded by his son, Fulk the Red, whom Louis Halphen, the historian of Anjou, calls 'the true founder of the Angevin dynasty', and whom Charles the Simple, King of the Franks, made *vicomte* of Angers, conferring upon him also two religious houses in the same city. We should note in passing the phenomenon of lay abbots as the type of abuse and exploitation of the Church by secular lords which will lead in the fullness of time and the eleventh century to the cry that the Church must be free, though we should avoid black and white categories by noting also that Fulk the Red's son and successor, Fulk the Good (941–60), was by reputation a particularly pious prince, said to have delighted in taking part in choir services with the canons of Tours. Meanwhile Fulk the Red soon changed his title from mere *vicomte* to the more elevated *comte* or count, and he also married well, Roscilla, daughter of a rich lord in neighbouring Touraine, who brought her husband several lordships including that of Loches. If we pass over the next two generations after Fulk the Red, *i.e.* Fulk the Good (already mentioned) and Geoffrey

[1] For what follows, see especially R. W. Southern, *The Making of the Middle Ages*, pp. 81–90, and, behind that, the three excellent local histories of Anjou—L. Halphen, *Le comté d'Anjou aux xi siècle* (Paris, 1906); J. Chartrou, *L'Anjou de 1109–1151* (Paris, 1928); J. Boussard, *Le comté d'Anjou sous Henri Platnagenêt et ses fils* (Paris, 1938).

'Greymantle' (*c.* 960–87, and destined to be a legendary hero, appearing in the *Song of Roland* as the standard-bearer of Charlemagne), we must nevertheless observe that in practice son is succeeding father even though in principle hereditary succession and primogeniture are scarcely yet established, before we pause awhile before one of the great figures of the later tenth and earlier eleventh centuries, Fulk Nerra, Fulk the Black, Count of Anjou from 987 (when he was 17) to his death in 1040. If his world was narrow he bestrode it like a colossus, and he has been rightly called 'the founder of the greatness of the county of Anjou'.[1] His earliest biographer, his grandson Fulk Rechin in the late eleventh century (and an example therefore of the literate laymen not uncharacteristic of that time), lists, amongst others, four achievements of Fulk Nerra especially worth our notice: he built thirteen castles which could be named as well as others by then forgotten; he fought and won two pitched battles against his neighbours to east and west; he built two abbeys, one at Angers and the other near Loches; he went twice to Jerusalem (in fact he appears to have gone three times), and died returning from his last pilgrimage there. Each of these recorded achievements is typical of Fulk's age and class, an emergent class of tough, virile, warlike and pious knights and feudal princes, and 'taken together they convey a vivid impression of a pioneer in the art of feudal government'.[2]

Thus Fulk Nerra was an early and a mighty castle-builder, so much so that Anjou in his day has sometimes been suggested, though probably incorrectly, as the very place of origin of the castle. In any case the new castles were the substance as well as the symbols, and the means, along with knights, of the new feudal lordship,[3] and though the fact may be accidental yet it seems entirely proper that the earliest stone-built keep or *donjon* now surviving in Western Europe is at Langeais in Anjou and is attributed to *circa* 994 and Fulk the Black. Castles riveted

[1] Southern, *op. cit.*, p. 87.
[2] Southern, *op. cit.*, p. 86.
[3] Cf. p. 122 above.

one's lordship on the land and were also the bases for expansion. They also 'made loyalty easy',[1] and under the protection of their palisades or walls townships grew up (as they did also under the protection of the new monasteries, 'the castles of God') as centres of population and prosperity in the economic revival that was also a feature of Fulk's age. Since castles dominated the land they also came to dominate warfare because, to control the land, one must first control the castles, and in this way siege-warfare became more common than pitched battles. Nevertheless, Fulk Nerra won both his battles, at Conquereuil (992) in the west against the Count of Brittany and at Pontlevoy (1016) in the east against the Count of Blois, and by his victories, his castles, his knights, and by judicious marriages, he was able to expand the confines of his county of Anjou especially in the east towards his enemy of Blois, in which direction the acquisition of Tours and the whole lordship of Touraine by his son and successor, Geoffrey Martel, was largely the result of his efforts. Within his county, his authority depended less on ancient rights and Carolingian comital power than on the hard yet sanctified facts of feudal lordship. He was the suzerain, the lord of lords, and the fiefs he bestowed or imposed brought him not only the essential military knight-service and other valuable services but also bound men to him as his vassals as closely as the age knew how. In addition they put into his hand the huge power of feudal patronage, the ability to make and break, to raise up and cast down, for the fief was held (not owned) precariously, conditionally in return for loyalty and service, and at this date no hereditary principle even guaranteed its transference from one generation of a family to the next.

Yet with all, this man of war and feudal autocrat (who is reported to have made his rebellious son proceed on all fours for miles with a saddle on his back in sign of ignominy) was a pious prince and patron of the Church. If his sins were many he was aware of them, and the pilgrimages to Jerusalem (themselves representative of a growing social custom of the time that

[1] Southern, p. 86.

will lead to the Crusades) that his grandson records were undertaken in expiation. So were his benefactions, as when in 993
he made a grant of privileges to the abbey of St. Maurice at
Angers for his soul's health and 'as penance for so great a slaughter
of Christians' at Conquereuil the year before. So, too, with
his foundations of new religious houses which were, amongst
other things, great chantries to pray for the founder, his kin, and
their souls. The two foundations with which Fulk's grandson and
biographer credits him were the abbeys of St. Nicholas at
Angers, and Beaulieu near Loches in Touraine, and in addition
he and his wife jointly founded a third, the nunnery of Notre
Dame de la Charité, also at Angers. But in this we may see much
more than personal piety. The Count of Anjou as a ruler had
other responsibilities, and ancient concepts of Christian Kingship
filtered down to the level of the feudal princes as did the inheritance of a close relationship of Church and State within their
principalities. Fulk like other rulers of the age sought to restore
the Church in his dominions, shattered by wars and invasions,
and to do it especially by the restoration and foundation of
monastic houses. Like other feudal lords also he was the patron
of the Church within his lordship, and the Church he thus
effectively controlled through patronage was his right hand in
his government and his ally in his wars. One can see again and
vividly enough the sort of thing the Gregorian reformers of the
eleventh century will have in mind when one finds Fulk's
bishop, Hubert, of Angers (the principal city of Anjou) riding
beside his master the Count at the head of a force of knights to
devastate the lands of a neighbour who is the neighbouring
archbishop of Tours. 'Madness has seized thee', wrote the outraged metropolitan, 'thou who hast become instead of a bishop a
leader of troops, thou who carriest fire and sword in our lands,
thou who menacest us with a thousand deaths!' Yet when bishop
Hubert died in 1047 he received a glowing eulogy from his
monks at St. Maurice at Angers, whose church he had rebuilt.
'More than any of his predecessors,' they declared, 'this generous
prelate, noble and enlightened, applied himself with zeal to

bring our chapter from the miserable state to which it had been reduced by the oppression of tyrants and the negligence of bishops, and to restore it to prosperity.' And so, of course, he did. Wherefore the grateful monks decreed special prayers for the soul of Hubert 'by reason of the benefactions of this venerable man and the eternal recognition to which he has a right'. In such a world, where most reality was local and immediate, Rome could seem far removed from the heat and burden of the day. It is instructive to listen for a moment to the voice of the next bishop of Angers, Eusebius Brunon, defending the next count, Geoffrey Martel, against the 'unparalleled presumption' of the reforming Pope Leo IX in summoning his master to Rome to answer an ecclesiastical offence (he had imprisoned and held in prison the bishop of Le Mans). 'Has the Pope forgotten', Eusebius wrote, 'that he has a pontiff more powerful than himself in Jesus Christ, and that his authority consists only in conforming to that of the Lord?' Count Geoffrey is far too busy with affairs of state to go to Rome, beset as he is with enemies at home who plot against him day and night. 'One wishes', he concludes, 'that he had released the bishop: yet it is a public enemy that he detains.'

The death of Fulk Nerra in 1040 did not end either the expansion or the development of Anjou. Touraine, as we have seen, was at length acquired by his son and successor, Geoffrey Martel, in 1044: Maine, wrested from the rival power of Normandy, in 1109. But by then (in Southern's phrase again) 'the swashbuckling days were over', and so was the first fine careless rapture of splendid irresponsibility. The mould hardened, frontiers were defined, established states, Normandy, Anjou, Brittany, Blois, Poitou, played the power game and made war upon each other like any other states in any other period. Internally, also, the apparatus of the state appears as government becomes institutionalized and ceases to be entirely personal and amateur, a matter of lordship merely Almost everywhere in Western Europe the age of bureaucracy begins in the eleventh century, as in Norman England Domesday Book remains prodigiously to prove. In Anjou, the count's seal to authenticate the increasing number of his written acts first appears in the time of Geoffrey Martel, successor to Fulk Nerra; the chancellor, as head of the count's secretariat, appears in the last quarter of the eleventh century; and in the localities the *prévôts* also first came upon the scene in the eleventh century as the local agents of developing comital powers. In the twelfth century horizons undreamt of opened for Anjou. In 1129 Fulk V was chosen for and accepted marriage to Melisande, heiress of the kingdom of Jerusalem, and through her became king in Jerusalem in 1131, leaving the government of his French county to his son, Geoffrey le Bel. And Geoffrey le Bel is that Geoffrey of Anjou who married Maud or Mathilda, daughter of Henry I, King of England and Duke of Normandy, and widow of the Emperor himself. Geoffrey and 'the Empress' Maud, as every schoolboy knows, contested the Norman inheritance with Stephen King of England (Stephen of Blois, and thus an enemy of the Angevin house), and took Normandy from him. Their son Henry was recognized as Stephen's heir, and thus in 1154 became, as Henry II, the first Angevin King of England, and was also Duke of Normandy, Count of Anjou, and, in right of his own wife Eleanor (the most beautiful woman of her day), Duke of Aquitaine also. 'Were it farther off. I'll pluck it down.' Henry II, like Fulk Nerra his ancestor, bestrode his world like a colossus, but it was a much wider world, and the history of Anjou has now become a large part of the history of Christendom. For exactly fifty years matters so remained until, as every schoolboy knows again, King John of England in 1204 lost his patrimony of Anjou, and also Normandy, to Philip Augustus, King of France—which is another story.[1]

Of course the histories and exact conditions of the several feudal principalities into which the France of the tenth, eleventh and twelfth centuries was divided differ from each other in particulars according to their several circumstances, yet in the broadest sense Anjou is typical enough for us, seeking simply to get the French history of this dynamic age into the right

[1] Cf. p. 188 below.

perspective, and differs, like Normandy, from the others only in the enormity of its success. One could and should go on—though Anjou we have seen and Normandy we will see, and both afford fleeting glimpses also of Maine and Touraine, Blois, Brittany and Aquitaine—to discuss at least Flanders and Champagne as further illustration. Thus the power of the Counts of Flanders rested securely upon wealth, and their wealth was derived especially and already from the wool trade and the Flemish cloth industry—still made manifest to us by Ghent and Bruges, the latter especially, being still almost wholly medieval, amongst the loveliest places in the West. Flanders was feudally tied to France but economically tied to England by wool, to form, so to speak, the eternal triangle of medieval European history. The Middle Ages were not magically immune from economic forces though they were happy in their comparative ignorance of them (yet a magic world indeed where industry could produce beauty such as Bruges, or Lavenham here in East Anglia), and the Counts of Champagne also derived power largely from commercial wealth, in this case through the great fairs of the county, which were the meeting places of the east-west trade via Ghent and Bruges on the one hand, Venice and Constantinople on the other. Yet surely by now enough has been said to show how misleading it is to speak or write of French history from the tenth to the twelfth centuries exclusively in terms of the kingdom as opposed to the principalities which comprised it, and how out of focus is the resulting picture of weak kings, overmighty subjects and private war, ever to be contrasted with the vision of a contemporary English kingdom where things were very different. It is with Normandy or Anjou that England is to be compared, its fortunes deeply involved with both, while warfare within the French kingdom is not something to be set on one side and deplored as 'feudal anarchy', but was a matter of wars between quasi-sovereign princes no different from wars between national states in the modern or the medieval periods. And lastly, the moral to be drawn from the history of France in these centuries, if seen in the right perspective, is that feudalism itself,

far from being anarchical and a centrifugal political force, is
centripetal and cohesive. Feudalism and the state are the very
reverse of contradictory terms. It was by feudal means above all
that the feudal princes of this period welded their feudal principalities together, just as, as we shall see, it was the potency of his
feudal rights and the potential of his feudal position as suzerain
that in the end transformed the king of France into an emperor
within his kingdom.

If then, we may ask, at any time within the tenth, eleventh and
twelfth centuries political reality in France was not the kingdom
but the feudal principalities into which it was divided, if many of
the feudal princes in material power were stronger than the king
himself, and if all of them by their position excluded him in
practice from any direct intervention within their lordships, so
that in terms of real government the king was confined within his
own demesne, the Ile de France—if all this was so, how did it
come about that by the late thirteenth century the monarchy was
master in and over all of France? A large part of the answer,
namely feudalism, we have in fact anticipated, yet that part
needs illustration and also there are other factors scarcely less
important. One such other factor is good fortune, for 'fortune
favoured the Capetians', and not least in that they lasted,[1] each
generation producing a male heir, until the late twelfth century
crowned in his father's lifetime (significantly the first king for whom
this precaution had not been taken was Philip Augustus in 1180),
and thus establishing the fact of hereditary succession by primogeniture before the principle. Further, the Capetian kings of
France were kings. This obvious statement is important, for it
means that they were always more than *primus inter pares*.
Everywhere in Latin Christendom kingship was older than feudalism, its majesty long-since sanctified by the Church, and in
France not even the Danes nor Gregory VII could wash the
balm from an anointed king. In point of fact, through both the

[1] Robert Fawtier, *The Capetian Kings of France* (London, 1960), p. 16.
This book, thus and now available in an English edition, is far and away the
best on its subject.

weakness and the sagacity of the Capetians there was to be no Investiture Controversy in France, and in the reign of Louis VII (1137–1180), long after Gregory's time, the abbot of La Chaise Dieu could write to the king in the unchanged spirit of the pre-Gregorian past, saying that his monks prayed for the monarch every day 'for two reasons: first because you are our lord the king; and second, because you belong to our order.' Gregory himself in seeking to deny that divinity of kings which the Church had once created, liked to point out the paucity of royal saints ('Where, amongst emperors and kings, can a man be found to compare through his miracles with St. Martin, St. Anthony, or St. Benedict, not to speak of the apostles and the martyrs? What emperor or king has raised the dead, cured the leprous, made the blind to see?') but the Capetian house remedied even this deficiency in Louis IX, St. Louis, in whose reign indeed in France 'the religion of the monarchy' (the phrase is Fawtier's) begins. In his reign (1226–70) the mystique and sheer prestige of the monarchy reaches a lasting culmination. St. Louis was 'the king who won and kept first place in French affections, who most strongly influenced the development of the French monarchy, and who obscured the glory of his forerunners and predecessors alike. After his time, men spoke not of the Capetians, of the royal house of France, of the throne of France, but of the line of St. Louis, the blood of St. Louis, and the throne of St. Louis;[1] 'Son of St. Louis, ascend into heaven': with this viaticum another Louis half a millennium later met his death on the scaffold of the Revolution.

Mounting prestige and the mystique of royalty, associated in men's minds with a growing sense of French nationalism which the monarchy personified, is not the least of the factors in the success of the Capetians, and to it they were able to add the further element of Carolingian legend, posing as the heirs of Charlemagne (inaccurately since in spite of subsequent marriages, their dynasty had displaced them), while Charlemagne himself was represented as Emperor and King of France. The biographer

[1] Fawtier, *op. cit.*, p. 29.

of Philip II, Augustus (1180–1223), addressed him as *Karolide*,
and the chronicler of the royal abbey of St. Denis observed of
the succession of Louis VIII (who did have Carolingian blood on
both sides) in 1223 that 'the line of the great Charlemagne, who
was Emperor and King of France, returned after seven generations.'[1] In this way therefore the monarchy 'stepped out of the
past trailing clouds of legendary glory' (Fawtier).

But the Capetian kings of France were not only heirs and
successors to an ancient and pre-feudal monarchy, they were
also feudal suzerains and thus feudal kings, with powers real or
potential thus doubled, and their feudal rights are the most
important of all factors—paradoxically at first sight, but not
when the process is understood aright—in their transformation
into national monarchs. Feudalism kept the monarchy viable
in the dark days of the tenth century and thereafter added greatly
to its powers, to provide, indeed, the principal means of the
future unification of the realm. Enough has been said already,
in this chapter and before, of the rights and powers of feudal
lords, and the king was potentially the greatest of them all, the
lord of lords, the feudal king becoming thus the New Leviathan.
All the great feudal princes of feudal France, the dukes of Normandy, counts of Anjou and Flanders, and the rest, were vassals
of the king, nor did they ever deny that their principalities were
fiefs. There were, of course, quarrels, as in any other relationship,
and, since feudalism is above all a matter of military lordship,
such quarrels often enough became wars between the king and
his great vassals—though never, it is to be noted, between him
and all of them combined. Feudal custom, feudal law, allowed
the confiscation of a fief for a vassal's default, as it allowed the
diffidatio, the formal defiance of a bad lord and the renouncement
of fealty and homage, in either case envisaging war to vindicate
the right. War, indeed, could become a form of judgement, a
means of seeking the judgement of God, like the legal ordeal in
lesser cases. To come to the point we want is, once again, a
matter of getting one's perspective right, and thinking not only

[1] Fawtier, p. 56.

exclusively of the rights and liberties of vassals (important though these are in constitutional history), but also of the rights and powers of lords, at all levels in this hierarchical society, including the highest level of the kingship. It is not only services, including vital military services, that are at issue, but also the taking of counsel and giving of judgement from and to one's vassals in one's court, the custody of fiefs during a minority, the escheat or reversion of fiefs through failure of heirs, the confiscation of the fiefs of defaulting vassals, the manipulation of marriages and inheritances, the huge powers of feudal patronage. One classic instance must suffice to show the relevance of these things to the expansion of the Capetian monarchy and the unification of the French kingdom in this period. In 1204 Philip Augustus obtained from John of England all Normandy and Anjou, Maine and Tourine, and other lands besides. He did it by defeating John in war, but the war was waged to give effect to the judgement of his court, condemning John to confiscation of his fiefs as a contumacious vassal.

Yet also there is more to it than this. Feudalism is a cohesive force, but that not simply as an imposition from above. No vassal, however great, could afford to play fast and loose, to act against feudal law and custom, in his relations with his lord, because of public opinion and because, more particularly, his power in the last resort was dependent on his own vassals observing their obligations to him. 'Do unto others as you would be done by' is a basic feudal principle (and is accordingly enshrined in Magna Carta). And further yet, the feudal bond is bilateral in every sense: of course a lord needs vassals, but so also does a vassal need a lord, and this, again, at all levels of the hierarchy including the ultimate. A surviving letter from the year 1023, in the name of Eudo II, Count of Blois, to the king, Robert the Pious, against whom he was then at war, speaks nevertheless in words sharply contrasting with those student essays, and even books, which talk only in terms of feudal anarchy and overmighty subjects. 'I am astounded', wrote the count (or caused to be written for him), 'I am astounded that without having heard me

in my own defence, you should hasten to pronounce me unworthy of the fief I hold of you ... If you will desist from your
attempts to take away my honour, there is nothing in the world
I should desire more than to be restored to your good graces.
For it is very painful to me to quarrel with you, my lord. From
the man who is at loggerheads with you are withheld the blessings
kingship bestows—justice and peace.'[1] The blessings which
kingship bestows, justice and peace—it was, and was increasingly
regarded as, the king's chief business to keep the peace and dis-
pense justice, and as his prestige increases, so his peace and his
justice are worth more than other men's. Society must have a
head to gain stability, the arch must have a keystone, and vassals
need a lord especially to get judgement. By no other means, not
even by the arbitrament of war, can right and title be so firmly
established as by the judgement of a superior court, and the
proper court for judgements affecting the feudal princes of
France, who were the king's vassals, was the court of their lord,
the king's court, where under his majesty their peers would be
assembled (hence trial by peers). By these means the kingdom
is held together and pulled together, and in this process there is a
snowball effect, since the more the king's power increases the
more readily men will seek his judgement and turn to his courts.
Just as Papal Supremacy in the post-Gregorian period became
real by the eagerness with which men turned to the Papal Curia
in all ecclesiastical causes, so the Capetian monarchy became a
reality throughout France by the dispensation of justice. 'Be so
just', wrote St. Louis in his *Instructions* for his son, 'that you never
deny justice to anyone on any account.'[2] Royal justice expanded
in the twelfth and thirteenth centuries in France as in England
because men wanted it, and it is as erroneous to think it an
imposition from above upon reluctant subjects liable to rebel in
consequence as it is to think of feudal kings pursuing anti-
feudal policies.

Again, if we wish to describe and measure the process of the

[1] Quoted by Fawtier, pp. 65–6.
[2] Quoted by Fawtier, p. 32.

expansion of the Capetian monarchy in the thirteenth century we can only do it in feudal terms, for the expansion of the monarchy is, almost literally, to be equated with the expansion of the royal demesne, as one after another the great fiefs fell in, until the demesne began to become almost coextensive with the kingdom, and the distinction almost ceased to matter. In the beginning the Capetian royal demesne consisted of the Ile de France and the country about the cities of Paris, Orleans and Laon—strategically placed, we can see, but very small in relation to the kingdom. Though technically to do so involves a contradiction in terms, the demesne may be thought of as in practice like one more of the great fiefs into which the kingdom was divided, whatever direct royal government there was being confined within it. Early Capetian history, before the late twelfth century, is customarily written in terms of the kings becoming first the masters of their own demesne, and exploiting its resources as a solid, material basis for their powers which were otherwise only indirect, theoretical and constitutional. Then the scene changes with dramatic suddenness as the workings of the feudal system (if the phrase may be allowed) brought about a huge expansion. Philip Augustus deprived King John of Normandy, Anjou, Maine and Touraine, thereby increasing the royal demesne threefold and the royal resources fourfold. In a continuation of the same conflict (since the English king did not recognize his deprivation until 1260), Louis VIII obtained Poitou. In the course of the thirteenth century also—though we mention only the most important instances—first Toulouse and then Champagne fell in through marriage and inheritance and the failure of other heirs. By the end of the century, only the special cases of Aquitaine and Flanders, the one held by the king of England and the other bound to England by economic ties, remained as fiefs on something like the old semi-autonomous model, and even there pressure and infiltration were increasing. Elsewhere those fiefs like Burgundy and Brittany which survived outside the royal demesne and the orbit of royal appanages were in practice so interlocked with royal government as to be more like the rare palatinates of England, administered for the king if not directly by him. The flood tide of monarchy was against them, and what we can only call the spirit of the age, as France becomes an entity in men's minds.

As the royal demesne expanded, so also of necessity did royal government to administer and control it. In this process also 'fortune favoured the Capetians,' for some of the great fiefs, notably Normandy, had a far more sophisticated administration than the demesne itself, and the king's government now profits from it. The thirteenth century especially, and the overall period of 1180 to 1314, saw the development and establishment in France of centralized monarchical government, the process noticeably accelerating in the reign of Philip IV, 'le Bel' (1285–1314), just when the demesne reaches its widest extent. The first royal Registers, in which the king's clerks kept copies of letters and written documents sent out or received, survive characteristically from the reign of Philip Augustus, and so do the earliest written accounts of the financial transactions of local officials, taken centrally after the manner of the English Pipe Rolls. By the turn of the thirteenth and fourteenth centuries we find all the specialized departments of the medieval state in being, and established at Paris which thus becomes a capital city in the true sense of the seat of government—a Chancery for secretarial business, the Chambre des Comptes to manage the royal finances, and the Parlement for the central dispensation of royal justice. That many of these developments in France came whole centuries later than their equivalents in England (though French historians commonly fail to mention it) is a measure of the difference in the histories of the two realms, and perhaps above all a measure of the difference in their size. The importance of justice in unification we have mentioned before, while with the Chambre des Comptes goes the appearance of something approaching national taxes exacted by Philip IV. These things are the sinews and manifestation, cause and effect, of a national unity, and mention should be made in this connection also of the occasional great assemblies, the precursors of the

States General and the equivalents of the contemporary English Parliaments, which figure prominently in the history of the reign of the same Philip. So too with legislation: in theory in the beginning the king of France could legislate direct only for his own demesne, and such legislation could be applied in the great fiefs only by the counsel and consent of the great vassals. But other forces were at work. Notions of Roman Law (*quod principi placuit, legis habet vigorem*) came in from the deep south now entering the royal orbit, and from the revived study of jurisprudence in this age. Beaumanoir wrote (*c.* 1283) that 'the king may make such statutes (*établissements*) as he pleases for the common weal'. St. Louis in his later years issued legislation intended for the whole kingdom without reference to his vassals, and under Philip IV we hear, as we have previously noted, of 'the plenitude of royal power'. Nor can the role of the new type of local royal officials be omitted from any account of the achievement of French political unity in the thirteenth century. *Baillis* or bailiffs in the north, *senéschaux* or seneschals in the south, more royalist than the king, they pushed their master's interests at the grass roots as far as they would go, and with less respect for the rights of others than their master would have had. About their importance French historians of the period wax almost lyrical: '*ces mystiques de la puissance royale*', wrote Fawtier, while Petit-Dutaillis referred to them as 'these ants which were gnawing away at the feudal structure' of the kingdom.[1]

Of course there were other factors in the political unification of France than the king's regality, his feudal suzerainty, and the expansion of the royal demesne, though these are the most important. There was also the Church, the ally of the monarchy within the kingdom in the interest of stability, and liable to think in larger terms than feudal princes, while in the Universal Church the Capetian kings, until the end, maintained good relations with the Papacy. The end, however, is significant, for

[1] Fawtier, p. 187, but better in the original French. C. Petit-Dutaillis, *Feudal Monarchy in France and England* (trans. E. D. Hunt, London, 1936), p. 301.

the first serious breach with the Papacy came between Philip IV and Boniface VIII and the former was triumphant. The king of France was emperor in his kingdom, and the new monarchy, it seems, could not endure an ultramontane order immune from the application of new notions of *raison d'état* and common weal. So henceforth Philip, like Edward I in England, could, amongst other things, tax the clergy on occasions of necessity, such necessity to be decided by himself. The historian, also, seeking to explain the development of this new monarchy in France, must fall back on intangibles in the last resort. There simply was, from at least the twelfth century onwards, a growing sense of French identity, and so of nationalism, overriding all particularism, reflected as early as *The Song of Roland* (*c.*1100?) with its reference to 'sweet France', or in Gerald of Wales' frightening experience as a young student in mid-century Paris on the night of the birth of a new heir to the throne, the future Philip Augustus. ('Two old hags who, in spite of their poverty, were carrying candles, and showing great joy in their faces, voices and gestures ... one of them looked up at him and said: "We have a king given us by God, an heir to the kingdom, who by God's grace shall be a man of great might. Through him your king shall suffer dishonour and defeat ...". For the women knew that he and his companions were from the realm of England'[1]). Contributing to this nascent nationalism was an awareness of French leadership, as a common attribute, in all aspects of an increasingly self-confident medieval civilization, from the tournament to art and letters and the intellectual achievements of the schools and universities. Thus the poet, Chrétien of Troyes, could write, about the year 1070, 'Our books have informed us that the pre-eminence in chivalry and learning [by which, combined, he meant what we mean by civilization] once belonged to Greece. Then chivalry passed to Rome, together with that highest learning which now has come to France. God grant that it may be cherished here, that the honour which has taken refuge with

[1] Geraldus Cambrensis, *De Principum Instructione*, Rolls Series, viii, 292–3. Quoted by R. H. C. Davis, *History of Medieval Europe*, p. 305.

us may never depart from France.'[1] Charles de Gaulle, one feels, and many a latter-day Frenchman would echo those sentiments, but we must also notice that much of this cultural pre-eminence is centred on northern France especially (and especially after the destruction of the brilliant southern culture by the Albigensian Crusade in the early thirteenth century). Paris, after all, the royal city, was the home of the earliest and most famous of the new universities in northern Europe, to which flocked the ambitious youth of Latin Christendom, and the confident splendours of Gothic architecture spread out from Paris and the Ile de France at the turn of the twelfth and thirteenth centuries to clothe much of the West in a robe of new churches. Henry III of England was so impressed by St. Louis' Sainte Chapelle in Paris that he wanted to take it home with him, but perforce instead rebuilt Westminster Abbey on French lines (at vast expense). Once upon a time, it may be remembered, two centuries before, it had been Norman churches in Norman Romanesque that had inspired Edward the Confessor to build the first Westminster. Though the Capetian kings of France, like most kings, were patrons of the arts and architecture, with much of this cultural fervour they were not directly concerned, yet they profited from it, for Fortune favoured them, as they became the personification of the new nationalism of France.

We may end this chapter, perhaps, with two considerations. The first is that because we end with a unified French monarchy it does not follow that this was the result of conscious and consistent policy, still less, as some books imply, that it was foreseen from the start and plotted and planned for by the Capetians from their very beginning in 987. Any lord, the king no less, is likely to exert his rights to the full, but is much less likely to look far beyond the exigencies of the moment, and it is always a mistake to suppose that an institution like the monarchy or the Church can somehow exist by other standards than those of its own time and place. It is, or should be, one of the prime lessons of history that what happens is not necessarily what was foreseen

---

[1] Quoted by Southern, *Making of the Middle Ages*, p. 14.

or meant to happen. As far as the great success story of the Capetians is concerned, something of the more complicated and fortuitous truth is at once apparent when we see that, even in the crucial matter of the demesne, what they received with one hand they often gave away with the other, and that alienations of the demesne are scarcely less common than acquisitions. Of the conquests of Philip Augustus from John of England, and his own of Poitou, Louis VIII granted out again all save Normandy, albeit to his own sons. In this way the royal 'appanages' of the textbooks were created, and for the most part it was merely luck if they and others came back again to the demesne. Those modern historians who bewail the unwisdom of those actions only show themselves out of touch with the period of which they write. Contemporary reality, untouched by anachronism, has never been better expressed than in the words of Fawtier:[1] 'No modern ideas of territorial unification lay behind their [*i.e.* the Capetians'] enrichment of the crown of France. They never sought to become the direct owners of all France, to remove all the great fiefs, to dismantle the feudal structure of the kingdom. As long as their vassals ... performed their feudal duties and services, the kings were well content. They were no different from other barons of the age, anxious to muster as many knights as possible under their banners and to see their *curia* attended by as many vassals as possible ... Nor were they even anxious to create an unchallenged despotism. Rather, they looked on their kingdom as a great domain, in which God had enfeoffed them, and which it was in no way wrong for them to entrust to their blood relations or to their loyal servants.' The second consideration is that the national monarchy which nevertheless emerges may not be pleasing to everybody's taste. The doctrine of necessity preached by Philip IV, and Edward I in England, has a very dangerous ring, and the former's proceedings against the Order of the Templars have all the distasteful modernity of political trials in Communist eastern Europe, including propaganda, the use of the media to smear, and 'confessions' ob-

[1] *Capetian Kings of France*, pp. 167–8.

tained by torture. It seems surprising that, living as we do in the age of the big battalions, we should nevertheless be out of sympathy with smaller units, though nostalgia for them might seem more appropriate. We are out of sympathy also with aristocratic privilege, though it is arguable that we owe more to it than to the overriding power of kings. One of the oddest paradoxes of history, at least as it is usually written, is that vices in lords somehow become virtues in princes.

CHAPTER X

Normandy and England

In this chapter we shall deal with the histories, separate and combined, of Normandy and England. Of the Normans it has been said that 'true medieval society is unimaginable' without their contribution,[1] while for England and Britain something more, however brief, than the incidental references so far made is necessary in a book whose purpose is to trace the origins of modern Europe and the West. Further, since Fortune brought the two together with momentous and lasting results in 1066, in the most formative epoch of our whole formative medieval period, it does not seem unreasonable here to bring the two together in one chapter. To do so may even help a little to dispel that insularity which does prevail among English historians and English history students, not least, however paradoxically, among those of the Middle Ages. It is ridiculous to talk and write of a Henry I or a Henry II as though they were only kings of England or to imply that they should have been, when the one was also, by great effort, duke of Normandy, and the other not only that but also count of Anjou and duke of Aquitaine. Yet it happens, and happens also, *mutatis mutandis*, with other post-Conquest medieval kings (who for long were not in fact English). While it is entirely justifiable and desirable, though going out of fashion, for history students to study in most detail the history of their own country, the academic and syllabus convention which results, of treating English and British history separately from something else called 'European', is very undesirable indeed.

In one sense the history of Normandy is by now familiar to us:

[1] J. M. Wallace-Hadrill, *The Barbarian West* (London, 1946), p. 146.

that is to say, the duchy was one of those feudal principalities into which the kingdom of the West Franks became divided in the course of the tenth and eleventh centuries. If, therefore, there is one instance above all others to drive home a principal message of our last chapter, that political reality in the France of this time is not the kingdom but the principalities, and that to concentrate upon the kingdom to their exclusion is to omit most of the relevant history of the age, this must be it. For having established themselves in Normandy to make of it one of the most powerful states in Latin Christendom, the Normans from about the middle of the eleventh century broke out and moved on, to conquer first neighbouring Maine and then England (thence to overflow ebulliently into Wales, Scotland, and ultimately Ireland), to conquer also and at the same time southern Italy and Sicily, and in the van of the Crusade, before the century was done, to carve out and establish the crusading state of Antioch, in Outremer, the Middle East. Moreover, since they thus became a dominant force in Western Europe and beyond, their exploits and achievements have to be set in the whole context of medieval history, and were potent and often determinant factors in the great movements of the age, whether it be the turning back of Scandinavian influence from which, paradoxically, they themselves were sprung, the cultural predominance of northern France which, in part, results, the turning back of Islam also from the West, and the Crusades which follow, or the expulsion of Byzantium from Italy and the advent of a far more forceful relationship (leading on to 1204) with that hitherto overwhelmingly superior power. They enlarged the bounds of Christendom as well as the area of French culture, and wherever they went they took feudalism with them. Nor are even these things all, for though the Normans were not an originating race they were above all active and efficient: they made things happen, and thus made a quite disproportionate contribution to almost every achievement of that developing society in which they played a leading part, in religion, monasticism and the revival of the Papacy, in government, administration and warfare, in architecture (characteristically not only great churches but castles also), in learning and in the renaissance of this age. If it is acceptable to speak, in modern jargon, of the take-off point of medieval society in the West, then we reach it in the mid-eleventh century, and the Normans were a crucial element in the combustion.

A full and satisfying explanation of the mystery of how this extraordinary race of men were able to do what they did will probably always elude us, however many factors the historian may patiently analyse and tabulate, and perhaps in the end it matters less than the realization that they did it. Up to a point, after all, the Normans in Normandy were the same as everyone else in France, subject to similar circumstances and conditions, and with similar interests and needs. Why, then, the Normans? Why not the Bretons or the Angevins, the men of Champagne, Blois or the king's men of the Ile de France? If at the outset we thus seek a fundamental difference, we meet at once the Scandinavian origins of Normandy, and though in fact not even the Viking element was unique to the future duchy it must be counted in as one possible, partial explanation of that extra measure of adventurism, wander-lust, land-hunger, energy and ferocity of the future Normans. For the Normans, as their name betrays, were Norsemen in the beginning,[1] and the history of Normandy is taken to begin with the so-called Treaty of St. Clair-sur-Epte in *c.*911, when the Frankish king, Charles the Simple, granted to a band of Vikings operating in the Seine valley under their leader, Rollo, a parcel of territory which will become Upper or Eastern Normandy. Normandy thus begins as a kind of Frankish equivalent of the English Danelaw, though with a future very different. Yet here, as with the Danelaw, the area was scarcely a vacuum or *tabula rasa* when the Vikings settled it, nor do we really know, at least for Normandy, the density of that settlement, nor the proportionate influence upon the future of Viking and pre-Viking, Frankish and Carolingian elements. Further, what we do know is that the Normans

[1] Cf. p. 100 above.

from the beginning exhibited one of their most marked characteristics, that of adoption and adaptation, adopting the Frankish Christian religion, Frankish laws, Frankish feudalism, and Frankish warfare, the new monasticism, the new learning and the new architecture, to become, as it were, by the mid-eleventh century more Frankish than the Franks, more French than the French.

The earliest history of Normandy after 911 is obscured by an insufficiency of evidence, but it is known that the original grant at St. Clair-sur-Epte was supplemented by others adding Lower or Western Normandy in 924 and 933, so that by the latter date the future duchy was territorially complete. Further, this territory and principality of Rollo and his successors coincided almost exactly with the pre-existing ecclesiastical metropolitan province of Rouen. The results of this were two-fold: it made the frontiers of the duchy far more precisely defined than was usual in this age of overlapping and competing lordships, and this in turn contributed significantly to its unity and cohesion, while also it established from the beginning that close and intimate relationship of 'Church and State' characteristic of the age but more particularly characteristic of Normandy in the great age of her expansion. And that great age, roughly the period 1050 to 1100, it is certainly to be noted, begins only a little more than a century from 933, and less than a century and a half from the first foundation in *c.* 911. Clearly development from these beginnings, not markedly auspicious, had been rapid and dramatic, even though we have little detailed knowledge of what was going on before the eleventh century itself.

If we seek to analyse and explain something of Norman power and capacity in the mid-eleventh century, when the evidence is more abundant, we can without much difficulty list certain basic factors, not all of which are new and some, though reaching their culmination and their apogee in the time of William the Conqueror, must be the developing themes of pre-Conquest Norman history. Thus it is with the then all-pervading ecclesiastical revival, which it is not paradoxical to place high on any list. This, in the broadest sense, begins early, and is a remarkable instance both of poacher turning gamekeeper and of the Norman-Viking powers of assimilation and adoption, since the Norsemen were pagans when they came and had so far spent much of their energies in burning and looting churches. All the great monasteries of the province had been destroyed by 911—Les Deux Jumeaux, Mont St. Michel, St. Wandrille, St. Evroul, Fécamp and Jumièges—and the fabric of the secular church shattered. Nevertheless, Rollo accepted baptism in his part of the bargain of St. Clair-sur-Epte, and his successor, William Longsword (927–43), has left a reputation as a pious prince and the refounder of Jumièges, where, it was said, he wanted to become a monk himself. These things could not but matter in a society increasingly hierarchical, and the pattern of the conversion of a people from the top downwards was both common and logical within the Church of Rome. But the Norman ecclesiastical revival proper may be said to begin in the reigns of Richard I, the Fearless (943–996), and Richard II, the Good (996–1026), and more especially in the time of the latter, and there are three notable features about it—that it was under ducal patronage; that, typically of the age, it concentrated first and foremost on monasticism; and that it drew its inspiration and direction from the main centres of the general monastic reform movement of this time, and more particularly from Cluny.[1] Richard I, who refounded St. Ouen at Rouen, Mont St. Michel, St. Wandrille and Fécamp on the model of the reformed monasticism of Ghent, is said to have tried and failed to get monks from Cluny for the last, but Richard II in 1001 obtained the services, as abbot of that house, of William of Volpiano, a notable Cluniac from Dijon (where he was abbot of St. Bégnigne). William hesitated at first to accept the invitation, remarking that he had hitherto supposed the Normans were more apt to destroy than build the Temple of the Lord, but come he did, and from Fécamp his reforming Cluniac zeal spread out over Normandy, not only to those houses then in existence, but to others yet to come. By the accession of

[1] See pp. 131–6 above.

the future William the Conqueror in 1035 there were ten monasteries in Normandy and all were the foundations of the ducal family, but at that point the movement was taken up by the new Norman aristocracy, following the duke's example. While William and Mathilda his duchess made their two great foundations of St. Stephen's and the Trinity at Caen (their churches still intact today) as penance for their marriage, the rest of the twenty or more religious houses founded in Normandy between 1035 and 1066 were the foundations of other Norman lords, who, in a famous passage of the chronicler Ordericus Vitalis, 'seeing the great zeal of their princes for holy religion, urged themselves and their friends to similar undertakings for the good of their souls. They vied with each other in taking the lead in such good works, and in the liberality with which they made ample endowments. The most powerful nobles held themselves cheap if they had not on their domains some establishment of monks or clerks provided by them with whatever was necessary for the service of God'.[1]

Revival and reform of the secular Church came later, scarcely beginning before the reign of the Conqueror himself (1035–1087), the turning point usually taken to be the appointment by him of the reforming Maurillius to Rouen in 1055. But by 1066 the Norman Church was fully organized on the latest model, its dioceses re-established, great new cathedral churches rising up to rival or excel those of the monasteries, and its bishops never less at least than vigorous and efficient. These things matter especially to us because at every point the Norman Church contributed to the strength of Normandy and the potency of the Normans. It was both a cohesive and an expansive force, at once a principal bond of society and a principal inspiration. Closely controlled by the duke, the Church and clergy stood at his right hand in government and administration. The duke and the great magnate families were the patrons of the monasteries, frequently entered and not infrequently ruled by their own sons (and daughters), and the bishops were mostly drawn from the same top

[1] *Historia Ecclesiastica*, ed. A. Le Prévost (Paris, 1838–55), ii, 12.

level of this closely integrated society. The monasteries in particular brought respectability, prestige and fame to their patrons and the duchy, and they also brought learning in their schools, notably those of Fécamp, Jumièges, St. Evroul and, above all, Bec, which achieved a European reputation in one generation through the work and teaching there of Lanfranc. As for the intangible element of inspiration, if we use the phrase 'muscular Christianity' of the Normans, both dusty and anachronistic though it is, we may sense a little of the ethos of this society, so different from our own. Certainly the role of the Normans in the emergence of the concept of Holy War in this period has often and rightly been pointed out. To fight and win salvation, to enjoy yourself and yet to do good, to win both spiritual and material gain, this was a near-irresistible combination for the new Norman chivalry of knights, born and bred to war in a prevailing climate of accepted piety. The developing notion and ideal of Holy War is present in all the Norman exploits of the age, not only and most obviously in the First Crusade, but also in the conquest of Sicily from the Moslems and the activities of individual Norman adventurers in Spain, and also in the expulsion of Byzantium from southern Italy and the conquest of England in the interest, among other things, of the reformation of her Church. It is relevant at this point to note that the Normans in Italy became the allies of the Papacy and that the Papal blessing and a Papal banner went with Duke William to England in 1066.

If the Church was one bond and sinew of Norman society, feudalism was another. The American historian, C. H. Haskins, wrote long ago of Normandy in the mid-eleventh century that it was 'one of the most fully developed feudal societies in Europe', and work since his day has done everything to confirm, and nothing to refute, that conclusion. Feudalism, also, with militant Christianity (for the two were integrated), goes far to explain and define the ethos of contemporary Normandy, and feudalism too was much of the substance of the power of Norman duke and aristocracy alike. The growing power of the Norman duke, indeed, is another of the dominant themes of Norman history from the beginning, and by the middle of the eleventh century it was both great and doubly based. If on the one hand he was vassal of the king of France, on the other he was also suzerain of his duchy, with all that that implied, and in addition, like his princely peers in France, he was the successor of the Carolingian counts, whose once delegated powers or royal sovereignty he thus inherited and usurped. Though we speak always of the dukes of Normandy it is significant that 'count' [*i.e.* of Rouen] is often the title most favoured by contemporaries down to 1066 and beyond. By the 1060s, in all but name the duke was sovereign in his duchy, whose small size was commensurate with the personal rule and lordship of the age. By then he also had a developing government apparatus in his household and the Church which he controlled, control of the provinces through the *vicomtes* his officials, the great amalgam of services and rights and the huge powers of patronage which accrued to feudal princes, wide powers of justice, wide lands in his demesne, and rich resources including tolls and taxes. In the person of William the Bastard, after his dangerous minority and the triumph of 1047 with which it ended, he also had a growing personal ascendancy, as well as feudal lordship, over the new Norman aristocracy, his vassals.

Clearly the contribution of the Norman aristocracy to the Norman political achievement was immense. They, even more than the duke (who was yet one of them), were responsible for it. They shared the lordship and the land of Normandy with him: they shared the triumphs and the spoils of England, and there became, as he did, even greater than they were before; and they also conquered southern Italy and Sicily and Antioch far beyond the orbit of the duke's control. Here, then, we come up against, once more, the mystery of *Normanitas*. How did they get away with it? We can go some way towards an answer, if no further. They were vigorous and virile—though not unique in being either. They were pious and loved fighting—though those characteristics too they shared with others. They also shared in, and contributed, perhaps even disproportionately, to an expanding population, and though again this feature of the times is not confined to Normandy it is certainly a factor explaining Norman emigration. We are told that Norman lords in this age prayed for sons, and their prayers were evidently answered in abundance. Twelve sons of Tancred of Hauteville set out for Italy,[1] and we meet in the pages of Ordericus Vitalis with the seven sons (and four daughters) of Giroie, who were 'a race of knights', the five sons (and four daughters) of Roger of Montgomery and Mabel de Bellême his wife, and also with the 'almost forty' knightly kinsmen of Robert de Witot. Everywhere in northern France in the tenth and eleventh centuries a new feudal ruling class of knights was in process of formation, new men in the ascendant, but in Normandy, which made a late start only in 911, the ruling and knightly families were even newer than elsewhere, more *arrivistes*. Even the greatest names of Norman history, for example—Montgomery and Montfort, Beaumont and Ferrers, fitz Osbern and Mowbray, Tosny, Warenne, Hauteville—scarcely emerge into the light of history before the eleventh century. The particular combination of common social factors in Normandy was evidently particularly explosive. New men rising to eminence through ducal patronage and preferment, but some falling by the way and others cast down (our age is not the only one to have a rat-race though the prizes differ and diminish); an open society still, with room at the top, but that room progressively narrowing, and the supply of fiefs running out as sons multiply and the feudal solution in the duchy reaches saturation point. Add the cult of knighthood, the profession of arms as the only alternative, for the gentleman, to the Church, the love of war, and small wonder if they, and they were many, who were younger sons, who fell from grace, who missed their fief at home or yearned for more and better, took their service and their arms, and sought their fortunes somewhere else. Much of all this Duke William harnessed to his English cause together with the loyal support of his established but ambitious vassals—though once again we pull up short to notice

[1] Cf. below p. 208.

that he took into his service in 1066 others than Normans, as volunteers flocked in from other lands to join an enterprise thought to be beyond even the capacity of Normandy. Meanwhile others had gone off to Spain and more to Italy, and Italy became in late eleventh-century Normandy, for the dissatisfied and dispossessed, the unofficial Promised Land. 'Unofficial' seems, indeed, a keyword in any account of the Norman conquests in Italy and Sicily, for they were the extraordinary achievements of private enterprise, of individual knight-adventurers. From the beginning, too, we hear in Italy of political exiles, like the forty knights, 'most skilled in the use of arms', who may have begun it all, whom the Lombard notable and rebel, Meles of Bari, met at Capua in the second decade of the eleventh century, and took into his service against Byzantium.[1] Nor is it likely to be coincidence that much of the earliest Norman enterprise in Italy took place during the 'anarchy' and social upheaval of the young Duke William's minority, and the suppression of discordant elements which followed it.

Out of this jostling, jingling company of bellicose knights and magnates in process of becoming the ruling class of Normandy and much else besides, the leaders under whom these things were done emerge. Nothing could be more important in an age of personal rule and personal lordship, and with the Normans the age produced the men. We know little enough about them as persons, and can only judge them by their acts; but it was their acts which chiefly made them, for it is significant that few of them save Duke William himself and his kinsmen were born to great place, but achieved it by their own endeavours. As for William the Bastard (son of Duke Robert the Magnificent and Arlette, allegedly a tanner's daughter at Falaise), we may feel with hindsight that all his career before 1066 had been a purpose-designed experience to equip him for his greatest act in England. Yet close behind him as outstanding figures in the Latin Christendom of their day, were the Hauteville sons (and grandsons) of a minor

[1] See D. C. Douglas, *The Norman Achievement*, p. 37, citing the chronicle of Monte Cassino.

2

lord on a small estate at what is now Hauteville-le-Guichard near Coutances: Robert le Guiscard, Roger and Bohemund, rising by their own prowess and audacity to be princes in Italy, Sicily and Antioch.

Two other factors yet remain, and though in these the Normans obviously shared with much of Western Europe that economic expansion and increased wealth which underlies their enterprise, and though their upper classes shared also with the rest of feudal France their love of war and dedication to it, yet in their outright excelling in contemporary warfare we find another difference peculiar to them which obviously goes very far indeed to explain the facts of their achievement. Adopting and adapting, they borrowed from the Franks at an early date the techniques of Carolingian warfare, not least of mounted warfare. From heavy cavalry, *i.e.* knights, and castles, they had forged by the mid-eleventh century a war machine which waged the blitzkrieg of their age. The war they loved they fought like other feudal societies in France, but fought it better. The charge of their knights (which they combined, of course, with infantry) was their ultimate offensive (and at times defensive) weapon, and their castles made their conquests permanent. When all else is said and done, the extraordinary Norman political achievements of the second half of the eleventh century are the direct result of military prowess, that prowess combined with an audacity to which history can afford few parallels. Mere squadrons of knights, hundreds at most, not thousands, took over southern Italy, and the conquest of England was achieved by a country little bigger than the single English province of East Anglia. 'The Normans are good conquerors, there is no race like them': thus Jordan Fantosme the poet in twelfth-century England. Before them, declared a Lombard prince in eleventh-century Italy, the enemy were 'as meat to the devouring lion'.

The first arena to be substantially and lastingly affected by Norman arms and Norman prowess outside Normandy was Italy. The end product was to be the foundation and establishment of the Norman kingdom of Sicily and southern Italy, the kingdom 'of the two Sicilies', whose last and most famous monarch in our period was that medieval Frederick the Great, King of Sicily, King of Germany and Emperor of the West.[1] The process involved the expansion of Latin Christendom and the defeat thereby of the two most formidable contemporary powers, Byzantium and Islam, whose ancient hegemony was broken for all time in Italy and Sicily respectively. Yet all this was done, as we have seen, by private enterprise, by individual Norman knights and lords. Because this is so, moreover, the achievement is piecemeal and untidy in the beginning, and the details missing or confused. Norman involvement in southern Italy, where the political situation of rival and competing powers and influences (Greek, Moslem, Lombard, Roman) was ripe for exploitation, first began, traditionally through pilgrims returning from Jerusalem, but perhaps more probably through exiles seeking their fortunes and military employment in new fields. The first Norman contingents were evidently in action about 1017, aiding the Lombard rebel Meles against the Greeks.[2] The price exacted for this and other military compacts was to prove prodigious as the momentum of events increased and news got home to Normandy of opportunity in the south. One Rannulf, established as a mercenary ally in the hill fort of Aversa by the Lombard prince of Naples, died in 1045 as count thereof and duke of Gaeta, while his nephew and successor, Richard of Aversa, soon became prince of Capua. Meanwhile further south the Hauteville brothers had arrived, to establish themselves in Apulia—William 'Bras de Fer' and Dreux and Humphrey—the second of them, Dreux, recognized as count by 1047. In that year also another of them, Robert Guiscard (the Wary) arrived in Italy. Operating at first in Calabria as little more than a successful brigand, by 1059 he had become, together with Richard prince of Capua, the ally and the vassal of the Papacy, and was recognized by the startling and post-dated title of 'duke of Apulia and Calabria by the grace of God and of St. Peter, and with their help in future,

[1] See p. 167 above.
[2] Above.

duke of Sicily'. In the event, however, while Robert Guiscard took Bari, the seat of Byzantine government on the mainland, in 1071, it was his younger brother, Roger, who came to join him in 1056, who was principally responsible for the conquest of Moslem Sicily. Beginning in the autumn of 1060, the conquest of the whole island was more or less complete thirty years later by 1090, in which year Roger, 'the Great Count', also captured Malta. Robert Guiscard died in 1085 at the age of seventy, by then (on his epitaph) 'the terror of the world', and Roger I of Sicily in 1101. It was the latter's son, Roger II, who brought under his sole rule all the Norman Italian principalities and lordships, to be crowned and anointed in 1130 at Palermo, King of Sicily, Apulia and Calabria. In this way there was created the most brilliant, advanced, and probably the richest, of all the kingdoms of the earlier Middle Ages, where the three worlds of Greek, Moslem and Latin civilizations met and cross-fertilized each other. They had come a long way, those dusty Norman adventurers and hard-riding knights, like so many cowboys in a Western film, and the Hauteville brothers, whose undistinguished village, church and manor still lie off the main road in the Cotentin, and whose descendants henceforth ruled in Oriental splendour in Palermo as monarchs of the Norman kingdom in the sun.

Perhaps the most impressive single feature of the Norman conquests in Italy and the Norman Conquest of England is that they both took place together. While private enterprise in Italy was winning prodigious profits as a kind of underground Norman venture, Duke William was harnessing the official resources of his duchy to vindicate his English claim. As every schoolboy really does know, he landed with his army at Pevensey in the autumn of 1066, and had the victory in one of the few decisive battles of Western history outside Hastings two weeks later. Decisive though that victory was, it did not end the Conquest in the sense of the occupation and control of all the English kingdom, but that was completed by 1071 at latest, when the capture of the Isle of Ely ended the thuggery in the Fens of

Hereward the Wake, afterwards romanticized as the last hero of Old English resistance. If we ask how on earth it happened, then as for Italy (and Antioch) so with England, we have to add to Norman prowess the negative factor of weakness and disunity in the conquered land. To appreciate this element of English weakness we must go back, however briefly, to earlier British history.

In England, unlike the rest of the Roman Empire, there seems to be no direct connection between the Roman period and the future, so that medieval, and therefore modern history begins to all intents and purposes with the settlement of the Germanic races, the Angles, the Saxons and the Jutes, in the fifth and sixth centuries, after the departure of the Roman legions. Thereafter, of course, the conversion of these 'English' heathen to Christianity by Roman and Celtic missionaries, and more especially the eventual monopolistic triumph of the Roman Church,[1] brought the legacy of classical and Latin civilization and reattached England, and ultimately Britain, to Western Europe once again. Politically, however, the early Anglo-Saxon centuries are the period of the so-called Heptarchy, of seven (or more, or less) independent kingdoms—Northumbria, Mercia, Essex, East Anglia, Wessex, Kent and Sussex—at times subject to the fluctuating overlordship (*bretwaldaship*) of one or other of their number, but otherwise autonomous. Even the Church, though it must always have been a powerful influence for unity, in practice was bent in its organization by the prevailing political facts of life. This situation was, however, dramatically ended by the Danes. The ninth and tenth centuries were no less a watershed in England than in France, but herein lies the paradox of early English history, that whereas in West Frankia they brought about the collapse of central authority and the disintegration of the state, in England they eventually brought about the opposite result, the achievement of political unity for the first time. It was only just so, but it was so. All the English kingdoms except Wessex (and a part of Mercia) fell before the Danes, but the

[1] Cf. above p. 68.

ultimate claim of Alfred King of Wessex to be 'the Great' in English history is that he alone held out. Not only this, but the main theme of subsequent history is of the reconquest of the Danelaw, the huge area to north and east originally conceded to the Danes, by Alfred and his successors, and this achievement, literally in other words, is also the expansion of the Wessex kingdom to the point where it becomes the kingdom of England. The consequence was that here in England (as in Germany) ancient, Germanic and quasi-Carolingian kingship survived and prospered, and something like a national state emerged. Nor was this basic situation altered by the second and successful round of Danish onslaught in Ethelred II's time at the turn of the tenth and eleventh centuries, for Swein Forkbeard and Cnut his son conquered all England, and the latter as king from 1016 preserved its unity until, after the brief reigns of his sons, Harold 'Harefoot' and Harthacnut, the Wessex line was restored again in the person of Edward the Confessor (1042–1066). This survival and, indeed, development and expansion of ancient monarchy explains, amongst other things, the absence of feudalism in pre-Conquest England, for monarchy in Western Europe is older than feudalism, and feudal society was established in France only with the breakdown of central, monarchical authority in the ninth and tenth centuries. In this as in all other ways the Old World survived in England to 1066, when it went down before the new.

The unity of England in 1066, however, is less impressive on closer examination than at first sight it appears. It was, in any case, comparatively recent, scarcely achieved before the death of Eric Bloodaxe, the last and Norse independent King of York, in 954. Further, the Danelaw, if reconquered, yet remained, an area comprising more than half England beyond a line drawn from the Thames Estuary to Chester, settled by Danes to a numerical extent that is controversial but certainly dominated by them, and under Danish law and custom since King Edgar (959–75) granted legal autonomy to them. This very real dichotomy between the Danelaw and 'English England' could scarcely not matter politically when the danger of renewed Scandinavian invasion prevailed at almost any time between 980 and 1086, and was especially important in the north, where the main centre of Danish influence reinforced the latent particularism of ancient, pre-Viking Northumbria. Every Scandinavian adventurer trying his luck in England, from Swein Forkbeard in 1013 to Swein Estrithson's sons in 1069, and including Harold Hardrada in 1066, sailed up the Humber to York in the expectation of support upon arrival. It was the Northumbrians also who in 1065, the last year of the Old English state, revolted against their southern earl, Tostig, Harold's brother, and forced a reluctant king to banish him, and the Northumbrians who at first in 1066 refused to accept Harold's kingship. It is easy to forget how much the Old English monarchy, to the end, remained the Wessex monarchy, King Edward never venturing beyond the Humber, and there is no doubt that the proven danger of Northumbrian particularism underlies both the Conqueror's devastation of the north in the grim winter of 1069–70, and Lanfranc's assertion of the superiority of Canterbury over York thereafter.

There were other troubles also. England was rich, undoubtedly, but her wealth in the tenth and eleventh centuries evidently did more to attract invaders than to enable her to repel them. It is worth reflecting that the conquest of Cnut took place only fifty years before the Norman Conquest as a kind of historical precedent. It also established an alien dynasty on the throne for thirty years, and though it did not bring settlement on the scale of the Danish and Norse settlements in the ninth century, it did go far towards establishing a new Danish aristocracy of earls and housecarls. These redoubled Scandinavian influences make one ask whether Anglo-Scandinavian rather than Anglo-Saxon is not a more accurate description of Old English society on the eve of the Norman Conquest: meanwhile they tied England to the Scandinavian world which, with Germany and the Rhineland, was her main affiliation, whereas the future lay with northern France. Mention of an Anglo-Scandinavian aristocracy must bring us also to the matter of the Old English earls. If ever there

were over-mighty subjects in England it was before and not after
the Norman Conquest, and the internal political history of the
kingdom in the fifty years before 1066 is of the rise to dominance
of the house of Godwin to the point of seizure of the crown itself.
The strains and stresses thence resulting have to be half guessed
at, but the enigmatic references of the Anglo-Saxon Chronicle
leave no doubt that they were there, and the events of 1051-2 are
not to be shrugged off. Earl Godwin and his sons rebelled against
the king in 1051, and were banished: the following year they
came back again in arms, thereafter to rise yet higher than
before. As for King Edward, though recent writing has done
much to strip away the legendary veils of hagiography, to reveal a
king devoted to the chase who could be leonine in his wrath,
nevertheless weak kingship seems the only verdict on his acts, to
be so dominated by a noble (albeit *parvenu*) house he did not
like, even to the point of marriage into it. Edith, his queen, was
Godwin's daughter, packed off to a nunnery at Edward's bid for
liberty and her father's fall in 1051, brought back again to court
the next year on the earl's return. Of that presumably less than
satisfying union there was no issue, and this in turn occasioned
the Great Matter of the succession to the throne, paramount in
politics at least from 1051, and the great conflicts of 1066.

English historians in the last half century have tended mis-
leadingly to exaggerate the unity, and therefore strength, of the
Old English kingdom on the eve of the Norman Conquest,
mainly through an over-emphasis upon the alleged but dubious
sophistication of royal administration and government techniques. Sealed writs and the geld system, law codes and sheriffs,
may be made to sound impressive on the printed page, but are
not all that much more advanced than the means of Norman
government in Normandy, and in any case do no more than
paper over, as it were, the dangerous cracks in the fabric of the
English state, which we have tried to indicate, however briefly.
Nor have we quite finished yet. Duke William was able to
muster on his side in 1066 the public opinion of Latin Christendom and the approbation of the Papacy not only on the grounds

of the justice of his claim to the English succession (which by contemporary standards, *i.e.* those that mattered, was the strongest), and of the perjury of Harold, but also in the interests of the reformation of the English Church. The condition of that Church, no doubt, was nothing worse than old-fashioned, with a loosing of momentum and direction since its own revival in the last century, but in the position of Stigand, its archbishop, it harboured a scandal of European proportions sufficient to be one cause of the Conquest in itself. He, a creature of the Godwin faction, had been uncanonically appointed to Canterbury, in plurality with Winchester, in 1052, after the equally uncanonical expulsion of the Norman archbishop, Robert of Jumièges, and so remained in spite of successive papal excommunications until his deposition in 1070. Finally, when the armed conflict came in the autumn of 1066, a military deficiency in the Old English kingdom also revealed itself. Of course in the event the Normans were aided by the closely preceding invasion of Harold Hardrada, the Norwegian claimant to the throne, as they were aided also by the impetuous bad generalship of Harold. Of course, too, Harold's army fought well at Hastings on the 14th of October, as they had done previously at Stamford Bridge three weeks before. But whereas they could win in Yorkshire against the Norse where the tactics of the opposed forces were the same, in Sussex they met for the first time the Norman and French cavalry of knights. A defensive position on the hill at Battle, the static and time-honoured tactic of the shield wall, the lethal wielding of the dreaded two-handed Scandinavian battleaxe, and courage—all this enabled them to stand and fight all day until dusk and Harold fell, but they could not prevail. The absence in pre-Conquest England of what we call feudalism meant the absence on the battlefield of cavalry, *i.e.* of knights, the new specialists in mounted warfare of the age. It meant also the absence of castles, and as the Norman knights (albeit with infantry support) won Hastings, so the Norman castles made their conquest permanent and made their settlement of England viable. English warfare in 1066, like English society (for the two things go together), was obsolescent by the new standards of Normandy and northern France.

To attempt now a full rehearsal of the results of the Norman Conquest of England would require another book rather than the residue of this chapter. In a real sense those results are with us still, for 1066 has never been reversed and was a turning point in English history after which nothing could be, or was, the same again. Amongst the most important one must place the wresting of England from the comparatively barren Scandinavian connection and its attachment to the world of feudal France. The Conquest also brought a new, immensely capable ruling dynasty, and a new and not less capable French and Norman ruling class. This total social revolution at the top, as complete in the Church as in the state, involved also the feudalization of society with all that that entails. It entailed amongst other things a huge increase in the power of English monarchy through the acquisition of feudal ties and services and feudal rights and patronage. No over-mighty subjects now, and from 1066 there rapidly develops a strong centralized, feudal monarchy, precocious in the development of the means of government, and therefore arousing periodically, from an early date, a not unjustified political opposition. There is little of the French religion of the monarchy in thirteenth-century England, but, rather, Magna Carta, the Provisions of Oxford and the *Confirmatio Cartarum*. Meanwhile England achieved rapidly a degree of unity unknown before: the submission of the north to the monarchy of the south begins in 1070; and the new and bellicose warrior-aristocracy overflows into Wales, Scotland (chiefly at this time by peaceful penetration) and, in the twelfth century, into Ireland. As from 1066, also, the kingdom of England was not only subject to the full impact of Continental influences, it also played a leading role in European affairs, in contrast to the comparative isolation of the late Old English period; nor could it have been otherwise since her kings now bestrode the Channel. This consideration brings us finally to what may be the most important result of all. War in and against France (that sweet enemy) is a constant feature of English and European history from 1066 to 1815 and beyond. War is the great catalyst of change, and here therefore is a thought to conjure with whether our concern is constitutional development, or social development, economic, technological, or whatever. Mary Tudor was wiser than most students of her period when she said Calais was written on her heart, for she stood closer to the Middle Ages.

The third Norman conquest in the eleventh century, of Antioch in Syria, in Outremer, is part of the general history of the First Crusade as well as of Norman history. Yet obviously we must note now, that when in 1095 Pope Urban II at Clermont preached the Crusade, and his appeal was taken up, perhaps more ardently than anticipated, by the new French chivalry, the Normans were soon in the van of a movement they had done much to pioneer as the self-appointed champions of Holy War. A powerful contingent set off from Normandy itself under duke Robert 'Curthose', eldest son, and successor in Normandy, of the Conqueror, and a still more powerful one, to prove yet more important, joined in from Norman Italy under Bohemund. Bohemund (who took with him his nephew Tancred) was an Hauteville of the second generation, son of Robert Guiscard himself and his second wife Aubrey,[1] and no less avid for fiefs and lordships than his father and uncles, though now they were harder to come by. On the Crusade he showed himself the best soldier in that martial company, but he did not reach Jerusalem, for on the way he set himself up as Prince of Antioch, the capture and retention of which city the Crusaders owed, indeed, more to him than anyone. Thereafter the Norman principality of Antioch characteristically became the strongest and best governed of the Crusader States of Outremer and as such it lasted almost to the very end.

---

[1] He 'was baptized Mark, but ... on account of his size when in his mother's womb was to receive the nickname of the giant Bohemund, which he later made famous throughout Christendom', Douglas, *Norman Achievement*, pp. 41–2.

By the year 1100 there was thus a kind of Norman common-wealth of Norman states, inter-connected and extending over-all from the Marches of Wales to Syria. Set in the wide span of European history it did not long endure. Specifically Norman history ends in 1204 when, following John's defeat by Philip Augustus, the duchy was reabsorbed into France,[1] while in their far-flung conquests the Normans of the eleventh century were to adapt themselves out of existence. Yet not before they had moulded to their wills much of Latin Christendom which they expanded, and in so doing they affected its whole course. Nor even now, almost a millennium later, have even the physical traces of these men vanished, for wherever they settled in their formative and constructive period they also built, with results yet more permanent than their other achievements. From Saone to Durham and the Tower of London, via Monreale and Palermo, Bayeux and Caen, we may follow them monumentally, and the epitaph *si monumentum requiras circumspice* is not the least of our tributes to them.

[1] Above, p. 188.

CHAPTER XI

Expansion and Consolidation

So far in this book we have by now rehearsed almost all the events, factors and developments required to lay the foundations of modern Western Europe, to set the pattern of the future, and, it may be hoped, to substantiate the 'relevance' of so-called medieval history. In this last chapter, in addition to rounding off and tying up loose ends, there are, however, certain omissions to be inserted, most notably the Twelfth-Century Renaissance, the Crusades, and the Christian reconquest of Spain. All three are connected, not least by having a common context or origin in the eleventh and twelfth centuries, each being a manifestation of the expansionism and dynamism of that period, of all ages in the history of the West perhaps the most formative. Of the twelfth century, which in all senses proceeds from the eleventh, it has been written, by an historian whose view is professionally broader than most, that it 'was one of the great constructive ages in European history' and 'has a relevance and actuality today which few other periods of European history share in equal measure'.[1] We have already noted that the passing of the Viking, Magyar and Moslem threats from the West in the course of the tenth century[2] ushered in a great period of revival and expansion, development and change, across the whole board of human endeavour from monastic reform, through the development of feudal society, to the revival of the State and Papacy, and in all this the eleventh and twelfth centuries are paramount.

[1] Geoffrey Barraclough, *History in a Changing World*, pp. 78, 79 (from a lecture first given in 1955).
[2] Above, p. 108.

Crowning their activity and achievement as a lasting symbol of them is the surviving architecture of those centuries, its best creations still almost universally respected as amongst the wonders of the world. This, after all, is an age of the great cathedral and monastic churches, passing through the final grand solidity of Romanesque to the first poised equilibrium of Gothic, from Durham (1093) to Notre Dame at Paris (1163) and to Chartres (1194).[1] If Chartres is not amongst the finest buildings in the world then no other building can be, and all of them represent not only faith and vision but also affluence, organization and technological achievement. Nor did the age, of course, build churches only. Though most of their palaces are now gone, Rufus' great hall at Westminster is still an ample setting for many English ceremonies of state, while amongst the castles Richard I's Château-Gaillard, on the frontier of Normandy above the Seine, is still technically amongst the most advanced in Western Europe, though built a century before the culmination of medieval military architecture at Edward I's Conway and Caernarvon, Harlech and Beaumaris. If these and other great buildings are the crowning glory, underlying the achievements of the time as an essential precondition of them there was economic expansion, accompanied by an expanding population and made manifest in the revival and growth of trade and industry, the development of urban centres (not least in the Italian cities which successfully defied the Emperor himself[2]) and the taking in of waste. These factors lead on, as we have seen, to a territorial expansion of Latin Christendom, in the eastward expansion of Germany against the heathen Slavs,[3] the Norman conquest of southern Italy and Sicily at the expense of Byzantium and Islam respectively,[4] and also, as we have yet to see, in Spain and in the Middle East, again at the expense of Islam. It should come as no surprise if these centuries witnessed

---

[1] The dates are those of their commencement.
[2] Above, p. 165.
[3] Above, p. 168.
[4] Above, p. 208.

also, as horizons widened and inquiry grew, an intellectual movement, a renaissance of classical studies, a great expansion and extension of learning, more especially as much of the new learning came from new contacts with the Greek and Arab worlds via Italy and Sicily and Spain.

The word 'renaissance' can be misleading if it is taken to imply the rebirth and revival of classical culture formerly dead, and the title 'Twelfth-Century Renaissance' can be doubly misleading since the movement to which it is applied began in the eleventh century and ran on into the thirteenth. What happened (as in the fifteenth century) was not a sudden transference from dark to light, nor could it have been so since from the beginning medieval culture was based upon the classical inheritance, and there had been other revivals and other 'renaissances' before, including the Carolingian and Ottonian Renaissances and the remarkable intellectual and cultural achievements of England and Northumbria in the seventh and eighth centuries.[1] Now in Latin Christendom (but centred significantly in northern France) in the period of the eleventh to the thirteenth century there was certainly the re-acquisition of ancient learning, notably Greek, formerly lost to the West, and newly enriched with Arabic additions, but there was also an extension and expansion of existing knowledge, an intensification of intellectual activity, new questions and new answers, development and progress in the arts—a whole movement, in short, intellectual in essence yet more than that in practice, which is part cause and part effect of the spirit of the age, and in the end is manifest in almost all its activities. In the last resort, as always, no amount of historical analysis can completely sever one aspect of society from another, and what we call the Twelfth-Century Renaissance finds its expression in the developing bureaucracy of the Papacy or the Anglo-Norman state as well as in the theology of an Anselm or an Abélard or the splendours of the cathedral church of Chartres.

Any short account of the so-called Twelfth-Century

[1] Above, pp. 47-9, 67-8, 160-1.

Renaissance must necessarily be confined to its more narrowly intellectual and cultural aspects, though at every point these overflow into the wider world. Such a treatment also the more easily enables us to distinguish between the Roman and the Greek sides of the movement. The former was the earlier and included the study of grammar and rhetoric and the classical Latin authors, pagan no less than Christian, poets as well as prose writers. This is the literary side of the renaissance, producing such cultivated men of letters as a William of Malmesbury or a John of Salisbury, producing also better histories for the use of modern scholars than any other medieval period can show, and finding expression in a Latin style and syntax as elegant and as accurate as anything to be found amongst the products of the better known renaissance of the fifteenth and sixteenth centuries. This, too, is the humanistic side, the sovereign antidote to any ill-formed judgement of the Middle Ages. Any student or any other reader with a lingering concept of the Middle Ages as the Dark Ages or an age of plaster saints may be urgently recommended to plunge into the heady waters of the lyric poetry of this period and the inspired translations of the late Helen Waddell—or for that matter, to read her novel, *Peter Abelard*, better than another dozen textbooks for a knowledge of the period.[1] 'Bliss was it in that dawn to be alive,' and, surely, 'to be young was very heaven'.

> If you were April's lady,
> And I were Lord of May—

or again

> Of all things the beginning
> Was on an April morn;
> In spring the earth remembereth
> The day that she was born—

[1] *The Wandering Scholars* (London, 1927: reprinted 1966: also in Pelican Books, 1954). Cf. *Medieval Latin Lyrics* (London, 1929: reprinted 1966); *Peter Abelard* (London, 1933 and many times reprinted).

and again

> God who hath made all things in earth that are,
> That made my love and set her thus afar,
>   Grant me this grace,
> That I may some day come within a room,
> Or in some garden gloom
>   Look on her face.

Some fragments of all this still remain in circulation, like the great drinking songs (*Mihi est prepositum in taberna mori*—In the public house to die, is my resolution), and 'Take thou this rose', which may be Abelard's. Abelard's also is one fragment surviving from his songs and verses for Heloïse, destroyed when their love was crucified.

> Peace, O my stricken Lute!
>   Thy strings are sleeping.
> Would that my heart could still
>   Its bitter weeping.

It seems right that one of the greatest love stories in the world should come whispering down the ages from this period. Yet he who wrote these verses and loved this woman was also the leading teacher and scholar, theologian and philosopher ('Verily Christ's philosopher', the abbot of Cluny called him) in all France. Here clearly are 'Renaissance' figures, but from the twelfth and not the fifteenth or the sixteenth century, and Heloïse not less than he. In one of her surviving letters, written when they were separated and she was abbess of the Paraclete, she speaks with a dreadful honesty of putting Abelard even before God. 'In the whole of my life (God knows) I have ever feared to offend thee rather than God; I seek to please thee more than Him. Thy command brought me, not the love of God, to the habit of religion.' Greater love, one must feel, could no woman have than this.

In these sad and enchanted places we cannot linger, but must move on to note that another important aspect of the 'Roman' side of the Twelfth-Century Renaissance, and one with great practical consequences, was the study of law, the study of Roman law especially, and of jurisprudence. The age sought order perhaps above all other things, and law and order go together, to find expression at this time in the growth of states as also in the development of Papal monarchy. 'Of all centuries the most legal', wrote Maitland of the twelfth, and 'in no other age, since the classical days of Roman law, has so large a part of the sum total of intellectual endeavour been devoted to jurisprudence',[1] while Haskins added that by the end 'for good or ill the lawyer had come as an active element in the world's government, and he had come to stay.'[2] By the end also the great law schools of Bologna were established in what had become one of the earliest of the new universities, but it must be further emphasized that there is more to this aspect of the renaissance than the rediscovery of Justinian's *Corpus Juris Civilis* of the sixth century, and the academic study of Roman law which is based upon it. England, for example, which did not take to Roman law as such, was nevertheless steeped in the legalism of the age, and the twelfth century sees the first great leap forward of the English Common Law, as it also ends characteristically with the first systematic, scientific exposition of it, in that 'Treatise on the Laws and Customs of England' written late in Henry II's reign and attributed to Glanville, the king's justiciar. So too in the Roman Church, as we have seen,[3] the eleventh and twelfth centuries are marked by a great development, expansion, and systematization of canon law, the law of the Church, which in turn is a fundamental part of the Gregorian reform movement and the revival of the Papacy. Much of the theory of Papal Supremacy will find practical expression in a universal jurisdiction, and it is no coincidence at all that much of the friction

---

[1] *History of English Law* (1895), i, 88.
[2] *Renaissance of the Twelfth Century*, p. 222.
[3] Above, p. 141.

between Church and State, both of them now developing and expanding, will come on the boundaries of jurisdiction—as witness Henry II and Becket.

When we turn to the Greek side of the Twelfth-Century Renaissance we turn to the realms of science, mathematics and philosophy. Here the word 'renaissance' may to a larger extent be allowed its literal meaning of rebirth since here we are much concerned with the rediscovery and revival of classical knowledge formerly lost. In these realms the original inheritance of the early Middle Ages was comparatively slender: with little or no Greek, men drew their classical culture via the Latin language from Rome, which was itself deficient in the higher flights of Greek thought, and they had access to Greek learning only through a few translations, notably those of Boethius. Even now in the twelfth century the new Greek knowledge causing intellectual ferment in the West did not come direct from the surviving Greek world of Byzantium, but via the Arab world, through Sicily which the Normans took from Islam, and especially through Spain where the Christian kingdoms were expanding southward against the Moors. This double transference might seem less than perfect, but in practice brought to the West the bonus of Arabic additions to the original, for the Moslem world, absorbing some of the most advanced Greek provinces of the former Roman Empire,[1] had not only assimilated Greek culture but augmented it, not least in science, mathematics, medicine, and even in philosophy via Averroës (1126–98). It is probable that, like the rest of medieval history, the debt of the West to Islam is nowadays insufficiently appreciated. In arithmetic, for example, our very numerals are Arabic, and the fundamental importance of this alone is soon made clear to anyone who tries to do sums in Roman figures.

'At no point', wrote Haskins, 'is the intellectual revival of the twelfth century more marked than in the domain of science', a just judgement which may seem the less surprising if it is accepted that science includes mathematics and, in this age, overflowed

[1] Above, p. 28.

into philosophy of which indeed it formed a part. It is we who have narrowed the usage of the word 'science' which formerly meant knowledge, and still has in the dictionary a root meaning of systematic and formulated knowledge, as in 'political science', 'moral science' and the like. In the twelfth century when, as in the earlier seventeenth, it was still possible for a man to take all knowledge as his province, philosophy (increasingly dominated by logic and dialectic, the reduction of things to order by the use of reason) was the 'supreme integrator', the 'sum and system of all the sciences'.[1] In the sciences in the attenuated sense, the period (more especially when we include the thirteenth century) saw important advances in astronomy notably, and in zoology and botany, as well as the absorption of Aristotle's *Meteorology* and *Physics*. In medicine the twelfth century achieved a dramatic advance, derived from Hippocrates and Galen among the ancients and from the Arab physicians including Avicenna. It is also marked by the flourishing period of the University of Salerno, 'the earliest medical school in modern Europe'.[2] In the fundamental discipline of mathematics there was the most important advance of all. The twelfth century absorbed the whole of Euclid, so that by its end geometry had developed to a point not to be passed until quite recent times. Algebra, also, reached a position not to be improved upon until the sixteenth century, and, for trigonometry, Adelard of Bath brought the tables of al-Khwarizmi to the West as early as 1126. It is often said, and with some justice, that this period, and indeed 'the Middle Ages', acquired thus scientific knowledge without the scientific spirit and method of experiment and inquiry; yet one should be wary of such generalizations and, still more, of their implications. Medieval architecture gained its achievements and progressed by bold experiments in applied science and mathematics, and scientific technology could also be applied for something that was wanted, as in the development of mechanical, weight-driven clocks at least from the thirteenth century.

[1] Haskins, *op. cit.*, p. 341.
[2] *Ibid.*, p. 322.

In philosophy, the prestige subject next to theology, to which it was inevitably related, and the growth point, so to speak, of contemporary education, the twelfth century absorbed before its end (again via Arabic sources) the whole of Aristotle's logic, to add to the meagre translations of a small part of Aristotelian logic which it inherited from Boethius. Aristotle thus became 'the Prince of Philosophers' in the schools, and the passion of the age for logic was amply fed. The twelfth century 'was pre-eminently an age of logic',[1] nor is it surprising that this should be so, for logic, with its allied subject dialectic or logical disputation, was above all systematic, rational, reducing things to order. It was, in short, that which the age most wanted, 'an instrument of order in a chaotic world'.[2] Not all was gain, for logic drove out literary and humanistic studies from the curricula, to the alarm of civilized men like John of Salisbury, and could and did lead to arrid logic-chopping amongst mediocre minds. Meanwhile it produced those *Summae* and encyclopaedic systematizations of knowledge which scholars and the world needed, like Gratian's *Concord of Discordant Canons* or Peter Lombard's *Sentences*, a systematic theology in four books. It also produced, as these works exemplify, and as does Peter Abelard's *Sic et Non* which antedates them, the new scholastic method of inquiry and arrangement of one's material, proposition, opposition and solution, to advance the truth—though in Abelard's case the solution is left wanting, often with devastating effect upon received authority. Meanwhile, also, we should surely notice this devotion to reason in an age of faith. And certainly when the new schoolmen's logic and the new methods were applied in theology, the queen of subjects, the results could seem dangerous to some, and there were conflicts and controversies, most notably between Abelard and St. Bernard. St. Anselm (*d.*1109) had written, 'I believe in order that I may know: I do not know in order to believe'. With this we may contrast Abelard (*d.*1142), 'By doubting we are led to inquire: by inquiry we perceive the

[1] Haskins, *op. cit.*, p. 355.
[2] R. W. Southern, *Making of the Middle Ages*, p. 179.

truth': and again, 'How far are they worthy of attention who assert, that faith is not to be built or defended by reasoning?' For St. Bernard, on the other hand, this was an assertion: 'he held that to discuss the mysteries of religion was to destroy the merit of faith'.[1] Yet if Bernard prevailed against Abelard in his lifetime, it was precisely the latter's methods and the application of reason to substantiate faith that were triumphantly used by St. Thomas Aquinas in the thirteenth century. We touch here upon timeless questions, and perhaps we may leave them by setting down, in Abelard fashion, a quotation from a once distinguished historian describing the Middle Ages as 'a millennium in which reason was enchained, thought was enslaved, and knowledge made no progress'.[2]

Finally the Twelfth-Century Renaissance is an expansion of knowledge also in the sense that it expanded its dissemination, and in so doing brought it more into the world, if not into the market-place. It begins with the monastic and cathedral schools and ends with the universities which, institutionally at least, are its most valuable bequest to us. Further, in spite of the initial pre-eminence of Bec, and the distinction of other monastic schools in the eleventh century (some of which were open and not merely confined to the monks and novices of their own community), the renaissance was germinated in the secular cathedral schools of northern France especially, Chartres and Rheims, Laon and Tours, Orleans and Paris. The palm of learning thus passes from the monasteries in this period as one aspect of the decline of monasticism from supremacy. From the early thirteenth century the new orders of the friars became the new élite of Christian society, and while the Franciscans as well as the Dominicans became a learned order in the end, it is characteristic of the age that the latter were founded with that intention from the beginning. But if the Dominicans were in this

[1] R. L. Poole, *Illustrations of the History of Medieval Thought and Learning* (New York, Dover Publications, 1960), p. 138.
[2] J. B. Bury, *History of Freedom of Thought* (London and New York, 1913), p. 52.

respect one end-product of the Twelfth-Century Renaissance, the universities were another, as institutions, that is to say, devoted to the expansion of learning and its dissemination, and knowledge of all kinds, both sacred and profane. The first and earliest universities—Salerno and Bologna, Paris, Montpellier and Oxford—have their origins in this period and are entirely medieval innovations. 'From these the continuity is direct to our own day, and there was no other source. The university is a medieval contribution to civilization, and more specifically a contribution of the twelfth century.'[1] It is paradoxical that youth today, for the most part ignorant of, and even taught to be contemptuous of, 'the Middle Ages', should nevertheless so strenuously compete, urged on by equally unknowing parents, for attendance at institutions which we owe wholly to the medieval past.

The physical expansion of Latin Christendom beginning in the eleventh and twelfth centuries we have already noticed piecemeal and in part in the eastward expansion of Germany[2] and the Norman conquests of southern Italy and Sicily.[3] If we now add the further instances of the Crusades and of the first and major phases of the reconquest of the Iberian peninsula we may the better appreciate the degree to which expansion is a feature of the age, and to what an extent it is a manifestation of the revived strength and affluence of the West, and the consequential shift in the balance of power as between the hitherto weaker world of Latin Christendom and the hitherto vastly superior worlds of Byzantium and Islam. The eastward colonization of the German peoples was at the expense of the heathen Slavs or Wends, but the settlement of the Normans in southern Italy was in Byzantine territory, nor did their subsequent aggressive activities and their alliance with the Papacy do anything to repair the widening breach between Greek and Latin,

[1] Haskins, *op. cit.*, p. 369.
[2] Above, pp. 168–71.
[3] Above, pp. 207–9.

while the Fourth Crusade in 1204 will see at least the temporary conquest of the Greek Empire by the Latin West. The Crusades proper, and the Norman conquest of Sicily, are, amongst other things, also an intervention by the West in former Byzantine territories and spheres of interest, while they and the Christian reconquest of Spain represent a dramatic rolling back of the former Moslem menace, and the adoption, and for a time the triumph, of the new concept of Holy War.

The Crusades to the Holy Land were in the end abortive, and, in the whole perspective of medieval history, the end was not long in coming. Jerusalem, taken—or liberated, as we might say—by the Western knights in 1099, fell again to Saladin and Islam in 1187, less than a century later, and the end of all Outremer came with the fall of Acre in 1291. Nor is it any longer customary among historians to exaggerate the direct effects of the Crusades upon the West, which had other and in the main more fruitful contacts with the East. Was all that prodigious effort and achievement therefore wasted? Whole kingdoms and principalities—Jerusalem, Antioch, Tripoli, Edessa—set up only to be lost again? Perhaps. Yet 'whether we regard them as the most tremendous and most romantic of Christian adventures or as the last of the barbarian invasions, the Crusades form a central fact in medieval history. Before their inception the centre of our civilization was placed in Byzantium and in the lands of the Arab Caliphate. Before they faded out the hegemony in civilization had passed to western Europe. Out of this transference modern history was born'.[1] The crusading ideal, too, so entirely appropriate as it seems to the bellicose piety and militant Christianity of western chivalry, though emasculated by the growing demands of nationalism and *raisons d'état*, will long outlive 1291 and its last expression in the Holy Land. Like other human ideals, also, it will be early bent, polluted and debased. The Fourth Crusade in 1204, before ever it reached Jerusalem, turned its arms upon Constantinople, that other city of the world's desires, and for a time brought down the Eastern Empire,

[1] Steven Runciman. *A History of the Crusades* (Cambridge, 1953–4), i, xi.

though this too was abortive. Crusade also was proclaimèd against the heretics of Languedoc in the early thirteenth century, destroying them and their brilliant southern culture in a prolonged agony which remains a stain on medieval history. And yet, of course, no age should preen itself upon the tragic follies of its predecessors, least of all ours, which has seen Belsen in the cause of racial purity, Hiroshima for peace on earth, or peasants burnt in Vietnam in a modern crusade against Communism.

Christian expansion into the Iberian peninsula, though at times it can be seen as a further manifestation of crusading endeavour, was something else again, and more lastingly momentous. Here are the origins, the forceful creation, of modern Spain and Portugal, and without them the modern history of both the Old World and the New would be very different. Our English schoolboy student of the Tudors and the Stuarts, for example, who so often casts his shadow across these pages, would be utterly at a loss without Spain. And, once more, the die is cast, the pattern of the future set, by the mid-thirteenth century, and more especially in the course of the eleventh and the twelfth. To all things there has to be a beginning, and in fact the overrunning of the Iberian peninsula in the eighth century by the Moslems[1] (more especially by the Berbers of North Africa) had left Christian communities surviving unconquered in the far north in the Pyrenean mountains, in the Asturias which will be the kingdom of León, while Charlemagne's expeditions into Spain at the end of the same century had set up a Christian Spanish 'March', the future county of Barcelona in Catalonia. These meagre territories for long remain, however, mere outposts of a hard-pressed Latin West, and the long epic of expansion and reconquest does not begin until the middle decades of the eleventh century, and more precisely in *c*.1031. In that year the formerly brilliant and successful Omayyad Caliphate of Cordova collapsed, and Moslem Spain disintegrated into the warring Moorish kingdoms of Seville, Granada, Malaga and

[1] Above, p. 28.

Valencia. The Christian states of León and Castile, Navarre, Aragon and Barcelona, were to prove equal to the opportunity, though not without rivalries of their own, which may seem to us a marvellous irresponsibility but mean in fact that they had other motives than the grand designs of modern historians, anxious to see Spain united. It should be noted also that, great as the achievement nevertheless remains, Christian success in Spain, like the huge success of the First Crusade, owes much to the disunity of Islam. The later eleventh century thus begins an era of piecemeal advance, here a little, there a little: in 1085 Toledo fell to Alphonso VI of León, and Tarragona, in *c.* 1091, to the count of Barcelona. It was also a period when the Spanish Christians received help from bands of individual Frankish knight-adventurers from the north, not least from Normandy, seeking military employment, fiefs and fortune, and salvation by the good work of Holy War. It was the period also of El Cid, the legendary Spanish national hero, who in practice seems to have combined the new chivalry with a good deal of self-interest and fought variously on both sides. In the twelfth and early thirteenth centuries the pace quickened both in terms of military success and in the coalition or emergence of larger Christian principalities. Portugal evolved from Castile in 1139, and its new king captured Lisbon (with the help of a crusading fleet from the Netherlands) in 1147. In 1140 Aragon was dynastically united with Catalonia or Barcelona, and in 1230 Castile and León were finally combined into one kingdom. Also these expanding principalities are more closely drawn into the society and politics of Latin Christendom. Portugal became a vassal-state of the Papacy in 1143. Alphonso VIII of Castile (1158–1214) married a daughter of Henry II of England, Anjou and Normandy, and also married one of his own daughters to Louis VIII of France. When after the defeat of the same Alphonso at Alarcos in 1196 the king appealed for aid to all Latin Christendom, the outcome was a special Crusade proclaimed by Pope Innocent III, and a total victory of the Christian forces at Las Navas de Tolosa in 1212. In 1236 Cordova fell to Ferdinand III of Castile, followed by Seville in 1248, and the submission of Cadiz. James the Conqueror of Aragon captured Majorca and the Balearic Isles between 1229 and 1235 and in 1238 took Valencia on the mainland. By the mid-thirteenth century Christian and Catholic Portugal was more or less complete, and only one Moorish kingdom, Granada in the south, remained in Christian and Catholic Spain.

In this book the phrase 'the pattern of the future' has often been employed, and by the end of the thirteenth century that pattern has been surely set. We have seen, above all, the emergence and evolution of Latin Christendom out of the former Roman Empire, and Latin Christendom is, or was, that Western Europe which becomes in turn the heart and kernel of the wider twentieth-century West to which we all belong. Within the outline pattern, we have also seen much of the detail which no less surely moulds the future. We have seen the developing unity and strength of France and England, together with their mutual rivalry, and we have also seen the disunity, and thus political weakness of Germany and Italy, the latter divided between northern Italy, subject to German intervention, a southern kingdom, and the Papacy and the Papal States between them. Future history, modern history, will be predetermined scarcely less by the negative factors, so to speak, of Italy and Germany, than by the very positive factors of England and of France. To this familiar political framework we add the emergence of Spain and Portugal in the west, and round off Latin Christendom to the north with a Latin and Christian Scandinavia as the dust of the Vikings settles, and, to the east, a Latin Prussia, Poland, Bohemia and Hungary. East again, and south, of those last four principalities, the line came to be drawn between Latin Christendom and the Greek Orthodox territories of the Byzantine Empire and her religious and cultural satellites of Bulgaria, Serbia and Russia. The division between the Latin and Western, and the Greek and Eastern worlds we have seen continually to harden in these pages, as we have also seen the

dramatic advent of the third world of Islam, and watched also
its subsequent fragmentation as well as its huge achievements.
The Moslem world is still a force today, territorially almost
unchanged, and still given reality in the last resort by the faith
preached by Mohammed. The division between Western and
Eastern Europe is very much still with us also, but the lines were
then different, based ultimately on religion and therefore culture:
the contrast seems to emphasize the artificiality of the present
political division, symbolized, it may be, by the Berlin Wall,
unless, as seems unlikely, either communism or democracy or
both become substitutes for faith. Indeed, one lesson which
emerges from so-called medieval history is the pre-eminence
of faith as a creative factor—nor, for that matter, does the
potency of that factor diminish until the so-called modern period
is well advanced. Certainly it was the Christian faith in Roman
fashion that made Latin Christendom an entity, moulded its
culture into something distinct, and gave it a real measure of
self-conscious unity. That unity gained its fullest and most
prolonged expression in the medieval Papacy, but also, although
by the end of the thirteenth century the forces of nationalism
together with the hostility of Rome itself prevented a more
directly political expression in a viable Western Empire, men
felt themselves to be members of a Christian society which
existed in unity in spite of internal political divisions, and whose
essence was the Catholic, Roman, Christian faith. If, therefore,
we must have a separate period called the Middle Ages, and
cannot think of anything more sensible to call it, then it ends with
the Reformation, though he would still be rash indeed who
called the Reformation 'modern'. Whether it is now possible to
recover anything of the former unity of the Western Europe
which was Latin Christendom through a Common Market
without any unifying faith save economic and political advantage,
is a question which the historian must ask and to which the
medieval historian, perhaps, may be inclined to give a pessimistic
answer.

But these speculations are not the way in which this book was meant to end. Its purpose was to demonstrate the relevance of medieval history and to show that the origins of modern Europe lie in the Middle Ages. These propositions ought to be self-evidently true, and when they again become so the sheer folly, for anyone wishing to be educated and to understand his world, of starting in the middle of the story when all that matters most is past, will also, one may hope, become apparent. This book also began as a series of lectures, which used to end with a great cry of 'Damned is he (or she) who knows no medieval history'. That cry still seems to be the only possible conclusion.

Suggestions for Further Reading

Almost the whole period of this book is covered, between them, by two very excellent, and eminently readable, works, *viz.* H. St. L. B. Moss, *The Birth of the Middle Ages, 395–814* (Oxford, 1935), and R. W. Southern, *The Making of the Middle Ages* (London, 1953), the span of the latter being from the late tenth to the early thirteenth century. Covering almost exactly the same period is R. H. C. Davis, *A History of Medieval Europe from Constantine to St. Louis* (London, 1957), while for reference purposes rather than sustained reading there is *The Shorter Cambridge Medieval History* of C. W. Previté-Orton (Cambridge, 1953), a remarkable compendium of information, lavishly and well illustrated. In addition to those four general works, the following books or essays will be found of particular relevance to individual chapters, as under:

INTRODUCTION

Geoffrey Barraclough, 'Medium Aevum: Some Reflections on Medieval History and on the Term "The Middle Ages",' in his *History in a Changing World* (Oxford, 1957).

CHAPTER I

Edward Gibbon, *The Decline and Fall of the Roman Empire.*
Bernard Lewis, *The Arabs in History* (London, 1950, 1958).
Henri Pirenne, *Mohammed and Charlemagne* (trans. Bernard Miall, London, 1958).

236   *Further Reading*

CHAPTER II

Robert Latouche, *Caesar to Charlemagne: the beginnings of France* (trans. J. Nicholson, London, 1968).

J. M. Wallace-Hadrill, *The Barbarian West 400–1000* (London, 1952).

J. M. Wallace-Hadrill, *The Long-haired Kings* (London, 1962).

F. L. Ganshof, *The Carolingian and the Frankish Monarchy: Studies in Carolingian History* (trans. Janet Sondheimer, London, 1971).

W. Ullman, *The Carolingian Renaissance and the Idea of Kingship* (London, 1969).

R. E. Sullivan, *The Coronation of Charlemagne* (Problems of European Civilization, Boston, U.S.A., 1959).

CHAPTER III

R. W. Southern, *Western Society and the Church in the Middle Ages* (The Pelican History of the Church, vol. 2, London, 1970).

Geoffrey Barraclough, *The Medieval Papacy* (London, 1968).

CHAPTER IV

R. W. Southern, *Western Society and the Church in the Middle Ages* (as above).

Dom Cuthbert Butler, *Benedictine Monachism* (2nd. edition, London, 1924).

Dom David Knowles, *The Monastic Order in England* (2nd. edition, Cambridge, 1963).

CHAPTER V

Gwyn Jones, *A History of the Vikings* (Oxford, 1968).

Johannes Brondsted, *The Vikings* (trans. E. Bannister-Good, London, 1961).

Bernard Lewis, *The Arabs in History* (as above).
Karl Leyser, 'The Battle at the Lech, 955. A Study in Tenth-century Warfare', *History*, 1, 1965.

CHAPTER VI

Marc Bloch, *Feudal Society* (trans. L. A. Manyon, London, 1961).
F. L. Ganshof, *Feudalism* (trans. P. Grierson, London, 1952).
R. Allen Brown, *The Origins of English Feudalism* (London, 1972).

CHAPTER VII

G. Tellenbach, *Church, State and Christian Society at the time of the Investiture Contest* (trans. R. F. Bennett, Oxford, 1940).
Rose Graham, *English Ecclesiastical Studies* (London, 1929).

CHAPTER VIII

Geoffrey Barraclough, *The Origins of Modern Germany* (2nd. edition, Oxford, 1947).
James Westfall Thompson, *Feudal Germany* (Chicago, U.S.A., 1928; New York, 1962).
Karl Leyser, 'Henry I and the beginning of the Saxon empire', *English Historical Review*, lxxxiii, 1968.

CHAPTER IX

Robert Fawtier, *The Capetian Kings of France* (trans. L. Butler and R. J. Adam, London, 1960).

CHAPTER X

C. H. Haskins, *The Normans in European History* (New York, 1915, 1959).
D. C. Douglas, *The Norman Achievement* (London, 1969).
J. J. Norwich, *The Normans in the south* (London, 1966).

R. Allen Brown, *The Normans and the Norman Conquest* (London and New York, 1969).

CHAPTER XI

C. H. Haskins, *The Renaissance of the Twelfth Century* (Harvard, 1927; New York, 1957).
Helen Waddell, *The Wandering Scholars* (London, 1927, 1966).
Helen Waddell, *Medieval Latin Lyrics* (London, 1929, 1966).
Helen Waddell, *Peter Abelard* (London, 1933).
Steven Runciman, *A History of the Crusades* (Cambridge, 1951–4).
W. C. Atkinson, *A History of Spain and Portugal* (London, 1960).

Index

Arnulfings, 41
Arezzo, 165
Arts, 83, 102, 173, 194, 220
Ascetism, 13, 75–6, 77–8, 79, 80, 88, 138
Astronomy, 225
Atlantic, North, 97, 103–5
Attila the Hun, 24, 65
Augustine, St., of Canterbury, 54, 59, 66–7, 80
Augustine, St., of Hippo, 25, 49, 90
Augustinian Canons, 88, 89–90. *Cf.* Monasticism
Aurillac, Gerbert of, 161
Austrasia, 40, 41
Austria, 47, 171
Avars, 47
Aversa, 208; Rannulf of, 208; Richard of, 208
Avicenna, 225
Avignon, 94

Balearic Isles, 232
Baltic, 96, 97, 171
Barbarians, invasion and settlement of, 3, 4, 18, 19, 20–2, 23, 24–5, 31, 32, 36, 39, 57, 58, 62, 64, 70, 93. *See also* Germanic races
Barbarossa, Operation, 5, 172. *See also* Frederick I
Barcelona, 47, 230, 231
Bari, 209; Meles of, 206, 208
Baronage, barons, 124, 127
Basques, 47
Bath, Adelard of, 225
Balkan States, 16
Bavaria, Bavarians, 47, 156
Bayeux, 99, 217; bishop of, *see* Odo
Beaulieu, abbey, 181
Beaumanoir, 192
Beaumaris, castle, 219
Beaumont, house of, 205
Beauvais, 99
Bec, Bec-Hellouin, abbey, 84, 203, 227; abbot of, *see* Anselm, Herluin; Compromise of, 150
Becket, Thomas, St., archbishop of Canterbury, 130, 224
Bede, the Venerable, 23, 40, 64–5, 67, 77, 83–4
Belgium, 34. *Cf.* Low Countries
Bellême, Mabel de, 205

Benedict, St., of Aniane, 131
Benedict, St., of Nursia, 28, 78–81, 87, 88, 90; Rule of, 25, 74, 76, 78–81, 83, 84, 86, 87, 88–9, 131, 132, 133, 134. *Cf.* Monasticism
Benefice, 112, 119, 122. *See also* Fief
Berbers, 230
Bernard, St., 89, 133, 226–7
Berno, St., abbot of Cluny, 133
Bishops, 38, 58–61, 65, 66, 67, 68, 113, 120, 141, 175, 181–2; appointment of, 139–4; archbishops or metropolitans, 60, 67, 68, 139; 'Caesarian', 150–1; Carolingian, 174; Gallic, 36; German, 158; monastic, 85, 135; Norman, 202–3
Bjarni Herjolfsson, 103
Bloch, Marc, 111, 175
Blois, 99, 180, 182, 184; count of, *see* Eudo II, Stephen
Boethius, 4, 21–2, 224, 226
Bohemia, 153, 159, 232
Bohemund, prince of Antioch, 216. *See also* Hauteville
Bologna, 223, 228
Boniface, St., 41, 43, 68
Boniface I, Pope, 59, 61
Boniface VIII, Pope, 73, 193
Bordeaux, 99
Boroughs, 95, 122. *Cf.* Fortresses
Botony, 225
Bourgeoisie, middle classes, 144, 165
Brandenberg, 168, 171; margrave of, *see* Albrecht
Bretons, 178. *See also* Brittany
Britain, British Isles, 16, 24, 44, 52, 64, 97, 103, 210; Roman Britain, 31, 102
Brittany, 176, 180, 182, 184, 190. *See also* Bretons
Brogne, abbey, 131, 134
Bruges, 184
Bruno, archbishop of Cologne, duke of Lotharingia, 160, 161
Bulgaria, 232
Burchard, 142
Burgundians, 24–5, 34, 36; kingdom of, 34
Burgundy, 40, 41, 120, 131, 133, 156, 159, 164, 190

Germany, 5, 16, 36, 46–7, 68, 70, 93, 94–5, 105–6, 113, 135, 136–7, 143, 145–6, 148–9, 152, 153ff, 173, 174, 211, 212, 232; eastward expansion of, 5, 46, 155, 159, 168–72, 219, 228. Kings of, *see* Conrad II; Frederick I, II; Henry III, IV, VI; Otto I, II

Ghent, 131, 134, 135, 184, 201

Giroie, house of, 205

Glanville, 223

Godwin, earl of Wessex, 213, 214

Gorze, abbey, 131

Goths, 34

Government, development of, 59, 153–4, 160, 182–3, 191–2, 198, 204, 213, 215. *See also* Charters; Kingship; Law; Taxation

Granada, 230, 232

Grammar, 85

Gratian, 226

Greece, 4, 8, 16, 71. *Cf.* Classical culture; Renaissance

Greenland, 96, 103, 104–5

Gregory I, St., the Great, Pope, 25, 49, 65–7, 68, 80

Gregory III, Pope, 71

Gregory VII, Pope, 1, 5, 65, 73, 136–137, 141, 142–3, 144–9, 151, 152, 162, 163, 185, 186. *Cf.* Investiture Contests

Gregory IX, Pope, 167

Gregory of Tours, 36, 39, 40

Guthrum the Dane, 9, 102

Hadrian, abbot, 64

Hadrian I, Pope, 46

Halfdan, 101

Hapsburgs, 164

Harlech, castle, 219

Harold I, Harefoot, king of England, 211

Harold II, Godwinson, king of England, 212, 214

Harold Hardrada, king of Norway, 212, 214

Harthacnut, king of Denmark and England, 211

Hastings, battle of, 55, 141, 209, 214

Hauberk, 117. *Cf.* Fief

Hauteville, house of, 205, 206–7, 208, 209; Bohemund, prince of Antioch, 207, 216; Dreux, 208; Humphrey, 208; Robert 'Guiscard', 207, 208–9, 216; Roger I, 'the Great Count', 209; Roger II, king of Sicily, 209; Tancred, 216; William 'Bras de Fer', 208

Hauteville-le-Guichard, 207

Heloise, 55, 222

Henry I, king of England, duke of Normandy, 197

Henry I, the Fowler, king of the East Franks, 94–5, 158, 159, 168

Henry II, king of England, duke of Normandy and Aquitaine, count of Anjou, 183, 197, 223, 224, 231

Henry III, Emperor, 143, 144, 145, 163

Henry III, king of England, 194

Henry IV, Emperor, 136–7, 145–8, 152, 163

Henry VI, Emperor, 164, 166

Henry the Lion, duke of Saxony and Bavaria, 168

Heptarchy, English, 210

Hereditary succession, 122, 139, 180, 185

Hereward the Wake, 210

Herluin, abbot of Bec, 84

Hermits, eremitical life, 77–8, 79, 88

Hildebrand. *See* Gregory VII

Hippocrates, 225

Hirsau, abbey, 135

Hohenstaufen, 164, 165, 168

Holstein, Adolf of, 168

Homage, 112, 121, 125, 128, 140, 150, 187. *Cf.* Commendation; Feudalism; Vassalage

Honorius III, Pope, 167

Housecarls, 212

Household, 175

Hubert, bishop of Angers, 181

Hugh the Great, duke of the Franks, 176

Humanism, 221–2, 226

Humber, 212

Humbert, Cardinal, 139–40, 144

Hungarians. *See* Magyars

Hungary, 94, 95, 153, 154, 232; king of, *see* Stephen, St.

Huns, 24